IndePenPress

First published in Great Britain by Indepenpress

All paper used in the printing of this book has been made
from wood grown in managed, sustainable forests.

ISBN13: 978-1-907172-79-3

Printed and bound in the UK
Indepenpress is an imprint of
Indepenpress Publishing Limited
25 Eastern Place
Brighton
BN2 1GJ

A catalogue record of this book is available
from the British Library

Book layout and design by Geoff Beckett

Foreword

I was born three months before the first Miles M2 Hawk flew and spent my first sixteen years in Berkshire, living almost on the outskirts of Woodley aerodrome.

The first time that Geoff and I met – that we are aware of – was when he came down to Shoreham Airport, where I was working on the design of the M100 Student, to do a cutaway drawing for the magazine 'Aeroplane'. As Geoff was a pupil at the Miles Aeronautical Technical School at Woodley and I used to attend – at the behest of my parents – some of the general information lectures presented by people from outside, it is possible that we saw each other at that time, but neither of us has any recollection of it.

I used to visit the Woodley factory quite frequently in the school holidays – I had a pass which gave me entry even into the Experimental Department – and have memories of some of the projects which Geoff describes in this book so vividly in words and in pictures. Although war is not a pleasant thing, for me as a small boy with no real understanding of the darker side, it was exciting. I remember one day hearing a strange aeroplane flying over and saying to my mother, "If it were night time, I would say that was a German." "Nonsense," said my mother, "everyone knows that you can't distinguish them from the noise alone and, in any case, if it were we would have heard the bombs." Five minutes later my father telephoned from the factory to tell my mother "Keep the children indoors, a stick of unexploded German bombs has just been dropped on the aerodrome."

Geoff's story lights up the aviation history of Berkshire, peering into all sorts of unusual corners, far beyond anything that I knew from my years there. Even so, there are bits which extend from Berkshire into later life.

When I was living at Woodley my father, my uncle George and Don Brown used to give me the occasional lesson but it was not until my National Service that I learned to fly. Whilst in the Fleet Air Arm I flew the Firefly – assembled at White Waltham – and the Balliol, the latter only once when a ferry pilot delivered it by mistake to the airfield where I was based and the temptation was beyond resisting!

This book has two parts; one is Geoff's delightful autobiography, and the other is his broad and deep history of aviation in Berkshire. In the historical part, he goes back to the very beginnings of aviation, a surprising amount of which took place in Berkshire. He brings us through balloons to gliders and on to powered aeroplanes in the first decade of the 20th century and through to the developments of World War I. Many people do not understand the strides made in those few years; and that much of the infrastructure of aviation practices and regulations in use today was evolved within the first fifteen years after the Wright Brothers first flew.

Moving on through the inter-war period, which saw the foundation of Miles Aircraft and its growth from a few enthusiasts to a company employing seven thousand people, Geoff chronicles the astonishing amount of aviation activity in Berkshire during World War II. Not only were there substantial aircraft factories, producing most of the advanced trainers used by the RAF and Fleet Air Arm, but the county was dotted with military airfields, almost overlapping one another, from which Bomber Command and the airborne forces operated.

The whole book is illustrated by Geoff's exquisite paintings and a collection of photographs, many of which are rarely seen. The paintings in particular enlighten the narrative and make the book such a joy to read. I hope you get as much pleasure from it as I have.

Jeremy Miles

Upper Beeding, Sussex

Acknowledgements

In a book primarily about historic aviation, written in the 21st century, not surprisingly perhaps, very little, if any, is based upon original research. Over the years, it seems that there are no aircraft, no airfields, no manufacturers, no designers and, indeed, very few pilots that have escaped the attention of 'historians'. With the World Wide Web, the amount of available information has expanded to an incredible degree, although some of the 'information' must be treated with caution.

For my own part, although I actually played a very small part in the history recorded in this book, it was viewed many years ago, through very young and inexperienced eyes. I freely admit that most of what I have written or painted, has resulted from something I read somewhere, almost invariably, since 1985. That is why I must first acknowledge the part Julian Temple played in getting me started on my role as an 'aviation historian'. During the two or three years we worked together, he steered me in the direction of research into Berkshire's lesser known aviation personalities such as the Rev. John Bacon and the Holmes Brothers. He started me on my search to find a copy of Don Brown's book which, after five years or so—and a lot more money than it originally cost—I managed to obtain. Of course, Julian's own book was also a source for much of the Woodley story. Thanks Julian, I wish we could have worked together more than we did.

As soon as I learned that the lady I had sat next to at that first BAG meeting was the legendary Lettice Curtis and was able to obtain a copy of her book, 'The Forgotten Pilots', that too has been one of my most well-thumbed possessions. In July 2009 my wife and I met this grand old lady of British aviation again and showed her my précis of her incredibly detailed work from the 1970s that, in the following pages, tells the story of the ATA in Berkshire. We hope she was reassured that this story would be going on to inspire yet more generations.

But there's also the unknown young man at a print company who told me he had carried out all the typesetting for a book about aviation. He was so impressed by my reaction when he showed me his copy that he insisted I keep it. That book was Gordon Cullingham's comprehensive biography of Patrick Alexander and, by now, it has been so well used, it is just about in pieces. Then there was Judith Hunter, then honorary curator of the Windsor Borough Collection. We met back in the '80s, at a meeting of the Council for Museums in Berkshire and she kindly gave me back copies of the 'Windelsora' magazine in which Gordon Cullingham had written articles about early ballooning in Windsor. She also kindly provided photographs of Sidney Camm's early days in the town, as well as of that other Windsor resident, Patrick Alexander. Another lady, Susan Smith, played a part in my quest for information when, at the conclusion of a talk I gave to the Lower Caversham Women's Institute, when I mentioned the young lad from Reading who became Lord Hives, she told me she was one of his relatives and, soon after, provided me with useful press cuttings.

The Internet played its part when I discovered that Frank Poller, of the Hanney History Group, had written a booklet about the Holmes Brothers and Alan Cobham. I was lucky enough to get his very last copy, as well as copies of the very rare photographs he had reproduced. Many years before the Internet was available, and I confess I don't remember the exact circumstances, I managed to obtain information and photographs of Geoffrey de Havilland via Derek Lessware from Newbury. While, from John Baker of the Balloon Society, I obtained information about the Rev. John Bacon and Violet Kavanagh. The John Bacon story was later augmented by staff at the West Berkshire Museum. Then there was the member of the Oxford branch of the Observer Corps who, after I had given a talk to them, thrust a really historic Imperial War Museum photograph into my hand, saying just that "it was taken at Wantage". It was at a talk I gave to the Ridgeway Aviation Group that I met Jonathan Sayers whose book 'In Defence of Freedom' provided me with much of the history of West West Berkshire's USAF bases. Thanks to Jonathan, I was also able to include some relevant photographs. I must also mention a friend from the Guild of Aviation Artists, Graham Cooke, who consulted his huge collection of historic aviation magazines and provided me with copy from a 1935 edition of 'Flight' which explained exactly how FG Miles beat Edgar Percival in the Elimination Race in that year's King's Cup Air Race. Slightly 'glossed over' by Miles folklore, it was a story that had puzzled me for many years. My thanks also go to Richard Poad, from the Maidenhead Heritage Centre, where one can find many ATA artifacts. In recent years he has provided really useful additional information about White Waltham and, also, about some of East Berkshire's really obscure historic aviation characters. While Jim Bell from Wokingham helped me with information and photographs of Winifred Spooner

Many people have contacted me after seeing my own web-site, but I must mention John Prytherch who commented on the story of the last aircraft to fly out of Croydon Airport, which is the subject of my painting reproduced on page 152. This story originated in a small book published in 1984, 'Croydon Airport Flypast' by Peter Cooksley, where it said that the aircraft flew to Gatwick and this was duly repeated in my web-site. John informed me that it actually flew to Biggin Hill and he should know—he was one of the passengers! Thanks John. At least the correct information was able to be included here.

Lastly, among all those who have contributed in some way to the content of this book, my sincere thanks go to two men intimately involved in the Miles story. Dennis Bancroft, the Company's chief aerodynamicist, kindly provided me with a copy of his incredible investigation into the Frank Whittle/M52 affair. He later approved my perhaps unconventional précis of his report. My thanks and best wishes go to Dennis and his charming wife Elizabeth. While Jeremy Miles, whose friendship both Val and I have valued for many years, has honoured me by writing the Forward to this book, and putting me right on a few points. Thank you Jeremy for your kind comments on my work, both with 'the pen' and 'the paintbrush'.

As you will find out, 'Brushes with Aviation' gradually evolved over many years without any clear plan for it to be published. It was early in 2008 when a business acquaintance of many years, Fred Clayton, first saw the scope of my aviation work and learned about my book. He encouraged me to complete the remaining paintings and text and gave me the opportunity to see a first–proof of the whole book. Later, his colleagues Chris Darling and Chris Jewell weighed in with a marathon scan of my later paintings. Thanks to you all for your invaluable assistance.

Last, but certainly not least, my sincere thanks go to Lynn Ashman and her team at Indepenpress for their encouragement and help in bringing 'Brushes with Aviation' into being. In particular, I must mention their Production Manager, Kathryn Harrison who, aided and abetted here in Berkshire by my daughter, Angela , as well as Gail Blackman of Auryus , with considerable patience from them all, turned my untutored digital efforts into the high quality litho-printed book you see here.

Geoff Beckett

October 2009

Dedicated to my darling Val
with all my love and thanks
for being with me all the way,
from the very first painting
to the very last word.
I couldn't have done it without you.

Brushes with Aviation

A personal perspective on aviation heritage

Geoff Beckett

The first of my brushes with aviation, so I have been told, was in July 1930, when I pursued the airship R100, as it flew over my home town of Reading.

I was in my pram, just a few weeks old, with my sister, Joyce, who was seven, in charge of me and my three-year-old brother, Gerry (Gerald). We were the youngest of the five children in the Beckett family, our two elder brothers, Harry and Leslie, being in their mid-teens.

It was a time when the sight of any type of flying machine was a comparatively rare event and it seems that, in my early years, whenever any aeroplane flew over, someone in my family rushed me into the garden to see it.

Many years later Leslie told me he well remembered seeing the R100 that same day in 1930. He also recalled how, at that time, he often cycled to the recently opened Reading Aerodrome at Woodley, about five miles from our home, sometimes with Joyce or Gerry perched on a cushion tied to the crossbar of his bicycle.

Sir Alan Cobham and his 'Flying Circus' visited Reading Aerodrome three times around 1930. On one visit Leslie was happy to hand over five shillings for his first ever flight. Harry was working away from Reading by then but, as he later told me, he also flew with Cobham's Flying Circus at a different airfield. The aim of Sir Alan Cobham was to make British people 'air minded'. Obviously, my family needed no such persuasion and I was brought up to feel aeroplanes were something very special.

I was five years old when I first went to watch aeroplanes at Reading Aerodrome – and I walked all the way.

A ten-year-old friend of my brother, who lived close by, said he could show me lots of aeroplanes on the ground. Sadly, his knowledge of local geography was rather limited. From Reading, the aerodrome could be approached via two different main roads. From the more northerly road, the present-day A4, minor roads led to the aerodrome's northern boundary, where the flying club, hangars and aeroplanes could easily be seen.

My friend and I walked along the other main road and eventually approached the aerodrome's southern boundary along a narrow lane with high banks and hedges. I saw no aeroplanes, on the ground or in the air, only a somewhat limp orange windsock high above me.

As we made our way back towards Reading, it was nearly dusk. The narrow lane seemed to go on for ever and, even today, I can still feel the relief when I could see the lights of the main road. My relief was even greater when my friend said we could go home on the bus. What my mother's reaction was when I finally returned home, I do not know. I was probably much too tired for it to have registered.

What I do well remember is that, shortly after, my mother took Gerry and me by Thames Valley bus to visit Reading Aerodrome. I recollect sitting on a large tree stump for a picnic, waving furiously at the planes as they came in to land, almost directly above us. Some of the people in them even waved back!

It was an absolutely splendid day!

I remember making only one other trip to Woodley in the late 1930s—to an 'Empire Air Day', with my brother Gerry and two friends. Sadly, in view of my later links with the airfield and its many aircraft, I confess to having absolutely no recollections of the aircraft flying that day although, for some inexplicable reason, I have very clear recollections of the bus ride back to Reading.

About the same time I remember going to a fete in a park in Reading and seeing Westland Lysanders from RAF Odiham dropping 'flour bombs' into the small arena. Another time, I was one of many children who ran to see a 'Flying Flea' that had landed in the same park.

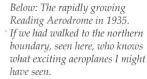

Left: This is me, about the time I walked all the way to Reading Aerodrome without seeing a single aeroplane.

Below: The rapidly growing Reading Aerodrome in 1935. If we had walked to the northern boundary, seen here, who knows what exciting aeroplanes I might have seen.

I was nine years old when World War II began and I suppose, like most children of that era, the potential for dangers and suffering were outside my imaginings. However, one particular misery I can still remember was when my elder brothers, Harry and Leslie, returned to their units after being on leave.

Before the end of 1939, Harry had volunteered for the Army, joining the Royal Army Service Corps. Eventually, he became a warrant officer, took part in the North Africa operations and then served in Italy until the end of hostilities.

Shortly after Harry enlisted, Leslie had joined the RAF as a wireless operator/air gunner. His flying log book showed wireless training in Airspeed Oxfords and gunnery training in Hawker Harts.

Above: It was in Hawker Harts like this that Leslie was trained in Air Gunnery. This 'acrylic sketch' was among my earliest paintings of six famous biplanes which were eventually published as a greetings card.

He was promoted to sergeant when he went to an operational squadron in the late summer of 1940, flying in Armstrong Whitworth Whitley bombers. Then, in December 1940, his aircraft failed to return from an operation and he spent the next four years in various prison camps.

He was promoted to warrant officer whilst a prisoner and, on his release, received the 'Oak Leafs' of a 'Mentioned in Despatches' — for working in the prison camps as a forger.

The war years left Reading surprisingly unscathed, despite the town having long had a large railway goods area and main line junctions. From the early war years, it had also developed into an important manufacturing centre, although most of the factories were small and widely scattered.

Even Woodley airfield, which had become an important production centre for Miles Aircraft, was only bombed twice, without any significant damage.

I remember a few personal scares from the noise of bombs, but my specific aviation memories are all about British and American aircraft, rather than the enemy's. The only German aircraft that I can be sure I saw was a crashed Heinkel 111 which was brought to the Odeon cinema car park to raise money for the 'Spitfire Fund'.

One particularly vivid memory I have of those early war years was seeing a giant Handley Page HP42 airliner as it flew low over Reading in a westerly direction. Even today I could return to the exact spot where I stood rooted as it appeared from the 'smog' above the railway goods yard and flew the length of Northfield Road until it disappeared beyond the roofs of Swansea Road. The memory stayed clear in my mind and the scene was one I knew I would have to paint one day.

Not long after seeing the Handley Page HP42 , I cycled with brother Gerry to the airfield at White Waltham, near Maidenhead. Unfortunately, the airfield police there were particularly vigilant and not even small boys were allowed to stop and watch the many different aircraft that flew there.

Above: I believe this photograph shows 'Heracles', from the Imperial Airways fleet of Handley Page HP42s, being flown into the 1930's Bristol Airport at Whitchurch by their senior captain OP Jones, in what I think may have been the end of the actual flight my painting commemorates. During World War II, Whitchurch became the No.2 Ferry Pool of the Air Transport Auxiliary and OP Jones was one of their senior pilots.

Below: Enemy aircraft that had been shot down were sometimes taken around towns such as Reading to help us all believe we were winning the war and to raise money for worthy causes such as the 'Spitfire Fund'. I well remember seeing a Heinkel 111 like this in the Odeon car park.

Painted in oils on canvas. 1998. 500mm x 750mm. Original painting in the collection of Mr & Mrs J. Sandrock

'End of the line?'

This painting was inspired by my own boyhood recollection of seeing one of these lumbering giants flying over Reading during the war years.

Eight Handley Page HP42s were built for Imperial Airways, in two slightly different versions. In many ways, they were 'dinosaurs' when they first appeared in 1930 because, although some up-to-date manufacturing methods were employed, the design thinking harked back to World War I.

At the outbreak of World War II, 'Heracles' and two other HP42s based at Croydon were flown to Whitchurch, near Bristol. Without the navigation aids enjoyed by today's flyers, the pilots would have flown visually, following the main railway line through Reading as shown in the painting. It is understood that one of the three pilots became lost in fog and the aircraft was destroyed in a crash landing. A few months later, 'Heracles' and the other aircraft were badly damaged on the ground when they were blown together during a severe gale. Neither ever flew again.

One HP42, 'Helena', was used by the RAF for transport duties until the middle of 1941 and a contemporary photograph shows its original silver finish repainted in wartime camouflage.

Modern research suggests it was 'Helena', in its camouflage, that I saw in 1941, probably en-route to Whitchurch from where it was flown to Scotland to be broken up.

However, 'artist's licence' surely allows my boyhood memory to be transposed to the earlier last flight of 'Heracles'.

3

Woodley airfield police were far more relaxed and it became a regular haunt for me. My most vivid memory from those visits, in the months just after the Battle of Britain, was seeing the M20 'utility fighter'. Despite the old fashioned appearance of its fixed spatted undercarriage, it looked every inch a fighter, so unlike aircraft you usually saw at Woodley.

Above: The remarkable Miles M20 'Utility Fighter', exactly as I vividly remember seeing it at Woodley airfield in late 1940 or early 1941.

I joined the Reading Air Spotters Club when I was twelve and, by then, I reckoned I could identify anything that flew over. However, I remember being initially baffled by the prototype Mosquito, which flew over Reading a few times before it was officially unveiled to the public. Yet, even from the first glimpse, its manufacturer seemed so obvious that Gerry and I called it the de Havilland 'Unknown'.

There had been a long association between the Beckett boys and the 1st Reading Scout Troop. I was the first member of the troop — and one of the first boys anywhere — to gain the air spotters badge, introduced mainly for the new troops of Air Scouts. Perhaps it looked out of place on my Sea Scout uniform because, some time later, it certainly confused the retired Admiral who carried out our annual inspection.

I was so besotted with aviation at that time that it caused me much heart-searching when the decision was made to become Sea Scouts. However, it helped to overcome my reservations when our troop leader arranged for me to meet occasionally with a new Air Scout Troop based near White Waltham airfield. Once a month, this troop was allowed to visit the airfield which was, by then, the headquarters and No.1 Ferry Pool of the Air Transport Auxiliary (ATA) and there was always a great variety of aircraft to be seen there.

It was certainly an air spotter's paradise!

One particular memory of those visits to White Waltham was seeing the airfield absolutely littered with a completely unknown type of aircraft. We learned they were Fairey Barracudas, awaiting delivery to their Fleet Air Arm squadrons.

Above: When seen on the ground, the Fairey Barracuda was one of the oddest looking aircraft imaginable, with bits hanging off it everywhere. Perhaps this ATA pilot at White Waltham thought the same thing.

Handley Page Harrow

St Paul's Church, York Road, Reading
I was thirteen when I began this as a pencil drawing in an art lesson by a visiting teacher, held in the playground of my school opposite. Wartime restrictions meant that we had no art teacher of our own. Although the drawing wasn't completed in the lesson, the visiting teacher encouraged me to return in my own time and finish it. Less than a year later, I was walking past the church, when low-flying American light bombers signalled the beginning of D-Day.

Some memorable 'brushes with aviation' around that time are shown here in the two paintings on the following pages. Another was during a Scout camping/boating trip along the Wye and Severn rivers over Easter 1945. I well remember, just after dawn, standing on a hill where the first Severn Bridge now crosses the river, watching spellbound as a Hawker Typhoon fired practice rockets at a target in the middle of the river.

Just before the end of the war in Europe, my brother Leslie was released from captivity and, after demobilisation, took up his pre-war job with Shell. He bought an ex-Army BSA motorcycle to commute to Oxford where he was based. In September 1945, I well remember riding with him to White Waltham, to the farewell airshow of the ATA, when it was disbanded. The highlight for me that day was a breathtaking display by Alex Henshaw in a Seafire. In my later life, I had the opportunity of meeting this superb pilot on two occasions.

Painted in oils on canvas. 2003. 450mm x 550mm. Original painting in the collection of Mr G. Turner.

'Just follow the river'

Many times, as I stood on the balcony of the Scout boathouse, overlooking the Thames, I saw American spotter planes, such as this Piper Cub, flashing by just a few feet above the water. Many years later, I learned that the aircraft were shipped to the UK in crates and were then assembled at Grove airfield, near Wantage. Perhaps the pilots collecting them were told "Fly due east to the river, then follow it all the way down to Reading where, if necessary, you can follow the railway wherever you want to go." It seems they just couldn't resist following their instructions very closely indeed.

Painted in oils on canvas. 2004. 600mm x 900mm.

'D-Day memory'

It was the day before my fourteenth birthday, early in the morning when I was on my way to begin my paper round. I was walking past St Paul's church in York Road, Reading when, suddenly, a squadron of American light bombers thundered overhead. They were very low, at just a few hundred feet and the direction in which they were flying suggests they were navigating by following the River Thames. At that time I had seen very few American bombers over Reading and I cannot be absolutely sure they were A20G Douglas 'Havocs' of the US 9th Air Force, as I have shown in this painting. Nevertheless, I well remember, as a fourteen-year-old, thinking that this squadron must be part of something special and it came as no surprise when, later that day, it was announced that D-Day was underway. The thrilling sight and sound of that squadron made such a lasting impression on me that, ever since I took up painting, I knew I had to try and capture it on canvas. I eventually began work early in 2004 on researching the background as it had been at the time and working up the overall composition, without even thinking that, later in the year, it would actually be the 60th anniversary of D-Day. But, somehow, I just couldn't get the painting to work. Twice, I scrapped all my efforts and started again. Somehow, it only began to work as publicity about the official commemoration of D-Day began to build. So, perhaps, this painting was always destined to be completed, signed and dated on 6th June 2004, exactly sixty years after that day I still remember so vividly.

Early in 1945 I had become a student at the Miles Aeronautical Technical School, taking my first steps to becoming an aircraft designer, as I thought then. For some years this had been my youthful ambition, but I must retrace my steps for this part of my story.

I was about twelve when Leslie Howard's film 'The First of the Few', the fictionalised story of Spitfire designer, RJ Mitchell, fired my ambition. From that time, aeroplane designs of all kinds literally poured from my pencil — fighters, bombers, transports and trainers.

Encouraged by his mother, Geoffrey Beckett (aged twelve) sent a design to Miles Aircraft. It was accompanied by (and I still blush to recall it) an excruciating poem likening me to RJ Mitchell.

Shortly afterwards a letter arrived from Miles Aircraft, signed by Don Brown, (assistant to the chief designer), inviting me to visit the factory on a forthcoming Saturday — a working day in the war years, of course. As I was to learn many years later, Don Brown had played a part in the story of Miles Aircraft from its very earliest days and, at the time, was an important figure in the company's design team. Many aviation enthusiasts will remember him as the author of probably the best book about Miles Aircraft, published in 1970.

On that Saturday morning in 1942, Don Brown met me with great courtesy, seriously discussed my design and then took me down into the factory to show me the construction of their Martinet target-towing aircraft, which were then in full production.

The encouragement shown by Don Brown to a twelve-year-old epitomised the company's approach to education. To quote from his later book, they were "convinced that the average youngster has, latent in him, much greater potentialities than he ever gets the opportunity of developing and using".... "students had to be paid a living wage, otherwise the school would be restricted to those who could afford it".... "formal instruction was to be kept to a minimum".... "Let the youngster find out for himself the direction in which his talents lay and then be given the opportunity and facilities for pursuing and developing them".... "encouraged to see a job through from beginning to end, that is to say, draw a component, make it and install it on the actual job".

This philosophy was put into practice in 1943, with the formation of the Miles Aeronautical Technical School (MATS) and, by the summer of 1944, the possibility of gaining a place there was an exciting topic of conversation for many boys at my school in Reading.

Once again, encouraged by my mother, I wrote to Miles Aircraft. This time, I did not include an excruciating poem!

At the culmination of my time at school, despite being some eighteen months younger than the average age of the class, I had passed the Oxford Schools Certificate, with a respectable number of Credits. No doubt influenced by this, I was granted an interview at MATS, even though there was a nominal minimum age of sixteen for students. I was delighted when the headmaster offered me a place at the school the following spring, which would still be a few months before my fifteenth birthday.

Below: The pioneering moving final assembly line at Phillips & Powis in 1939, showing Miles Master I trainers being completed. By 1942, when I was shown around the factory by Don Brown, the later Martinet target-towing aircraft were being built on this line.

He suggested that, in the meantime, it would be useful experience to work in a factory and to study technical drawing at evening classes. At the age of fourteen, working as a 'gofer' in a wartime factory mainly staffed by women, was certainly an experience and an education, although I don't remember it as a particularly academic one!

In the spring of 1945, I again began pedalling from home to Woodley, but now as a first-year student of MATS.

By this time the great days of aircraft production at Woodley had already ended. The important wartime contracts for the Magister, Master and Martinet designs, which had seen almost six thousand aircraft produced by the Miles company, were long since completed.

Another major contract, for three hundred twin-engine, target-towing aircraft known as the Monitor, had been cancelled as the war neared its end. Just seventeen were completed and, later in my time at the school, I well remember the sad sight of them parked around the airfield waiting to be broken up.

However, in those early years after the war, Miles Aircraft faced the future with a great deal more confidence than many other aircraft manufacturers. It appears there had even been talks with two other aircraft manufacturers, Folland and Boulton & Paul, with a view to Miles taking them over. The aim was to increase production capacity and to add more designers experienced in metal aircraft construction.

By then, despite the cancellation of the M52 project, which would have seen Britain fly the world's first supersonic aircraft, Miles had the contract from the Ministry of Aircraft Production for the Marathon airliner, as well as three smaller successful types already selling reasonably well in the private and commercial sectors - the Aerovan, Messenger and Gemini. With Miles's already well established history of innovation, there were, of course, many other designs 'on the drawing board'.

Gemini, Aerovan and Messenger.

After a few months at the school, the very familiarity of seeing aircraft every day had perhaps already begun to erode something of the 'magic' I had felt as a child. I also learned very quickly that designing aircraft was considerably more complex than lying on your back on the cliff top, gaining inspiration from seagulls as, a few years before, the Spitfire's designer, R J Mitchell, had been depicted in the film 'First of the Few'.

Right: At the Miles Aeronautical Technical School, the hangar that would eventually house the Museum of Berkshire Aviation, was where I and other students attempted to build a twin-engine aircraft known as the Venture. In my last year at MATS I particularly remember some of the students who were working towards being 'stressmen', testing it to destruction.

At the airfield the Miles types were seen most frequently, of course. A few Masters, Martinets and Magisters still but, increasingly, Aerovans, Geminis and Messengers. Tiger Moths from the RAF Flying School and the occasional Harvard or Anson were 'regulars', but there was nothing particularly 'exotic'.

However, two particular flying memories stand out, both so unusual that virtually every student at the school stopped whatever they were doing and rushed out to the airfield boundary fence to watch. The first was a visit by a Lancaster bomber, which arrived one day about lunchtime.

For whatever reason the pilot landed — and it was no mean feat to land a Lancaster on Woodley's small grass airfield — he did not intend staying long. Some twenty minutes after arriving he taxied the Lancaster as close as he dared to the eastern boundary fence, close by the school, to prepare for take-off. Unfortunately, this part of the airfield was a wartime extension and had a restricted width. The pilot attempted to make a very tight turn by braking the starboard wheel and revving the two port engines, but the wheel began to dig into the ground and, the more he tried, the deeper the wheel went.

Silence descended as he gave up trying to extricate the aircraft and, later in the afternoon, earth-moving equipment and scaffold planks appeared, the plan obviously being to dig down to the wheel at an angle to form a ramp. Sadly, I missed the final escape. When I arrived the next morning, the unexpected visitor had gone.

The other unusual visitor that excited the whole school was a Vampire, one of the RAF's first jet fighters and certainly the first jet aircraft to appear at Woodley.

Painted in oils on canvas. 2005. 400mm x 500mm. Original painting in the collection of Mr & Mrs J Beckett

'Unexpected Guest'

The Lancaster that spent a longer time than originally intended at Woodley is seen approaching the airfield from the east. In the left foreground can be seen part of the technical school and the windtunnel. Two of the oak trees close to the windtunnel are, nearly sixty years later, in the garden of the house owned by my son, Joe and his family.

During my third year at the technical school an interesting month was spent on secondment to the company's Aerodynamics Department. At that time, flight tests were being carried out on the prototype Miles Marathon airliner. Tests included one for an aborted take-off from a concrete runway, which Woodley airfield never had, therefore an abandoned wartime base near Thame was taken over for the day. An Aerovan was used to transport cameras and other equipment, plus a few department personnel — including me! It was the very first time I had ever flown. I remember the pilot was 'Red' Esler who sadly lost his life some years later, testing one of the experimental aircraft of the 1950s — a Handley Page one, I think.

The Aerodynamics Department was situated close to the Experimental Department and, one day when passing the door, I caught a glimpse of something that looked very exciting. However, as unauthorised personnel were not supposed to even look in this most hallowed place, I didn't dare ask what it was. Many years later, I learned it was the wooden mock-up of the legendary Miles M52, which would have been the world's very first supersonic aircraft — if the Government hadn't cancelled the contract in 1946.

In retrospect, joining MATS at the age I did was not a success. I know now I was far too immature and, as time went on, I couldn't really handle the vast differences in educational styles between the regimentation of an old-fashioned war-time state school and the unique self-motivated application needed at the technical school.

On the positive side, I had gained an insight into aerodynamics and stress calculations and built up practical experience of woodworking, sheet-metal working, machine shop practice and engine maintenance. However, my main interest centred around the drawing office and, by my final year, I was well on the way to becoming a competent design draughtsman.

However, in the late summer of 1947, there came the completely unexpected announcement that Miles Aircraft had been forced to cease trading. I confess I have no recollection of my personal feelings at that time, even though the collapse of the company I seemed to have known and loved all my life was sending shock waves around the local area.

Above: The prototype Marathon. In 1947, I played a miniscule part in its flight-testing programme.

Below: Part of the wooden mock-up of the legendary Miles M52, that I guiltily glimpsed in 1947.

It was some years before details of the collapse began to emerge and, by then, I was working in a different industry and Miles was just one of the many British aviation companies being consigned to the dustbin of history by politicians of the day.

It would be another forty years or so before, with a considerable amount of business experience behind me, I looked at the details of the Miles collapse and, even over that span of time, a rather unsavoury 'odour' still lingered.

Back in 1947, to many students of the technical school, the main impact of the collapse was the termination of our 'employment' by Miles Aircraft, although we were informed that we would be allowed to complete our courses — without pay — under the banner of the embryo Reading Technical College. My own future at the school must have been in doubt, until my brother Leslie offered to make good the meagre contribution to the family income that I had been making.

For the following year or so life at the school continued much as before and, in the spring of 1948, I was, perhaps unwisely, entered for the first stage examinations for Associate Fellowship of the Royal Aeronautical Society. I failed miserably.

I was just eighteen and it was time to start earning a living.

At the time, the British aircraft industry in other parts of the country didn't seem to offer a particularly glittering future for a barely experienced draughtsman, although many MATS students of my time — no doubt much more academic than me — did manage to carve out successful careers in aviation, both in the UK and abroad. On the local job market, however, the demise of Miles Aircraft still created many problems.

For a very short time in the summer of 1948 — and for the only time in the near fifty-year career that followed — I was a small part of the unemployment statistics.

The prospect of National Service had beckoned of course and, I suppose inevitably, I had opted for the RAF. Not in a flying job, even if I could have got one, but as an electrical mechanic, hoping to catch up on what I perceived as a gap in my technical education.

Judging by the experience of many of my friends, it is probable that I would have been sent into the Army instead, as a cook or a hairdresser! However, an injury to my arm at birth meant that I couldn't hold a rifle according to King's Regulations. So I never did get the chance to learn cooking or anything else at the Government's expense.

In September 1948 I obtained a job as a draughtsman in a Reading-based firm specialising in the design and manufacture of tubular structures. My immediate boss encouraged me to continue studying and to enrol at Reading Technical College.

It was to be many years before Reading Technical College boasted an actual building of its own and, of course, at that time there was no such thing as day-release schemes or company sponsorships. For three evenings each week, students like me crammed into children's desks at various schools around the town. At least my academic efforts at MATS gave me a flying start and, in two years, I obtained the ONC in Mechanical Engineering.

I was marked highly in the final examinations and my tutors were keen for me to go on to the Higher National Certificate, but — and it was a very big but — there were no facilities to study to this level in the Reading area. It meant a fifty-mile round trip to either Oxford or Kingston, at your own expense, for three evenings each week for two years. By public transport it was impossible and I know of only one of my contemporaries, with his own motorcycle, who was able to gain the Higher National Certificate.

By this time, aged twenty-two, I was beginning to question my role as a design draughtsman and having, on a number of occasions, used perspective drawings for assembly instructions of structures I had designed, I began to consider a move into technical illustration.

To me, this increasingly looked like an interesting job. In fact, when I was about fourteen, I well remember being fascinated by a cut-away illustration of a Zundapp motorcycle engine in one of Leslie's books. So, perhaps, I was always destined to be a technical illustrator. Letters to a number of engineering companies in the local area eventually led to an offer from Handley Page, who had taken over the aviation interests of Miles Aircraft. Once again, I set out to Woodley — this time, to be a technical illustrator.

The Miles Marathon had become the Handley Page (Reading) HPR1. Some went into airline service, but most were being converted to navigation trainers for the RAF. Much of my work for the first year or so was producing illustrations for instruction books and maintenance manuals for the RAF conversion of the HPR1.

Later, I produced the very first perspective illustrations of the HPR3 Herald - the original version with four Alvis Leonides radial piston engines. Even then, in the very early stages of design, many people within the company felt it should be designed around the already proven Dart turbo-prop engines fitted many years later.

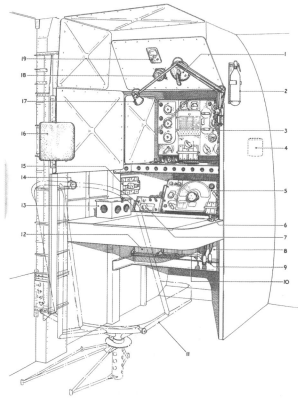

FIG 2 —WIRELESS OPERATOR'S STATION.

Above: One of the many illustrations that I produced for instruction manuals for the Handley Page HPR I Marathon.

At that time the 'Mecca' for any aspiring illustrator was a job with either of the two publishers of technical magazines, Temple Press and Illiffe. Within two years of first becoming an illustrator, I applied to both publishers and, soon afterwards, became one of the youngest staff artists with Temple Press. It was the first of many years I spent commuting daily from Berkshire into London. It was also the start of one of the most interesting - but relatively poorly paid - periods of my life.

Certainly, Temple Press and, probably, Illiffe too, had worked for many years on the principle that, because the job was so interesting, they really didn't have to pay their artists much money.

Working for all of the magazines published by the company, which included 'Motor Cycling', 'Motor', 'Commercial Motor', 'Motor Boat and Yachting', 'Farm Mechanisation', 'Nuclear Engineering', 'Plastics' and, of course, 'Aeroplane', my own engineering horizons expanded quickly.

For 'Aeroplane', I twice visited Shoreham, where the Miles brothers had established a new business and were building their typically advanced-for-its-time jet trainer, the Student. I produced a number of illustrations and then a full cut-away drawing.

The Student prototype later flew successfully, but no Air Ministry orders were secured and, later, it was sold to a private owner. In the late '80s, more than thirty years after it first flew, it appeared at various airshows but was, unfortunately, badly damaged in an accident. As I write, the Student now resides at the Museum of Berkshire Aviation where it is being rebuilt to static display standards.

In the mid-1950s, with my first marriage forcing me to think more of salary than job interest, I moved to a commercial technical publications studio in Maidenhead. Although I hadn't anticipated doing so, over the next few years, I handled even more interesting and challenging illustration projects and my engineering and business horizons expanded still further. Major illustration projects included a series of power stations for ICI, the new Bessemer plant at the Port Talbot steelworks for British Steel and, for Orient Lines, the first liner *Oriana*.

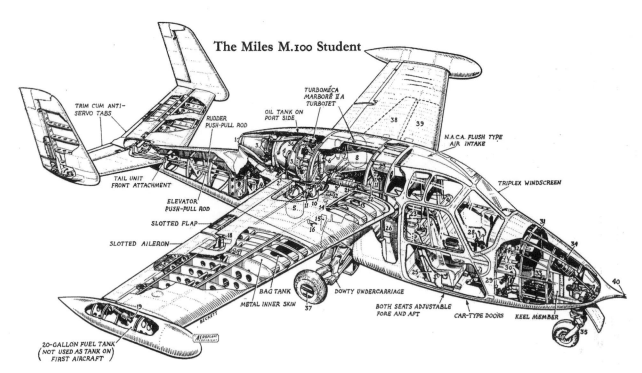

The Miles M.100 Student

Above and Right: On my first visit to Shoreham I produced a number of drawings showing design details of the Miles Student, such as the one on the right, which were published in Aeroplane magazine. Some months later, I returned to produce the full cutaway illustration of this very interesting aircraft shown above.

By the early 1960s my career had developed into publicity management and then account management in a major London advertising agency.

By the late 1960s I was in executive positions with two London-based major construction industry groups, responsible for advertising, printwork, exhibitions and all aspects of PR.

In 1975 I created my own advertising, design and PR consultancy, later known as The Publicity Mill, which remained the core of my working life until my retirement in 1996.

My direct involvement with the aviation industry had begun and ended with Miles Aircraft. The 1957 cut-away drawing of the Miles Student for 'Aeroplane' proved to be my 'swansong'.

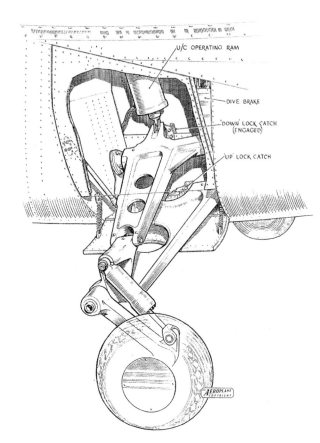

For well over twenty years, aviation played very little part in my life, other than as an occasional passenger. I admit I still felt something of a 'buzz' when I went to an airport but, if I had seen the aircraft flying above me, I doubt I would have recognised most of the ones I flew in. One exception, of course, was the Dart Herald, in which I flew a number of times as a passenger.

In my private life, airshows were an occasional day out, particularly when my children were young. Like everyone else, I gasped at the 'Red Arrows', was awestruck at the first sight of Concorde and marvelled at the Harrier, but most modern aircraft left me relatively uninspired. It was only when the 'rebuild and replica' movement began to gain pace and one could see aircraft from the '20s and '30s flying again, that something of the old 'magic' I had felt as a child returned.

My brother Gerry, who had shown only limited interest in aviation in his younger days, joined the Royal Observer Corps in the late 1960s and remained involved until they were disbanded in the late 1980s. Despite the Corps' changed role during the Cold War years, individual members had retained something of their original interests. A good relationship was maintained with local RAF stations and Gerry enjoyed many interesting flights in service aircraft. He certainly knew more than I did about service and civilian aircraft of the last thirty years.

By the early 1980s, my own slightly renewed interest in aviation was almost entirely nostalgic, particularly leaning towards the '20s and '30s, as the pictures on my office wall testified!

I did have one brief flirtation with flying around that time, when I was persuaded to help an aerobatic team obtain sponsorship. It cost my company a lot more money than I was able to obtain for them, but an aerobatic flight in one of their Pitts Specials, when I actually handled the controls, remains one of the highlights of my 'flying career'.

Pitts Special

However, my business activities were generally very demanding and, even at the level of a hobby, aviation played no real part in my life.

But that was about to change.

I suppose it began when friends who had lived for many years within a few hundred yards of the old Woodley airfield, proved woefully ignorant of its history. Was this typical of most local people? To me, it wasn't just local history, it was also my personal history. No matter how small a part I had played, I was actually a part of Woodley's aviation history. It was then that I first began to think I should record it in some way.

Then, sometime in 1982, I found out that I was not alone in my interest in local aviation history. My wife, Valerie, came home from Reading having seen a poster from the Berkshire Aviation Group, advertising a talk about Miles Aircraft by someone she thought was called Don Brown. I had never heard of the Berkshire Aviation Group but, obviously, the name Don Brown instantly took me back forty years.

It was good to meet Don Brown again after so many years, even if, not surprisingly, he didn't remember the twelve-year-old boy he had inspired. At the meeting, I was also very happy to meet a few of my old MATS colleagues again.

However, Valerie and I moved house soon after and, before really getting to know them, I lost contact with the Berkshire Aviation Group.

A few months later my company staff gave me a present to mark the purchase of our own premises. It was the book of Michael Turner's excellent paintings of the RAF's aircraft in service from 1918. I turned the pages eagerly to see how he had treated the Miles Magister and Master - and was dismayed to find that, despite their importance to the RAF, particularly in the war years, neither was included.

Thus it was that, in 1984, I first began to think about recording local aviation history by a series of paintings.

However, it would be some twelve years before I took up my brushes to begin. I was side-tracked by an aviation museum, the demands of my business and, finally, by the desperate times as the recession of the early '90s hit me hard.

As I suppose such things sometimes do, the idea of a local museum initially took flight over a couple of beers. In the case of the Museum of Berkshire Aviation, it was in my lounge at home, when Julian Temple and I first swapped ideas in May 1985.

Since its inception, certain members of the Berkshire Aviation Group (BAG) had been collecting various artifacts relevant to Miles Aircraft. However, no really practical ideas seemed to have emerged about what to do with them.

Julian Temple had been one of the founder members of the Berkshire Aviation Group, and its first chairman, when he was an archaeological student at Reading University. Following a post-graduate year at the Ironbridge Museum, he had returned to Reading and had been commissioned by the Adwest Group - which had developed out of Miles Aircraft's activities with electric actuators - to write a book about Woodley airfield and the various companies it had spawned.

He interviewed as many people as he could find who had been involved with Woodley airfield and someone I had once met, who remembered I had worked there, had given him my name. For nostalgic reasons I chose to meet Julian at the Adwest head office at Woodley and found him closeted in a small office a few yards from where I had first met Don Brown more than forty years before.

Right: The Adwest main office in Headley Road, Woodley, originally built as the Miles Aircraft headquarters.

Julian was surrounded by archive material such as photographs, drawings and press-cuttings that I would have thought had been lost years before. Pride of place went to a large parcel of blueprints and dyeline prints of the original drawings of the Miles Hawks which first flew between 1933 and 1935 - many of them drawn by F G Miles and his wife, Blossom. There was also a full set of drawings of the Blackburn Cirrus engine. These parcels had been in the vaults of Barclays Bank, Reading since 1935!

Above: The parcels of fifty-year-old Miles' prints as I first saw them in Julian Temple's office in 1985.

It was on that day in Julian's office, when I first handled those fifty-year-old blueprints and read some of the contemporary press-cuttings, that my slowly reviving interest in aviation was firmly set on its course. I was hooked on aviation again – at least, local aviation history. Julian was relieved to find someone who could interpret the drawings and I agreed to identify and catalogue them.

It was when he delivered all thirteen hundred of the prints to my home a few days later, over a couple of beers, we kicked around the first ideas about a local aviation museum.

During his time with Adwest, Julian arranged various 'get-togethers' of old Miles people, sometimes including a fly-past of the few Miles aircraft still flying. I got more involved in BAG activities by improving their display of photographs and other items.

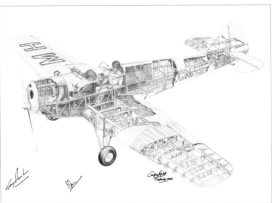

Left and below: The work I put into cataloguing the fifty-year-old prints enabled me to produce definitive cutaway illustrations of the Miles Hawk (left) and the Miles Hawk Major (below) that were both published as high quality posters. The original Hawk drawing was signed by George Miles and Don Brown at one of the 'get-togethers' in 1985. The Hawk Major drawing was signed just by George Miles a few weeks later when I met him in Sussex.

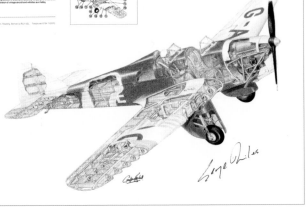

Below: About this time I also had the idea of producing 3-view general arrangement drawings in colour of all the Miles designs. Having completed the first four, it was another project abandoned in favour of the museum.

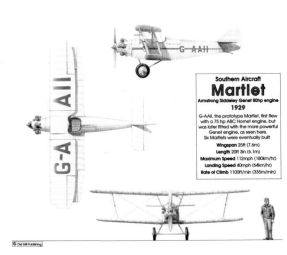

Suddenly, our ideas about a local aviation museum were given a firm focus, when Adwest said BAG could have an old hangar. Indeed, the hangar itself was of real historic interest – it had originally been part of the Miles Aeronautical Technical School. In reality, only the steel framework would be able to be used. The original cladding was beyond rescue and, since much of it was asbestos, it required special disposal.

Already, perhaps, I should have anticipated the demands the museum project would eventually make upon my already busy life but, as I have already said, I was hooked.

An even greater problem was the fact that the hangar was due to be demolished in a year or so, as the housing developments slowly swallowing up the old airfield spread ever further. If it was ever to be used again, it would require careful dismantling, refurbishment and skilful re-assembly. Much more importantly, for ideas about a museum to become a reality, we needed a new site for the hangar — and everyone involved felt it should be as close to the old Woodley airfield as possible.

So began my long involvement with Wokingham District Council.

I put together one of our 'improved' displays and acted as 'anchorman' when BAG members made the first presentation to the Council, to demonstrate the importance of local aviation history. About this time, one of the Council officers said they wished they had known us before all the roads on the new airfield housing estate were named—most of them after aircraft and aviation personalities that had nothing to do with Woodley airfield or, indeed, anything to do with Berkshire.

Not long after this presentation we were invited to discuss our requirements with the Council's recreation and amenities officer, Gordon Bendall, who suggested we might consider a Council-owned site, adjacent to what had been the southern boundary of the airfield.

Ironically perhaps, it was close to the place to which I had walked as a five-year-old, without seeing a single aeroplane! By the 1980s, it was part of a little used car park, on land that included old filled—in sewage beds.

Now, the BAG 'Museum Committee' had to begin to think very seriously about all the implications of creating an aviation museum. However, from its very first meeting, it was obvious that, apart from my own, real business experience was in short supply.

Below: The hangar that had originally formed part of the Miles Aeronautical Technical School, as it was given to the Berkshire Aviation Group in 1986. Other MATS buildings can also be seen.

Below: BAG members soon transported their Miles artefacts to the derelict hangar, one of the first being this Messenger wing.

I should perhaps make it clear at this point that, by choice, I am not a 'committee man'. For much of my working life I had, by the very nature of the job, been a 'loner'. Sadly, even in my later executive roles, I had often found the old maxim to be true— 'if you want a job done properly, do it yourself'.

I had also learned that 'playing politics', as one often had to do in bigger companies, was not something I enjoyed or thrived on. There's another saying about 'not suffering fools gladly'. That's me too, I'm afraid.

That early museum committee proved no different from others I had known. At the first meeting it was agreed we would individually prepare ideas for an 'action plan' to be presented at the next meeting. At the next meeting, my ideas were the only ones on the table. Perhaps I should have been warned but, as I said before, I was hooked on the idea of a museum.

In those early days, of course, the task was to 'market' the concept of a museum and that fell well within the scope of my main professional experience. Thus it was that, from the very beginning, the Museum of Berkshire Aviation became a 'client' of my own company, The Publicity Mill — albeit a non-paying one. Following some friendly 'arm-twisting' on my part, a number of my clients and suppliers also played their part.

Using my company resources, I produced a 'presentation brochure' for the proposed museum. A client's finance director helped me with the ten-year business plan it incorporated. I had also used my activities in the Reading Chamber of Commerce to secure inclusion in the brochure of Barclays as bankers and KMPG as auditors.

The brochure also included a list of BAG members with the relevant experience to create an aviation museum. I was impressed to learn that, as well as Julian, there were three others who had carried out historic aviation research and had their material published. This brochure was the basis of the group's first official request to Wokingham District Council for use of their site for an aviation museum. Later, it was the core of a presentation pack I sent to dozens of companies, both local and national, as well as every other local authority in Berkshire, in the hope of winning sponsorship.

Above: The design of the museum logo included many of the important elements in Berkshire's aviation heritage. In addition to the RAF roundel, there is the Star of the American Army Air Corps and the badge of the Air Transport Auxiliary.
The Hawk was the logo of Miles Aircraft and the yellow background was the colour for training aircraft, for which they were best known.
The different horizontal stripes include the black and white stripes painted on all D-Day aircraft, the red and yellow stripes of the original Reading Aero Club flag and the blue and gold stripes to represent the contribution to naval flying made by Fairey Aviation at White Waltham.
The curved outline reflects the elliptical shape of the Spitfire wing and commemorates the important part Berkshire played in production of this historic aircraft.

Below: Part of the original brochure promoting the concept of an aviation museum at Woodley.

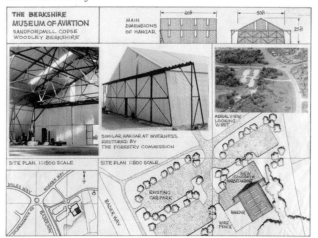

I designed a logo for the museum and 'persuaded' friendly printers to provide letterheads and leaflets without charge. Another client introduced me to the directors of a specialist construction company that was eventually to handle all the work on the hangar framework.

In addition to using my personal skills and company resources, the fact that I could, if I chose, use at least some of my time during the 'working week' was also a vital factor in the years of creating the museum. Increasingly, I met with other professional people, such as Council officers or the staff of potential sponsors, who were just carrying out their normal 9—5 job.

For the first year or so, Julian Temple was in a position to meet some of these demands. However, soon after his contract for the Adwest book was completed, he obtained employment as curator of aircraft with the developing Brooklands Museum. There would have been an obvious conflict of interests and he resigned from the BAG Museum Committee, although he kept an interest in our activities for some time. From that time on, for the next three years or so, I was, to all intents and purposes, on my own in pursuing Berkshire's aviation museum project.

I visited Brooklands Museum with Julian soon after his appointment and, when one considered its potential, with both its motoring and aviation heritage, I was not impressed. It had been in existence, I think, for almost five years, supported by the local council and including the employment of a full-time curator and support staff. However, to me, it was still so far from being a real museum that I was surprised. A 'Friends of Brooklands' group had existed for many years but, it appeared to me, its impact on the museum had been negligible.

Julian's appointment followed the end of local authority support and the establishment of the museum as a charitable trust, with the well known businessman, Sir Peter Masefield, as cp;hairman. The change at the Brooklands Museum under his dynamic leadership was to particularly influence my thinking about Berkshire's aviation museum in the coming years.

At every one of the BAG monthly meetings I reported on progress or, for the first year or two, lack of progress on the museum project.

Appeals to BAG members, particularly in fundraising, produced a couple of 'five – minute wonders', but that task too was soon back in my lap. Nevertheless, sometime later, when the hangar was about to be rebuilt on its new site, I was told by one member, Doug Rough, who hadn't actually been to many early meetings, that I had "kept things too close to my chest". Surprisingly, perhaps, we became, and still are, very good friends.

Looking back, perhaps my greatest contribution in those early days was to pass on my enthusiasm and dedication for the idea of an aviation museum to Gordon Bendall of Wokingham DC with whom I developed a strong bond.

Later, as the project developed, I also worked with other officers employed by the Council. Certainly, a mutual respect developed and, when they were faced with organising an exhibition at the official opening of the new Civic Offices in Wokingham, they turned to me to 'mastermind' and construct it.

It may sound arrogant, but it is a simple fact that, at any time in the late 1980s, if either Gordon Bendall or I had walked away from the project, the Museum of Berkshire Aviation would certainly not exist today. Sadly, having done far more than anyone else in Wokingham District Council to create the museum, Gordon never received the recognition he so richly deserved. Just a few days after the reconstruction of the hangar was completed, he was made redundant.

Did the frustrations encountered in those early years make me feel like giving up? You bet they did! But I can be an obstinate so-and-so when I really believe in something.

From, I think, my third meeting with Gordon Bendall back in 1986, through no fault of his, I was sent on a six-month-long 'wild goose chase'. When he presented the BAG 'presentation pack' to a Council meeting, a member suggested that a different site at Woodley should be considered. This site was not owned by the Council and so I was presented with additional problems.

When I did visit this site a short time later, it clearly had far more potential than the car-park site Gordon had first suggested. Adjacent to the original Falcon Hotel, with its close links to the history of Woodley and its airfield, in recent years the new site had been used as a car repair yard. There was room for the hangar to be rebuilt and there were also a number of small buildings that could prove useful.

Courage Brewery owned the whole site, although the hotel building had been leased as a rather notorious nightclub. With the advance of the new housing estates across the old airfield, the already vociferous complaints from local residents about the noise and other problems caused by the nightclub were bound to grow.

I reckoned that, if Courage leased the adjacent site for the museum and returned the Falcon to something like its pre-war character, it could be a real money-spinner for all concerned.

I redesigned the 'presentation pack' to incorporate the new site and set out to try and find whoever would be responsible for this sort of project within Courage. This task was made even more difficult by the fact that, within days of me starting in this new direction, Courage was suddenly being taken over by the giant Australian brewer, Fosters.

After months of contact, Courage declined my proposals, the reason given being that revoking the lease on the old Falcon would be too difficult. In fact, the night club soon closed and the Falcon, which many in BAG believed should be a 'listed' building, remained empty for years, was continually vandalised and was eventually burned down.

It was more than six months after the first suggestion from Gordon Bendall to look at the Falcon site that I went back to him to admit failure with Courage and ask if we could pursue the possibility of using the original site.

The 'presentation pack' was returned to its original form to include details of the Council-owned site and I began sending it to every local and national company that could possibly be interested in sponsorship, plus, as previously mentioned, all the other local authorities in Berkshire.

I became BAG's representative with the Association of Independent Museums and the Council for Museums in Berkshire. I presented the case for an aviation museum at every opportunity and began to give talks to any local organisation that expressed an interest in Berkshire's aviation heritage.

Gordon and I continued to meet occasionally for an after-work drink but, over the months that followed, I had to admit to him that, despite expressions of interest in the project and many congratulations on the quality of the presentation by a number of potential sponsors, my fundraising efforts were indeed fruitless.

Of course, Gordon and I had already discussed the fact that, even though Adwest had given the old hangar to the Berkshire Aviation Group, its eventual erection on Council land would, effectively, transfer ownership to the Council and, indeed, provide it with a potentially valuable asset.

The original 'Falcon Hotel', soon after it was opened at Reading Aerodrome in 1937.

The new housing developments were creeping ever closer to the old hangar and BAG was under pressure to dismantle it. There was, of course, the additional problem of its asbestos cladding that would need professional removal and disposal.

It was then that Gordon made his first move to provide funds for the Museum project, out of the budget he personally controlled. This allowed me to instruct the structural engineering company I had found to carry out the dismantling of the old hangar, and its directors also agreed to store the dismantled framework at their site in Hampshire, free of charge.

In the meantime, planning permission was sought for a museum to be built on the site. The planning rules were such that the application had to be in my name, not the BAG.

When the consent was granted, I was told that members of the Planning Committee wanted the hangar to be camouflaged so that it did not 'intrude' on the surroundings. Obviously they had not grasped the fact that camouflage was intended to be effective from a few thousand feet in the air, not from ground level. Gordon and I agreed that a dark green cladding would eventually satisfy the committee.

By now, Gordon was asking me to try and establish the final costs of the project. There were three main elements. The cost of refurbishing and re-building the framework was easily obtained from the structural engineering company.

The cost of the foundations and flooring presented me with a problem. Although, thanks to Julian Temple, I had a small wartime print showing the ground-fixing for the Robins-type hangar, I really needed a professional engineer to get involved. A good friend of mine, Rod Hayes, who had his own business, was ideal for the project but, with the amount of time it would involve, not to mention implications such as professional indemnity, he would need to charge a fee. Once again, Gordon agreed to cover the cost and, soon after, we were able to proceed with the groundwork design and eventually obtain quotes for its construction.

With the third main cost element – the hangar cladding - I was able to claim my first sponsorship success, apart from Gordon Bendall's vital contributions, of course.

An early wartime photograph of the airfield at Woodley. Impressions of country lanes and large trees were painted on the grass. Later, the large hangars were painted black and covered in camouflage netting.

The eventual site of the museum is about here.

Below: The original wartime Robins hangar foundation plan from which, in 1990, the engineer designed the new foundations and floor.

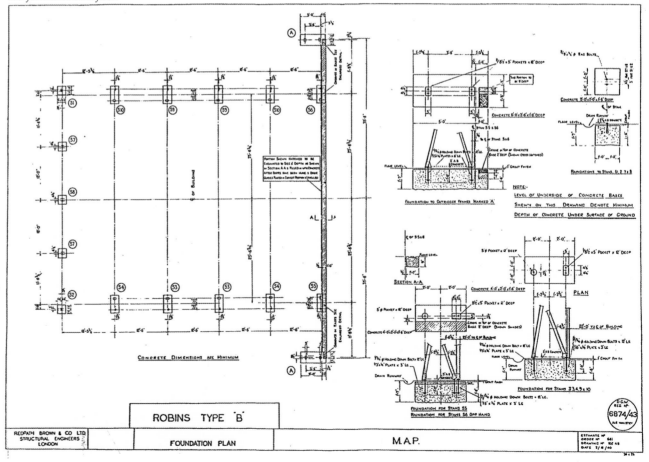

Redpath Brown, the original designers and builders of the Robins-type hangar, had, following nationalisation, become part of British Steel. The colour-coated cladding required for the hangar was a modern-day product of British Steel. I contacted their PR Department to see if they were interested in getting involved in the re-building of part of their own history and received an enthusiastic response.

Eventually, British Steel provided all the cladding at cost price and provided introductions to three contractors from whom I obtained competitive quotations for the cladding design and installation. The final cost I presented to Gordon Bendall was £60,000. In view of some uncertainty regarding the ground conditions, the engineer suggested a 10% contingency should be allowed

In the meantime, another organisation – the Air Training Corps – had been given permission to use the car park site for a headquarters building, close to the area planned for the hangar. The logic behind the Council decision was obvious but it was galling to see the speed at which the ATC project proceeded – thanks to its funding by the Ministry of Defence.

However, the problem of funding for the museum hangar project was also about to reach a dramatic conclusion.

In the spring of 1990 I was delighted when Gordon Bendall told me that he was proposing to the Council that BAG should be given a loan of £60,000. Soon after, when it was realised that, if BAG employed the various contractors, it would be unable to reclaim VAT, Gordon was the instigator in a number of the Council officers putting together a 'museum finance package' in what he claimed was a record time for any Council business – just two weeks until the Council's Recreation Committee 'rubber—stamped' the package.

For our part, BAG was to enter into a rental agreement, with an initial six-year rent free period. We also had to cover the £6,000 contingency sum.

Right: At the ceremony to officially hand over the museum site to the contractors, the chair of the Recreation Committee and the chairman of the main contractors are signing the contract. I am standing third from the right, with RBAS members, Doug Rough (extreme right) and Jean Fostekew (seated extreme right). Gordon Bendall, who played such an important part in creating the museum, is standing second from left, with other officers of Wokingham DC also in the back row..

I remember going along to the next monthly BAG meeting and making my report along the lines of Martin Luther King's famous 'I have a dream' speech. By then, the Berkshire Aviation Group had changed its name to the Royal Berkshire Aviation Society (RBAS) — just one of a number of changes in the preceding months as some of the more dynamic members finally began to believe that the museum project I had reported on month after month could actually come to fruition.

The main change, from my own point of view, was that I was joined in a Museum Management Committee by three or four members whose potentially useful experience complemented my own and whose enthusiasm seemed to equal mine. The first proof of this commitment came when the newly elected Committee chairman, Doug Rough, undertook to find enough members to guarantee the required £6,000 contingency fund. In fact, in just a week or so, twelve members, including me, provided funds to cover the sum.

It was on June 7th 1990, by coincidence my 60th birthday, when a ceremony was held at the Wokingham DC offices to officially hand over the site to the contractors. I was particularly happy that it featured, not only some of our museum Management Committee but also the Council Officers who had really ensured the success of our project. So often, on such occasions, the efforts of the Council's 'professionals' are relegated to the sidelines by the more 'public faces' of the Council.

My own workload now increased considerably as I took on the role of 'clerk of the works', liaising with the construction professionals — the engineer, and the three different contracting companies. Then, almost as soon as construction work began, we ran into a major problem. The ground where the hangar foundations were being excavated was found to contain too high a proportion of low-grade material used to infill the original sewage beds. Although we had known they were there, we had been unable to locate their exact location.

There was no alternative but to remove all the unsatisfactory material and replace it with compacted high-grade stone. With site-time being a major part of any contractor's cost, they had already removed the first lorry-load of waste from the site when, just before I was due to leave for work, I learned of the problem.

I was horrified when my engineer friend told me the estimated cost - the stone alone would virtually exhaust our £6,000 contingency. In addition, bringing in lorries to remove the waste, as well as its disposal charges, would double the cost.

There was nothing I could do about the stone, but I thought I could save the other costs and I ordered the removal work to stop. A telephone call to the relevant Wokingham DC planning officer, who I had got to know well, led to us meeting on the site within an hour.

We agreed to a redistribution of the waste-soil to form embankments around the site, which were later planted with shrubs and small trees. Construction work was underway again half an hour later. From then on, construction work continued without major problems.

With the hangar construction underway, Gordon Bendall suddenly threw another problem at me. How would the museum and the ATC develop the whole 'car park' site, if given the chance? Could I find out what the ATC would like and report back in time for a Recreation Committee meeting in three days time.

Over the years, the challenge presented by the re-building of the hangar alone had excluded any thoughts to its surroundings. Of course, with other BAG members, I had discussed what aircraft might be available to display at a Berkshire museum. But, what would we like to include on an enlarged site? Indeed, what would actually be feasible to do to the site itself?

A telephone call to the ATC's commanding officer revealed their surprisingly modest requirements. Just a concrete parade-ground in front of their building and a part-buried shooting range behind. However, I knew, even if it wasn't one of *their* main priorities, that the ATC had 'first call' on unwanted RAF aircraft!

The same day, I walked around the whole site, looking at it again but, this time, with a 'different eye'. That evening, armed with a site plan, a large drawing pad, pencils and cups of coffee, I thought about what might be done. The four small car parks included in the site were approached by a driveway across unused rough ground. Each car park was at a different level and this presented both a problem and, I realised, an opportunity.

My thoughts went back to the early morning meeting with the planning officer. Soon, a plan began to evolve using excavation to provide a large area for a hardstanding in front of the hangar and re-distribution of the soil to provide new car parks and embankments to screen the site. I was surprised when I realised that, with the site 'opened up' in this way, there was room for another hangar-like building, at least 50% larger than the hangar we were re-building.

I produced a drawing showing the plan of the enlarged site, together with elevations of the changed levels. Gordon Bendall presented it at his meeting and, whilst it impressed the Council members on the committee, it seems few of them really understood it. That was why, when we met a few days later, Gordon asked "could we produce a model?"

Luckily, a relatively new member of RBAS, John Kite, was a highly skilled modeller, so we tackled the job together. Using techniques that I employed years before when I built a model railway layout for my boys, I did the 'landscaping', while John produced metal scale models of three aircraft that were added as 'outside exhibits'. One of these was of a Handley Page Herald and, by then, a number of RBAS members were negotiating to obtain a particularly historic one for eventual re-building and display at the museum.

Above: The model I made with the invaluable help of John Kite. We hoped it would demonstrate the possible development of the museum site to both Wokingham District Council and various potential commercial sponsors.

The model was complemented by coloured drawings that I produced to show the possible layout inside the hangar. With this 'package' I hoped that anyone, particularly potential sponsors, could see what might be achieved within the finished museum.

Since my first presentation about the museum, some four years earlier, I had given many others, to almost anyone who would listen. It usually brought in a small donation to the funds. Following a 'Round Table' lunchtime talk, a local businessman, Mike Webb, who I had known for twenty years, offered to help.

The main services — electricity, water and drainage — had been brought to the site as part of the groundwork contract. However, the installation of lighting and electrical power inside the hangar was going to be required quickly once construction was completed. When I went to see Mike Webb, he undertook to pay for an electrician he used to supply and install our basic electrical needs. It was another important sponsorship success.

Towards the end of 1990, reconstruction of the main hangar shell was complete and, early in 1991, there was a ceremony on site, when representatives of Wokingham DC officially handed over the keys of the hangar to the Museum Management Committee.

Obviously, before the hangar could be thought of as anything like a museum, a lot more hard work — and money — would be required.

However, I hoped that my virtually solo performance as creator of the museum, was at last completed. Some relief from the responsibilities could not come too soon, because the pressure on my business life was increasing by the day. The nation-wide recession of the early '90s was biting deeper and deeper and, for Valerie and me, the future was more and more uncertain and worrying.

Re-building the Hangar

Above: The new foundations are to a much higher standard than the original Robins design.

Above: I always knew it would require real professionals to rebuild the hangar properly.

Above: A small group of RBAS members spent a weekend painting the completed structure.

Above: Unlike the original Robins hangar, a concrete raft was laid as part of the groundworks contract. The nearly completed ATC building can be seen in the background.

Above: With the right equipment and a skilled construction team, the steelwork contractor soon completed the assembly of the hangar structure.

Above: In its new life, the hangar is insulated to modern industrial building standards.

Above: RBAS members brought their Miles Magister back to Woodley, where it was built, as soon as the hangar was completed. Thanks to Julian Temple, it had been stored at Brooklands Museum since 1986.

Above: The new cladding has two skins of colour-coated steel and, thanks to British Steel, it was designed and constructed by a specialist contractor.

Above: I was included in one of the photographs taken by British Steel.

Before going on to tell how my personal hopes and dreams for the Museum of Berkshire Aviation were eventually eroded, I should perhaps put the whole eight years of my involvement into context with my work and other aspects of my life.

When I first met Julian Temple in 1985, I had been running my company for ten years. I had established it as the first company in Reading — and probably in the whole of Berkshire — to offer clients a total package of marketing services, namely advertising, PR and design.

Despite problems at various times, the company had proved profitable enough to allow the setting-up of my personal pension scheme and, just the previous year, for the first time, the purchase of premises – an attractive old water mill. I personally owned the property and its eventual sale was aimed to be the 'icing on the cake' for my retirement fund.

Essentially, the only thing my company ever sold was a person's time and skills and, as such, I was always the main 'breadwinner'. Over the years I was supported by a small back-up team whose loyalty is demonstrated by their average length of service of around ten years. I had employed other PR and design 'breadwinners' at various times without much success. Some, of whom I had high hopes, were tempted by 'greener grass'. Others, I am sorry to say, did not have the integrity to match their financial ambitions. I was presented with just such a problem on the very day we moved to our new premises.

Nevertheless, by 1985, The Publicity Mill - as my company was now known - was 'on a roll' and, somehow, for the next two years, I managed to keep 'six balls in the air' week after week. It was the most profitable time I had known , but I do not know how much longer I could have continued at that pace.

The business was always reckoned to be a 'young man's game' and I was already in my mid-fifties. Despite previous disappointments, I still thought I had to bring in younger, experienced 'breadwinners' who, with my existing back-up team, could carry the company on after my retirement. So began a sometimes hopeful, often frustrating four-year period when I employed five different senior design and PR 'breadwinners'.

Only two made any real contribution to even balance their salary costs and, after two sackings, another expensive defection and two mutually agreed departures, the attack on the company's profitability was near fatal.

Early in 1989, an approach by an acquaintance - the owner of a local advertising agency - led to discussions about merging our businesses at the Mill. Eventually nothing came of it, but it did cause me to investigate the possibility of building an extension to the Mill and I applied for planning consent. The value put on the Mill at that time absolutely amazed me and, even allowing for the cost of expansion and other improvements when we first moved in, if I had sold at that time, I would have easily doubled my money in just five years.

Some work of The Publicity Mill

1. Many projects were carried out for Reading Transport, including the livery design of their new buses.

2. Brochure and advertisement campaign for Marconi, a major contract gained by personal recommendation of an existing client. Marconi was the largest company for which I undertook work.

3. Brochure package for Victa - one of many projects for this Australian company, which was an important client for some seven years.

4. Many projects were carried out for Reading Borough Council. The brochure on the right was designed especially for the visit to Reading by HM The Queen and Prince Philip.

5. A major project for Trentham Construction was the concept, design and production of this comprehensive brochure package.

The merger discussions and the value of the mill perhaps brought a change to my thinking, although I was concerned about the future of my loyal back-up staff, who were all some years younger than me.

The loss of a major fee-paying client was followed by a costly defection by my PR member of staff and it all added to the financial pressures. I was still heavily involved with the fee-paying clients and still, by far, the biggest 'breadwinner'. Should I try again to expand? For about six months I delayed a decision — and it cost me dearly.

Looking back over this troubled time, I wonder why I kept pursuing – supposedly as a hobby - the dream of creating a professional aviation museum. At that stage, I was continuing to meet up with Gordon Bendall for an occasional after-work beer, but there seemed to be little, if any progress.

In February 1990, with the planning application for my mill looking as if it would fail anyway, I put the property in the hands of two commercial estate agents for whom I had previously carried out projects. I stressed I was in no particular hurry to sell because, for tax purposes, it would actually be better to sell after June, when I would be sixty. Nobody involved had any doubts that my very attractive mill would sell very quickly indeed.

By then I had reached an agreement to merge my business activities with a company in Maidenhead. I would continue to look after my fee-paying clients on a gradually reducing basis, leading to retirement in two or three years. Two of my back-up team joined the Maidenhead company. I negotiated a 'freelance' arrangement whereby I continued to be employed by The Publicity Mill Limited, although I had, effectively closed the company down and accepted personal liability for its bank loans and overdraft. The sale of the mill would easily cover these debts, everyone thought.

In fact, the sale of the mill *and* moving my business activities to Maidenhead proved to be nightmares I could not have imagined.

As many business people will remember, early in 1990, the John Major government was insisting that "we were talking ourselves into a recession". In fact, for the first time ever, a countrywide recession had actually started in the south of England and it was led by the previously 'invulnerable' high-tech

companies of the Thames Valley. It was many months before the recession took hold nationally but, when it did, it was the worst for generations.

Within a few weeks of my mill going onto the agents' books, the commercial sector of the property market was declining rapidly throughout Berkshire and, by June, my preferred sale date, the market was in a 'terminal dive'.

It was, of course, in June 1990 when construction work finally began on the museum site and I became the 'clerk of works'. By then, I had been working in Maidenhead for some months. It became a routine for me to travel via Woodley, to check on the progress being made. However, as the hangar was at last beginning to shape up to its new life, my own working life was changing yet again.

The situation at Maidenhead had proved to be very different from the picture originally painted and I became more and more unhappy. Finally, in early December, I withdrew from the arrangement and, with the agreement of my three main clients, began to work for them from home.

I equipped a small bedroom with a telephone/fax line and installed a new computer set-up. When I had bought my company's first computer, some three years earlier, it was mainly for use by my design staff. I had undergone basic training with them and had used the computer a few times since.

Basically, I just about knew my way around the keyboard and 'Pagemaker' software, but my typing and computer skills were limited, to say the least. I made a tentative arrangement for a friend and neighbour to carry out lengthy typing requirements, working from my hand-written text - the way I had worked with secretaries for very many years.

On Christmas Eve, I sat at my new computer to type a letter to my eldest son, Andy, who had been sent with the British forces to the Gulf. It was a 'fun' letter, showing him what my new 'toy' could do. But it made me think. Perhaps, with practice, I could type a lot of my requirements.

Three months later, for one of my main clients, I produced the next issue of their quarterly company magazine, which I had developed the previous year. It involved some ten thousand words — and I had typed every one of them! I never did call on the typing services of my neighbour.

For another client, my work included managing their annual participation in a major exhibition at the NEC in Birmingham. My computer skills were stretched even further when I used it to design the stand layout. My second son, Joe, the most practical of my boys, was happy to take a break from his desk-bound job and enjoy a 'paid holiday', helping me to erect the one-hundred-and-fifty-square-metre stand.

A revised version of a sixty-four-page technical handbook about animal feeds was a major project undertaken for another client and this involved, for the first time in many years, turning my hand to technical illustration again.

So this became the pattern of my work for the next three years or so, with many hours spent most days seated at my computer, on which I became far more competent and confident, to the benefit of the museum, as well as my paying clients.

Left: The mill at Woolhampton, Berkshire, home of my company, 'The Publicity Mill'.

So, what of the museum?

As I began what became an increasingly busy year working from home, the time I could afford to spend at the museum was limited. The Management Committee (MMC) had encouraged RBAS members to join in a weekly 'club night' at the hangar. There were a number of 'finishing off' tasks required to improve the hangar's insulation and weather-sealing. A start was made, but few members came and nobody seemed to want to take responsibility and complete a job. Time dragged by and the first seeds of doubt were sown in my mind.

Soon, every time I went to the hangar a new pile of 'junk' had appeared. No doubt the RBAS members meant well when, at work, they 'rescued' furniture, storage racking and such things from the rubbish tip. However, most items were, indeed, rubbish. I found this apparent attitude of 'anything will do for the museum' very depressing.

Up to that time, it was the work of Miles Aircraft that had dominated the planning of the museum's displays. However, as I had emphasised in the very first presentation pack, some of Berkshire's very earliest aviation history was worthy of commemoration.

Left: "The eyes of the world are on you tonight" was reported to be the rallying call when the Allies' Supreme Commander, Gen. Dwight D Eisenhower, talked to paratroopers of the 101st Airborne Division at Greenham Common on the evening before D-Day.

There were also two very important World War II aviation stories unique to Berkshire.

The D-Day assault by the American 101st and 82nd Airborne Divisions was built up and launched from West Berkshire. At the same time, airfields in North Berkshire played their part in the British airborne assault on D-Day.

The other story was the major part played by White Waltham airfield in the wartime Air Transport Auxiliary — at that time, a story not told anywhere else, except for a very small museum in the USA, commemorating mainly the American ATA volunteers.

At the Museum of Berkshire Aviation, we had a unique opportunity to tell these important stories in a way that would attract visitors from around the country and, indeed, from around the world.

Space inside the hangar was limited. However, very few aircraft associated with our three main stories were likely to be available to us. The presentation of these stories to a public ranging from schoolchildren to aviation experts, could only be told effectively with dramatic, imaginative displays of photographs, drawings, text and models.

As the only RBAS member with professional experience in such matters, I saw as my main task for months to come, the gathering of material, the writing of text and the design and production of the main displays. What is more, if the high standards of a really professional museum were to be achieved, as I had always advocated and worked towards, I would also require considerably more funding than I had previously been able to provide myself or to persuade other people or organisations to give.

By this time, I had found an effective use for at least some of the 'rubbish' that had been brought to the hangar. I designed a way in which sections of steel storage racking could be made into a structure, mounted on the hangar walls, which did not encroach on the floorspace. From this structure, I could attach what would appear to be 'floating' colour panels that formed the base for the photographic and text displays I developed.

A retired RBAS member, Mick Day, who was a skilled welder, spent many weeks shaping the 'legs' of the structure. For my part, I spent many a lonely 'club night' through the winter of '91/'92 rubbing down the old rusty storage racking shelves, before painting and assembling them into a structure which extended the whole length of the hangar.

During this time, I also built up a great deal of information on every aspect of developing and running a museum to the highest professional standards. I investigated the most modern types of lighting equipment and display cabinets. I made contact with the professional body — the Museums Association.

I knew the Miles Aircraft story well, of course, and had access to most of the available photographs. However, I also used various contacts to investigate Berkshire's earliest aviation history.

I visited the photographic section of the RAF Museum and found numerous Berkshire-related photographs. I visited RAF Abingdon, just before it closed, and obtained items for the museum.

As far as the MMC was concerned, the 'bible' by which we worked at this time was a very informative set of booklets from the Association of Independent Museums (AIM). We particularly noted their very clear recommendations regarding the proper relationships between trustees, their chairman, the curator(s) and 'Friends of the Museum'. All this was invaluable to my model-making colleague and new MMC member, John Kite, who led the efforts to obtain Charitable Trust status.

With their huge financial commitment to the museum, we felt that Wokingham District Council should be represented among the trustees and we invited them to nominate someone who, initially, would join the MMC.

They sent along Douglas Goddard, who I had first met when we sat him up in a JCB for a press photograph when we began work on the museum site. At that time he had been leader of the Council, but was no longer performing that role. But he was still a politician. We should have been warned!

In 1992, the Museum of Berkshire Aviation obtained Charitable Trust status, the first trustees being myself, Doug Rough, John Kite and the Wokingham DC representative, Douglas Goddard.

At our first meeting as trustees, Doug Rough, who was the MMC chairman, expressed his unwillingness to also be chairman of the trustees, due to the increasing pressure he was under in his job as a senior air traffic controller. He suggested that Douglas Goddard, with his Council experience and, being retired, with far more time available, should take on the role. At the time, with the job pressures we were all under, it seemed like a good idea. It didn't take long though, for me to realise it wasn't.

However, Doug, John and I made it abundantly clear that we considered that every one of these appointments was temporary, until the museum could attract trustees from local business and community leaders and, of course, major sponsors.

Remembering what had happened at the Brooklands Museum, we also stressed the need for a nationally known and respected chairman and a number of possible candidates were discussed. Eventually Raymond Baxter, the well-known broadcaster and ex-Spitfire pilot, emerged as the favourite. He lived in Berkshire, as I had discovered through a mutual acquaintance, and I could easily obtain an introduction but, when Douglas Goddard learned that he lived near Raymond Baxter, he quickly volunteered to approach him on our behalf.

Sadly for the museum, Raymond never became chairman, only a patron, but I truly believe that if I had gone to talk to him at that time, the museum would be a very different place today.

Right: The museum brochure I designed in 1992. Keen air-spotters may be puzzled by the small aircraft on the right - the 'Chevvron' microlight, then being produced in Berkshire. Anyone who has visited the museum in recent years will probably remember the helicopter-like machine shown above it. Made by ML Aviation of White Waltham, it was the 'Sprite' remote-controlled 'drone'. Really keen students of aviation history will, no doubt, pick up on my 'deliberate mistake'. At least, that's my story and I'm sticking to it.

At that first meeting, Doug, John and I outlined a complete management and personnel structure for the future museum, based upon the AIM advice. This included a 'Friends of the Museum' section that we decided to call 'crew members', taking into account the very necessary distinction between individual members and corporate members, including major sponsors. Once again, I set about designing a museum brochure, 'twisting the arm' of one of my business friends to print it free of charge

Sadly for the museum's future, none of these management plans actually came to fruition. Looking back, I can now see that not only were Doug, John and I politically naïve but, the fact that all three of us came under more and more pressure in our working lives, led us to 'let go of the reins' too quickly. By the end of the year, when we found we also had personal problems to add even more pressure, it was probably already too late to halt the museum's slide further and further away from the professional standards we had tried to establish.

Unfortunately, John suffered health problems which resulted in him reducing and then suspending his involvement with the museum. Doug's problems were mainly work related but it seemed he was often missing at critical times.

For me and, of course, my wife, Valerie, 1992 was definitely our 'Annus Horribilis'. The local property market was still at 'rock bottom' and my mill remained unsold. Although my decision to work from home had proved a successful and profitable move, every penny of profit I made just disappeared into the bank's unforgiving grasp.

As if the *financial* problems of the mill weren't enough, I also had to maintain it in good repair. In the summer I had to cut the grass and keep the long gravel drive and car park free of weeds. During one winter, a main water pipe burst and the insurers refused to pay for the damage because it was an empty building. On more than one occasion, I had to mend windows after local junior villains broke in.

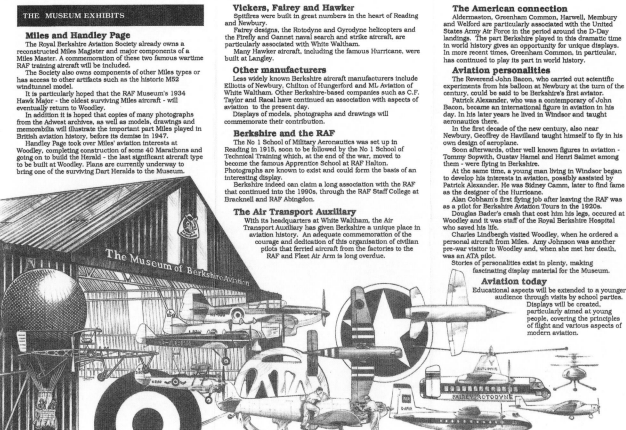

When, after nearly two years on the market, it looked as if my mill might at last be sold, albeit at a greatly reduced price, it was discovered that my original solicitor had made a ghastly mistake. He had failed to remove all the previous owner's Rights of Way through the property, making it virtually unsaleable. It took some three months for my current solicitor to solve the problem. It was the very lowest point for Valerie and me in what had become an extended nightmare.

That same year, just two years before my pension scheme matured, I could not afford the annual contribution and had to close it prematurely.

If we thought the failure to sell the Mill and my considerably reduced pension prospects were our only problems in 1992, how wrong we were! That was the year we first became aware of a subsidence problem at our house!

As far as the museum's future was concerned, when I thought about it during those lonely 'club nights' in 1992, its opening to the public was some years away. The agreement I had originally negotiated with Wokingham DC and was later ratified by the other trustees, gave the museum a six-year rent-free period, to allow for it to be developed. I was convinced that the completed hangar should be furnished with a brief but well presented outline of Berkshire's aviation heritage, with a few well displayed and documented exhibits and samples of the high quality display panels and cabinets we intended to use. This would certainly not be a museum itself, but it would demonstrate the very real *potential* for a new museum.

Later that year, particularly from newer MMC members not directly involved in the development of the museum exhibits, there was pressure for a partial opening to the public in the spring of 1993.

Suddenly it seemed that everyone except me believed the 'answer' to the museum's financial problems was to open the 'junk shop' we had to the public - albeit on a limited weekly basis, with a reduced entrance fee! All thought of finding commercial sponsors seemed to be abandoned. It was even claimed that paid school visits would bring in the revenue we needed. As far as real fundraising was concerned, it was just a 'cop out'.

Although I had many reservations and expressed them strongly, I eventually agreed, with a very small budget, to put together a *temporary* photographic display of the Woodley airfield story. Photographs and captions could be mounted upon the structure Mick Day and I had built over the previous months. My computer would allow a presentation of the text to a reasonably professional standard and the improving photocopy and laminating machines of the day would allow an acceptable quality of presentation. Compared to the highly professional standards I planned for the eventual displays in the museum it would be a second-rate presentation, but at least it was much better than the displays at the Brooklands Museum I had seen many years before. Little did I think then that this temporary display would set the standard for the museum graphics for years to come.

All thoughts of developing the proper management structure for the museum had to be forgotten as I began another concentrated effort over a number of weeks—and much of it had to be carried out in my already busy working day.

Early in 1993, the MMC was planning a limited public opening in March and I designed a poster that made it very clear it was a photographic display about Woodley airfield, to show why a museum should be developed. I was appalled when I was overruled and it was decided it should be a full opening of the Museum of Berkshire Aviation. In retrospect, I should have walked away then. It was a stupid decision that would permanently blight the museum. Certainly it was another factor that was rapidly unravelling all the energy and enthusiasm I had put into the project over the previous seven years. I didn't walk away though. I carried on creating the photographic display.

I played my part in the Opening Day, without much enthusiasm. The VIP reception was full of chairmen and their families from most of the other Councils in Berkshire, enjoying yet another 'freebie'. Previously, all had shown a marked parochial lack of interest in the museum project. There was a handful of other VIPs including Raymond Baxter, who had, it seems, been invited to be 'patrons'. Not one potential commercial sponsor was in sight.

At the opening I found the speeches turgid in the extreme, full of the speakers' own wartime activities. There was no mention of the aviation heritage of Berkshire, which had driven the idea for a museum in the first place. There wasn't even a mention of RBAS and its members who had actually set the project in motion. I seem to remember there wasn't even thanks to Wokingham District Council, who had finally made it all happen. And I certainly don't remember any of the really helpful Council officers being there!

Thankfully, the Spitfire pilot, waiting to entertain the public with an aerobatic display when the 'VIPs' went into the hangar, brought the speeches to a premature end.

For me, one pleasure in the day was to escort two distinguished ladies into the hangar. One was Lady Bader and the other ninety-one-year-old Mrs Winifred Brooks, who I had first heard about from her daughter, who had contacted me some weeks before. In 1913, as the eleven-year-old Winifred Antell from Reading, Mrs Brooks had actually flown from Woodley with Henri Salmet in a Bleriot. Over sixty years later, this remarkable lady was also one of the first 'civilian' passengers to fly in Concorde!

Within a few weeks of the Opening Day, I did walk away from any further part in management of the museum. I had lost all belief that it could be developed into the museum that I had always believed it deserved to be. Worse than that, without Doug and John's support and with a largely new and inexperienced MMC, who had not been involved in any of the original planning, I constantly found myself complaining about events that should never have happened in the first place, as I tried to save what was left of the museum's integrity. It was the sort of 'company politics' that, over the years, I had grown to hate and despise. This had all started for me as a hobby. Yet it was putting an extra strain on our life that Valerie and I didn't need. I resigned my position as a trustee and, for three years, aviation heritage played no part in my life.

In my working life, these were three years of challenge, satisfaction and considerable success. I was back to being a 'loner', without any staff to worry about and only regretting that I hadn't decided to do this years before.

Above: Eleven-year-old Winifred Antell, at Woodley with Henri Salmet in 1913. Eighty years later, she was my personal VIP at the museum Opening Day.

Above: At the museum Opening Day, left to right, Peter Potter, John Kenyon, John Wakeford, Jean Fostekew and me. In front of the hangar we had first entered around fifty years earlier as students of the Miles Aeronautical Technical School.

Above: A big smile from Geoffrey on the Opening Day! (I was always a good actor). But, when Valerie positioned me close to the Exit sign, was she trying to tell me something?

A few weeks later, in other aspects of my life, the gloom lifted slightly. After three and a half years on the market, I finally sold the mill. With the commercial market going from bad to worse, I had, some months before, placed the property with a residential agency. It would require a change of planning consent and a great deal of additional cost for the buyer to install a proper kitchen and a bathroom. However, that was how the mill was eventually sold – at a price less than half its original valuation. Every penny went to the banks.

At our home, after twelve months of monitoring, the subsidence problems had got worse. My friend, the consulting engineer, was now involved and we were faced with a series of investigations, including a hole being dug beneath our kitchen! Eventually, after months of stalling, the insurers gave the go-ahead for our house to have a completely new piled foundation to be designed and constructed.

In the summer of 1994, we moved out of our home for six months, to a rented house in a nearby village. Obviously, my working life and all the things that made it possible, such as my computer set-up, fax machine and telephone also had to make the move.

I was near my 65th year, when we finally straightened out our finances.

Below: For nearly six months in 1994, our house was just a building site. I visited it regularly to check on progress, but Valerie couldn't bear to go near until the construction work was completed. Even then we were faced with weeks of hard work to restore it to the home it had originally been.

This was the first of six stands that I designed annually for Dynopack at a major food-packaging exhibition. For five years running, until my retirement in 1996, my son, Joe, and I undertook the challenging task of constructing these stands at the NEC in Birmingham.

For my client, Dynopack, I continued to work on all their promotional activities, including the design and construction of their exhibition stands. Indeed, in the last year or so of my contract with them, I was frequently in a role more like one of their company executives. Among my varied tasks was the 'masterminding' of their parent company's international sales conference. I also investigated the bar code system and organised the company's first use of bar coding on their product packaging. I became involved in the development of a completely new product and organised the subsequent patent application. However, with a change in the company's top management and having just passed my 66th birthday, I decided it was time to retire. I had just returned home, after visiting Dynopack to be briefed on my very last project, when I suffered a thrombosis! So ended my working life.

About two years earlier, as the pressures of work had begun to ease, I decided to attend watercolour classes at the Reading Adult College. It was many years since I had painted and it proved an enjoyable and useful experience.

However, my thoughts were once again turning to aviation heritage and my original idea to tell the story in a series of paintings. Not only the story of Woodley airfield, as I had first thought about in 1984, but the whole of Berkshire, about which I had learned so much in the following years. Although I had never painted in oils, I felt this was the right medium for the task ahead. So, taking a fairly simple subject, a single aircraft, against a cloudless sky and desert-like ground, I began to paint.

Within a few months, with just three or four paintings 'under my belt', I went to the AGM of the Guild of Aviation Artists, which I had just joined. I took two of my paintings to the 'critique' by senior members. The kind remarks about one of the paintings made me think I was 'on the right track'. However, a few months later, when I saw my paintings with others being entered for the Guild's annual 'Aviation Paintings of the Year' exhibition, I knew they were really not good enough. The composition and accuracy of the drawing were fine, but it was obvious I hadn't yet managed to teach myself to paint in oils.

When all four of the paintings I had entered for the exhibition were, quite rightly, rejected, I set about 'reworking' them, as well as a couple of others I had completed. I also began to paint smaller aviation and motoring subjects in watercolour and acrylics – and soon I began to sell some! Then, I received my first commission for a painting in oils.

For the following 'Aviation Paintings of the Year' exhibition, in 1998, I once again entered four paintings. This time, three of them were selected, and two of these were among my Berkshire heritage paintings. It was a proud moment to see my three paintings hanging at this prestigious London exhibition, alongside work from some of the best professional aviation painters in the business, such as Gerald Coulson, John Young and Michael Turner.

The painting rejected in 1998, after just a little 'reworking', was one of four I entered for the 1999 Guild exhibition. This time it was accepted, along with another from my Berkshire heritage paintings. Even the small acrylic painting rejected for that exhibition was later sold through a local art gallery!

There was still a long way to go, but the journey I had begun back in 1984, to tell the story of Berkshire's aviation history in paintings, was well underway.

However, I never did manage to see my paintings on display at the 1999 Guild exhibition. A few weeks before it opened, I suffered a stroke that caused the left side of my body to be paralysed. As a result, I spent nearly three months in hospital, learning to walk and use my left arm again. At least, being right-handed, I was able to carry on sketching and painting in watercolours while I was in hospital.

It was also while I was in hospital that the seeds of the idea of writing this book were planted. As part of our rehabilitation programme, for anyone who had previously used a computer, a small PC was occasionally made available, the idea being that you could only use the left hand, to help in its recovery. For anyone with 'writer's block', starting your life story was the usual suggestion. A biography didn't really appeal to me, but I remembered how my own children had been really interested when my brother Leslie had prepared a 'what did you do in the war' audio tape for his grand-daughter's school project.

So the idea of what was originally a 'why I became an aviation nutter' story for my grand-children began its life on that hospital computer. In hospital, with just my left hand, my story got no further than "The first of my brushes with aviation, so I have been told, was in July 1930".

However, when I finally returned home, after a few adjustments to the way I worked, my painting of the story of Berkshire's aviation history was soon back in business. Now however, although it was indeed miniscule, my part in that history was also being put into words. By July 2002, I had completed and printed a thirty-eight-page book, complete with photographs and drawings and all my family had received a copy.

The more I had written, the more I began to think that I should expand my book to include all I had learned over the years about Berkshire's aviation heritage. After all, since 1985, I had talked about it on numerous occasions in Berkshire and Oxfordshire.

So that is how this book took shape.

About that time, I was given a copy of Tim Smit's excellent book about the creation of the Eden Project in Cornwall. Although his project was considerably more ambitious than mine, there was much in it that reminded me of my efforts to create the museum, some ten years earlier. It was particularly apposite when he recounted how he reached a point when he knew he and his earliest team-mates must draw back and hand over to a more effective professional management structure, including an appropriate Board of Trustees, with the right chairman.

At that point, our stories diverged. I failed to bring my dream to fruition, but Tim Smit succeeded in turning his dream into one of the leading public attractions in the UK or, perhaps, even in the world.

I have been back to the museum many times over the years and my feelings are mixed. There's pride, of course, that I succeeded in saving part of Berkshire's aviation heritage, particularly as it was part of the MATS history. But that pride is always mixed with sadness for what 'could have been'.

In 2001 the museum was the venue for an exhibition of the first thirty or so of my Berkshire heritage paintings and some of them are now permanently on view there. I thank my good friends Jean and Ken Fostekew for their help then and, more than that, I salute the way they have both put their unselfish best efforts into the Museum, rescuing it in its darkest days and pushing it up to it present level of success.

I still see my good friends, Doug Rough and John Kite occasionally. They both returned to make a contribution to the museum, sensibly doing the things they do best—and enjoying it.

I also salute the memory of my friend, Bob Brown, a colleague both at MATS and Handley Page. His untimely death in 2005 led to a substantial bequest to the museum, which has finally allowed a badly needed extension to be built.

At the Museum's 10th Anniversary celebration, with Bob Brown (centre) and Jeremy Miles (right). I first met Jeremy, the son of FG and Blossom Miles, when I visited Shoreham in 1957 to draw the Miles Student for Aeroplane magazine.

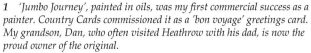

1 'Jumbo Journey', painted in oils, was my first commercial success as a painter. Country Cards commissioned it as a 'bon voyage' greetings card. My grandson, Dan, who often visited Heathrow with his dad, is now the proud owner of the original.

2 'Concorde Touchdown', now in the collection of Mrs A Jones, was selected for the 1998 'Aviation Paintings of the Year' exhibition.

3 This 'acrylic sketch' of a Swordfish is one of a number of paintings of aircraft, cars and even a motorcycle, completed when I first experimented with this medium in 1998. A number were sold through local art galleries. Six biplane paintings were published as a greetings card by Country Cards. The Swordfish was eventually selected for the 'Aviation Paintings of the Year' Exhibition in 1999.

4 I have completed many commissions for watercolours of planes, trains, cars and houses, sometimes for a local art gallery pleased to have found an artist "who knows what their customers are talking about".

5 This is one of a series of oil paintings of vintage cars celebrating the great days of the British manufacturers. They have proved popular and a number have been sold. The original painting of this Riley is now in Holland, in the collection of Mr Jan Rooderkerk.

6 With Valerie's insatiable love of flowers and her great skill as a florist, it is perhaps not surprising that I am occasionally 'persuaded' to paint watercolours of flowers, although my style is perhaps a bit bold for some.

7 With more than a nod in the direction of Jack Vettriano, this oil painting was given to our very good friends, Stuart and Sally Rolfe. We met on holiday, many more years ago than any of us care to remember.

Brushes with Aviation

A personal perspective on the aviation heritage
of the Royal County of Berkshire

Geoff Beckett

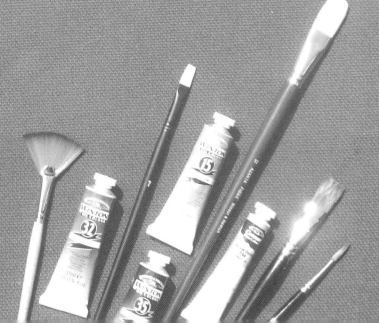

The historic boundary between the counties of Berkshire and Oxfordshire was the River Thames, flowing over a length of some one hundred miles from near Faringdon in the north-west to Windsor in the south-east. All this changed in 1974 when around forty per cent of Berkshire became part of Oxfordshire.

Sadly, this included some areas of ancient historical worth, generally still known as the Berkshire Downs. With those went parts of the ancient Ridgeway and the enigmatic Uffington White Horse and nearby Uffington Castle.

A notable part of the county's aviation history is to be found in this 'lost' area but, since the vast majority of this pre-dates 1974, it seems only right and proper that this book should tell the story of Berkshire's 'brushes with aviation' in the county boundaries that were there when they happened.

In 1974, Berkshire's famous White Horse at Uffington, near Wantage, galloped away into Oxfordshire. Berkshire's 'barnstorming' pioneers, one of whose aircraft is featured in this painting, were active in the area just after World War I. Their story begins on Page 52.

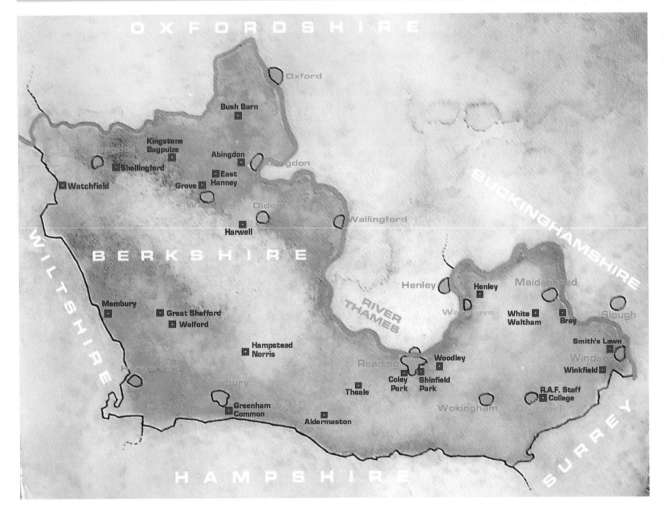

The Royal County of Berkshire, as it was before the 1974 boundary changes, showing the main airfields and sites of aviation interest.

In the Royal County of Berkshire, it is perhaps no surprise to learn that, in the pioneering years, most 'brushes with aviation' were associated with Windsor and the Royal family.

As far back as 1783, when George III heard of experiments in France with hydrogen-filled balloons, he wrote to the president of the Royal Society, Sir Joseph Banks, offering to meet the costs of similar experiments in England. Perhaps the King remembered that the discovery of hydrogen and its 'lifting properties' came from work by British scientists some ten years earlier. Sir Joseph, echoing the thoughts of many in the scientific establishment, replied that further experiments with hydrogen were worthless.

It should also be remembered that, at the time, mainly on religious grounds, the idea of man flying in the air was not a popular one and, surely, that was where the experiments in France were heading.

However, the King was not to be put off and when, on November 25th 1783, he heard that the first successful experiment with a small hydrogen-filled balloon had actually been carried out in England, he invited an eminent Prussian scientist, Professor Argand, who happened to be in the country, to visit him at Windsor.

The following day, Professor Argand made hydrogen by pouring sulphuric acid onto iron filings, the accepted method, and filled a one-metre diameter balloon with the resultant gas. Attaching a string, he presented it to the King who, with the Queen and Princesses watching from one of the castle windows, made it ascend and descend past them, before letting go of the string and watching the balloon disappear into the skies above Berkshire.

In fact, in France, just a few days earlier, on November 21st, a balloon big enough to carry two men into the air had made its first free flight. Constructed by the Montgolfier brothers out of paper and fabric, this was a hot-air balloon, the heat source being a pan of burning wool and damp straw in the balloon's platform. This was a potentially lethal arrangement, as Jean-Francois Pilatre de Rosier, one of the first men it carried, was to tragically discover just eighteen months later.

Throughout 1783 the two Montgolfier brothers had been experimenting with balloons and it seems they never realised it was the heat expanding the air that caused the balloon to rise. They were aware of other experiments being carried out with hydrogen balloons and assumed that the smoke that was produced by the burning straw contained some sort of similar gas.

In France, the development of hydrogen balloons had been led by a young physicist Jacques Charles and, just two weeks after the flight of the Montgolfier balloon, Charles and an assistant made the first flight in a man-carrying hydrogen balloon, watched by a crowd of four hundred thousand people. The hydrogen-filled balloon was recognised as the safer design, but the cost of producing hydrogen limited its use and balloons of both types were used until well into the next century

The first balloon flight in Britain was by a Mr Tyler of Edinburgh in August 1784, followed by the well documented flight from London in September 1784 by the Italian, Vincenzo Lunardi.

The French army used balloons for observation before the end of the century, but most balloons, whether tethered or free flying, became the province of the showman and, for many years, there were few public events that did not include a balloon ascent.

One of the most famous of these showmen was Andre Jacques Garnerin who, in October 1797 above Paris, became the first man in the world to successfully use a parachute. The following year his wife became the first woman to use a parachute and his niece became the world's first woman professional parachutist. They too were soon in demand as aerial performers. Garnerin made many balloon ascents in England and, in 1802, made the first parachute descent in this country, jumping from a height of nearly ten thousand feet over London.

Early in the 19th century the streets of London were being lit by gaslight and, gradually, this benefit spread to most towns in Britain, each one boasting its own gasworks. It was an English ballooning pioneer, Charles Green, who realised the potential of coal gas for making ballooning easier and cheaper and, in London in July 1821 during the celebrations for the coronation of George IV, he made the first ascent in a balloon filled with coal gas.

Thus the stage was set for ballooning to come to Berkshire.

By the 1830s a Mr and Mrs Graham were using the availability of coal gas to thrill the public with ascents in their balloon in and around London, often throwing out handbills to announce their own and forthcoming theatrical events. In September 1831, shortly before the coronation of William IV, they brought their balloon to Windsor. Heavy rain caused a day's delay and then the filling of the balloon was interrupted when all the gas was needed to light the streets. Despite supplementing the gas overnight with hydrogen from their own generator, when the King was ready to witness the ascent – he had requested it brought forward by a few hours before he left for London – the balloon was only sufficiently inflated for Mr Graham to make the flight alone.

In August 1837, this time as part of the celebrations in honour of the state entry into Windsor of the young Queen Victoria, the Grahams were back again with an even larger balloon. This time, although the arrangements made at the gasworks allowed a more efficient filling of the balloon, the heavy rain added so much to its weight that, this time, only Mrs Graham was able to make the flight. In fact, it was her 35th solo flight and she made a safe but thoroughly soaked landing at Pennyoaks Farm, appropriately perhaps, now part of Heathrow Airport.

An unexpected problem for citizen Garnerin

As a professional balloonist, Garnerin no doubt faced many problems. However, when he planned a balloon ascent in the company of an attractive young lady (and perhaps it was only his niece), he appears to have discovered a new problem, as can be seen in a French newspaper of 1797.

"The police have forbidden citizen Garnerin to make an air voyage jointly with a female since he could not prove that this companionship will in any way aid the perfection of the art. An air voyage undertaken by two members of opposite sexes must furthermore be considered quite improper and immoral."

As the second half of the 19th century began, ballooning was developing fast — in 'technology' and in popularity.

The Montgolfier type of hot-air balloon could still be seen, now with an enclosed straw-burning stove mounted in the suspended 'car' and a long chimney extending well into the 'envelope'. For gas-filled balloons, hydrogen was still being used when the cheaper coal gas was unavailable.

A number of professional balloonists were operating in the UK and, increasingly, ordinary citizens were paying to ascend in large tethered balloons or to experience the even greater thrill of a free-flying balloon. Even more adventurous people, providing they were also reasonably wealthy, were buying or hiring balloons to fly themselves.

Scientific research was being carried out from balloons, notably in the UK by the meteorologist, James Glaisher, between 1862–66, flying with the professional balloonist, Henry Coxwell. He was commemorated by the naming of Glaisher House in Bracknell, originally the Royal Meteorological Society's headquarters.

Various unsuccessful attempts were being made to control both motion and direction in balloons, by the use of 'paddles' or 'fans' and by elongating the shape of the 'envelope'.

France once again led the way in 'lighter than air' technology when, in 1852, Henri Giffard made the first flight in a small steam-engine-powered, gas-filled airship. Time would show, however, that it was work about that time with 'heavier than air' gliders, by the Yorkshireman, Sir George Cayley, that paved the way for the future of aviation.

This was the age then, when one of Berkshire's more colourful balloonists enjoyed his 'brushes with aviation'. 'Burnaby the Great', as he popularly became known, was an officer in the Royal Horse Guards, stationed in Windsor whenever the Queen and her Court were in residence at the castle.

At six-feet-four-inches and twenty-three stone, he was a man of enormous size, physical strength and courage, hence his popular nickname. He was a twenty-two-year-old lieutenant when, in 1864, he made his first balloon flight - one of ten young army officers invited by Henry Coxwell to be passengers in the trial flight of a new balloon.

Burnaby's enthusiasm was fired and, just a month later, he was in the air again. This time it was in a huge Montgolfier-type hot-air balloon brought to London from France where, unknown to the British authorities, it had been banned from flying. In fact, it proved to be the very last flight of any balloon of this type. On the next attempt 'The Eagle', as it was optimistically called, caught fire before leaving the ground and was destroyed.

Burnaby was soon attracted by another French balloonist's advertisement in which he claimed to have invented a 'controllable aerostat' – the term 'airship' was not yet in general use. Burnaby paid a £5 fee for the doubtful honour of turning the handles of the large 'fans' that were supposed to aid both lift and direction of the huge cigar-shaped balloon. Despite valiant efforts with the 'fans', the aerostat only ascended when Burnaby surreptitiously threw bags of ballast overboard.

Then he was horrified to see that the inventor had forgotten to remove a 'tie' which prevented surplus gas from escaping and it was now out of reach. The aerostat rose higher and higher, and the fabric of the 'envelope' became more and more taut, until it split and they began to plunge to earth. When it appeared nothing could save them, the torn fabric caught in the top ropework to form a large 'parachute' and they landed shaken but unhurt.

Surprisingly, Burnaby's enthusiasm for ballooning continued unabated although, from that time on, he made sure that he, or someone he knew and trusted, was in charge of the balloon. He made many flights in the company of other Guards officers, ascending from the cavalry barracks or the gasworks in Windsor, where they always attracted large crowds.

However, in 1882, by then a forty-year-old colonel holding a minor position in the Court, Burnaby attracted national fame by his flight across the Channel - only the third successful crossing and the first by a solo balloonist. He had been determined to test the theory of a professional balloonist who had recently failed in a cross-Channel attempt, the theory being that the direction of the wind varies at

different altitudes. Burnaby's lengthy but eventually successful flight proved the theory. However, it was the very last balloon flight of 'Burnaby the Great'. It seems Court officials, even minor ones, could not leave the country without permission. Reprimanded by his commanding officer, Burnaby was told "valuable lives should not be lost in such freaks".

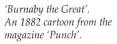

'Burnaby the Great'.
An 1882 cartoon from the magazine 'Punch'.

In 1866, when the Aeronautical Society came into being, Frederick Burnaby was a founder member. So too was Andrew Alexander, a Scots-born mechanical engineer, who lived in London.

Andrew Alexander passed on his interest in aeronautics to his son, Patrick, who, by the time he came to live in Windsor, his home for the last thirty years of his life, was one of the most respected figures in the whole world of aviation.

In 1878, when Patrick was eleven, his father took him to the Paris Exhibition, where they were passengers in a giant tethered balloon built by the veteran airship pioneer, Henri Giffard. It could carry fifty-two passengers and rose sixteen-hundred-feet above the city. That same year, Patrick successfully built and flew an elastic-powered model aeroplane, a growing source of interest and enthusiasm for many young people.

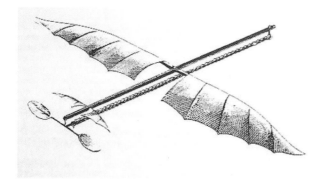

An elastic-powered model aeroplane of the type Patrick Alexander built when he was eleven.

By then, the principles of heavier-than-air flight, pioneered by Sir George Cayley some thirty years earlier, were well established. Models such as eleven-year-old Patrick built did much to make the youth of the day air-minded. Indeed, they helped to foster a worldwide interest in the possibility of man-carrying heavier-than-air machines, which grew rapidly during the final decade of the 19th century.

Otto Lilienthal, in Germany, Octave Chanute in America and Percy Pilcher in England, all developed what would later be called hang-gliders. In far away Australia, Lawrence Hargrave developed the box-kite, which would heavily influence the design of the very first successful flying machines.

More importantly perhaps, in Germany, the invention of the internal combustion engine provided the first really practical power-source that would enable man to 'navigate the skies' as he had long dreamed of doing. However, as the 20th century approached, it was the lighter-than-air solution — balloons and airships — that still seemed to offer the most practical answer to aerial navigation and, for a time at least, proved to do so.

In this exciting and challenging time, it was Patrick Alexander who, perhaps more than any other person in the world, came to research, record and promote the *science* of flight.

Despite his youthful interest in aviation, Patrick Alexander went to sea when he was just eighteen, sailing for Australia as an apprentice in a square-rigged barque. In rough weather, he fell from the rigging and broke his leg and, without proper medical attention for some weeks, it failed to set properly. Despite later treatment in England, he was left permanently disabled. His family had moved to Bath when his father retired and Patrick returned there to convalesce. Sadly, within just three years, he was alone, following the deaths of his elder brother, then his mother and, finally, his father.

Even before his father's death, Patrick had gained recognition for developments in the new science of wireless telegraphy. Suddenly, aged just twenty-three, he found himself a wealthy young man and began to pour all his energy and his money into scientific work. While he was always interested in different aspects of science, he became almost fanatical about meteorology and aeronautics — the youthful interests inspired by his father. After his father's death, he moved to a smaller house in Bath, but one that included workshops in its grounds.

He equipped these with the latest tools and machinery and soon employed two or three skilled men to assist in his experiments. It appears that Patrick Alexander, like many others, thought it possible to control the direction of balloon flights and his early experiments included the design of large fans and propellers. By the time he was twenty-five, he had also bought the first of a number of balloons he was to buy or, indeed, to build. He made many balloon flights in the Bath area that were extensively reported in the local newspapers. He even constructed a parachute and, despite his disability, actually used it, jumping from a balloon. In the early 1890s, this was still a very rare event.

Below: Guests at the weekend in Bath, hosted by Patrick Alexander in September 1902, include Samuel Cody, centre, in his distinctive 'cowboy' hat, and Colonel James Templar, of the Army balloon section, second right front row. Alexander himself is on Cody's right, next to Major Baden Powell, president of the Aeronautical Society of Great Britain, whose brother would shortly create the Scout movement. Second from the left in the front row is the Hon. Charles Rolls.

He soon began to widen his interests in aviation, in 1892 starting to keep books of press cuttings and other information from around the world. By 1913, this had grown to some one-hundred-and-twenty volumes and eventually became a highly valued archive in the Science Museum library.

He became friends with many in the British ballooning fraternity, one of whom was a young patent agent from Leeds, Griffith Brewer, with whom, in 1893, he collaborated in the publication of 'Aeronautics' — an abridgement and evaluation of aeronautical patents between 1815 and 1891.

What made Patrick Alexander perhaps unique in the world was the simple fact that he could use his wealth to back up his passion for knowledge about all things involved with aviation. He began to travel the world in pursuit of his passion as early as 1891, when he went to Germany to meet Otto Lilienthal.

Over the next twenty years or so, his reputation grew, perhaps even more abroad than at home. He became recognised as a leader in meteorological work using balloons. He was the first to demonstrate that wireless could be used for the remote control of flying machines. In Germany, he was invited to take part in prestigious balloon flights and, in 1903, was an official observer at the very first flight of the airship built by Count von Zeppelin.

At times, he was regarded abroad as an agent of the British government – which he never was. However, he certainly became closer to Army aeronautical work than a civilian could expect to be and played the major part in introducing Samuel Cody to the military.

Patrick Alexander regularly travelled to America and came to know the Wright brothers well. He regularly corresponded with them, after visiting them to see their early work on gliders. He was actually in America in 1903 when they made their historic first powered flights and, had he received a telegram sent to him, he would almost certainly have witnessed their triumph.

Left: Patrick Alexander was honoured by the Aero Clubs of America in 1908 when he was included in their book of cartoons of important figures associated with aviation. Others in the book included the Wright brothers, Henri Farman and Alexander Graham Bell.

Right: Patrick Alexander teaching boys the science of aeronautics at the United Services College, Windsor, before World War I.

In addition to his efforts as an aeronautical archivist, he was the first to appreciate the value of aeronautical archaeology and, in 1905, paid for the restoration of parts of Stringfellow's flying models from the mid 1800s. These are now also in the Science Museum. Later, he presented a substantial prize for the first British design of aero engine. The winning design, by Gustavas Green, was installed in one of Samuel Cody's most successful aircraft.

Patrick Alexander began his long association with the United Services College at Windsor in 1907 and, at the end of World War I, he took up residence there. He built and operated workshops at the college and constructed a full size glider and wind tunnel so that the boys could practise basic airmanship. He made substantial gifts to the college, just as he had to the Aeronautical Society, when it was in financial difficulties.

Indeed, his generosity was nearly his undoing. For some reason, he had expected to die before he was fifty and, five years after that, having given most of his money away, he was in danger of bankruptcy. He was rescued by his aeronautical friends and the college authorities, who allowed him to continue living there until its closure in 1942. He died in Windsor, just a year later.

The Reverend John Bacon, from Cold Ash, near Newbury, was Berkshire's first 'home grown' aviator and carried on the tradition of many early balloonists — carrying out scientific experiments from a balloon.

Although some twenty years older, Bacon was a contemporary of Patrick Alexander and is known to have been a passenger in the latter's large balloon.

John Bacon was born in 1846 at Lambourn Woodlands, the fifth son of the local vicar. At the age of nineteen he went to Trinity College, Cambridge and, five years later, was ordained a deacon.

Whilst at Cambridge, he saw his first balloon ascent and he said it remained an inspiration for him, even though it was to be another twenty years before he experienced his first flight.

After his ordination, he carried out a successful tutoring business at Cambridge with his brother for some ten years, before a severe illness forced him to move to the country. Eventually, with his wife and young daughter, Gertrude, he settled in Cold Ash. Despite his poor health, he entered fully into the life of the community. He assisted the local vicar. He organised an 'annual show' for local people – a new idea which spread around the country. He also formed a local team of bellringers.

He had pursued many different hobbies since his youth and now began to read widely on science and meteorology.

Eventually, he bought his own balloon and, in 1898, when he was fifty-two, made the first of a series of flights from Newbury gasworks, to carry out scientific experiments concerned with the travel of sound. Special arrangements were made with the sexton at Thatcham to ring the church's heavy tenor bell and also for artillerymen, some forty miles away at Portsmouth, to fire their guns at a given signal. He also carried out photography from his balloon. In all these flights his 'pilot' was his daughter, Gertrude, who later wrote a book about their experiences. Crowds gathered to observe the balloon flights and experiments, which proved to be a great success. The following year he took part in wireless telegraphy experiments. This was around the time Patrick Alexander was also experimenting in this field and it is interesting to conjecture that they may have been working together.

In 1900, the year that Patrick Alexander was elected a member of the Aeronautical Society, John Bacon was invited to present a paper at one of the meetings, 'Cloud Photography from Balloon', illustrated by lantern slides.

Ultimately, John Bacon's greatest contribution was to ballooning itself. With his friend, John Maskelyne from Bucklebury Common, he invented and patented a burner, fuelled by petrol, to create hot air. In principle, he had returned to the very first Montgolfier hot-air balloon but, more importantly, he had pointed the way to the success of modern-day ballooning. John Bacon first flew his hot-air balloon in 1902 and, the following year, achieved similar success with an even larger balloon.

However, by then, his life had nearly run its course. He died in 1904.

Below: John Bacon's balloon being inflated at Newbury gasworks.

Right: Using the petrol-fuelled burner to inflate his balloon, John Bacon can be seen bottom right.

Far right: A reproduction of the original John Bacon burner, on display in the West Berkshire Museum.

In 1898, the year John Bacon first carried out his experiments in his balloon at Newbury, a 12-year-old boy, Ernest Hives, began a three-year apprenticeship at an engineering company in his home town of Reading. There were still very few motor cars to be seen on the roads, but the company did occasionally carry out work on them and the young Ernest began to learn all he could about them. By the time he was fourteen, he was actually teaching customers how to drive!

In 1903, at the age of seventeen, with his apprenticeship completed, Ernest Hives was working in a bicycle shop in Reading, when fate took a hand.

At the time, the Hon. Charles Rolls was an importer and dealer in motorcars and it would be another two years before he met Henry Royce and their famous partnership was formed.

Charles Rolls was also a keen sporting balloonist and is known to have taken part in balloon events at the Reading gasworks. Perhaps it was such an event that brought him to the town. The fact is, the car he was driving broke down and, somehow, it was Ernest Hives who repaired it. Rolls immediately offered him a job as his chauffeur.

Although Ernest Hives left Rolls to extend his motorcar experience with two other dealers, in 1908 he applied for a job at Rolls Royce in Derby. In his own words, when he arrived at Derby station, "it was raining so hard and seemed so drab that I spun a coin to decide whether to go on to Rolls or catch the next train home". Fortunately for Rolls Royce and, indeed, the British aero industry, the coin came down the right way.

In the First World War, Ernest Hives led the team that developed the first successful British aero engine, the 'Eagle'. Between the wars, it was Hives and his team that developed the 'R' engines that powered the Supermarine Schneider Trophy seaplanes and the subsequent Kestrel and Merlin engines.

Ernest Hives was very influential in Rolls Royce developing the original Frank Whittle jet engine into full production and for the succession of world-beating Rolls Royce jet engines that followed.

He was elected to the board of Rolls Royce in 1937 and became chairman in the war years. He retired in 1956, by which time he had been knighted as Lord Hives. It was a remarkable achievement for that twelve-year-old boy from Reading.

Left: Ernest Hives (far left) around 1912, when he was in charge of the Rolls Royce rallying and racing team.

Below: Lord Hives, around the time of his retirement from Rolls Royce in 1956.

When twelve-year-old Ernest Hives began his apprenticeship in Reading, three thousand miles away, at Dayton, Ohio, in America, Wilbur and Orville Wright were running a successful business as bicycle manufacturers.

In 1898, as a hobby, they began to build kites. Soon these were developed into tethered man-carrying gliders, which they flew in the strong winds at Kitty Hawk on the Atlantic coast. Unlike many other aviation pioneers, they learned the rudiments of flight control from these tethered gliders before they began to make untethered flights. Indeed, by 1903, their glider was so successful that they applied for a patent on the design.

Later that year, having developed their basic glider design to be fitted with an engine and propellers, on 17th December 1903, the Wright brothers became the first men in history to fly a heavier-than-air machine. Four flights were made on that day, totalling ninety-eight seconds. The first lasted just twelve seconds and covered one-hundred-and-twenty feet at a speed of 8mph, although the strong headwind meant the actual flying speed was 30mph. Flyer I, as it was called, never flew again. From 1928 until 1948, it was displayed at the Science Museum in London before being given to the National Air & Space Museum, in Washington, where it is still proudly displayed.

The Wright brothers' remarkable success went virtually unreported by the world's press and, thanks to their increasing secretiveness, as they tried to protect their designs and benefit from their achievement, it would be another five years before they gained worldwide recognition. In 1904, with Flyer II, they could stay aloft for five minutes and first flew in a circle. The following year, in Flyer III, they were able to fly for well over thirty minutes and could perform perfect circles and figure-of-eights.

However, it became more and more difficult to avoid being seen by the public and some wild stories about their machines and their exploits began to appear in the press. As a result, from October 1905 until May 1908, the Wright brothers made no more flights. During this time they entered into discussions with the governments of America, Great Britain, France and Germany in attempts to sell their invention, but these negotiations all came to nothing

Above: Probably the most famous aviation photograph in the world. Wilbur Wright watches as his younger brother, Orville, flies for the very first time on 17th December 1903 at Kitty Hawk.

Above: The author, in May 1999, in front of the Wright brothers' Flyer I, hanging in the main hall of the National Air & Space Museum in Washington DC, USA.

By 1907, in France, hopeful aviators such as Voisin, Delagrange, Santos Dumont, Farman and Bleriot were making what were essentially all uncontrolled 'hops', yet claims were made that these were 'world records'.

That year the Wright brothers shipped an improved machine to France and, at the end of May 1908, Wilbur Wright arrived to assemble it in great secrecy. Finally, on 9th August at Le Mans, before an audience that included most of his rival aviation pioneers, he gave a perfect flying display that silenced the doubters forever.

To a large extent, the Wright brothers never did benefit financially from their pioneering achievement. Over the next few years around one hundred of their machines were built, mainly under licence, by companies such as Short Brothers on the Isle of Sheppey, which had started as a balloon manufacturer. One of their first customers for a Wright Flyer was Charles Rolls.

However, development of the Flyer was limited by its method of control, known as 'wing warping' and its complicated launching system. Within a year or two its French rivals were surpassing it, largely due to the 'designer/pilots' who were leading the field there.

By contrast, in Britain, many of the pioneers were originally 'amateur sportsmen', such as Charles Rolls, Moore-Brabazon, Claude Graham-White and Tommy Sopwith. Only AV Roe and Geoffrey de Havilland could be said to be cast in the French mould as 'designer/pilots'.

Left: Charles Rolls, in his Wright brothers' Flyer, built in England under licence by Short Brothers. Sadly, some of the modifications carried out were thought to be responsible for the aircraft crashing at a meeting in Bournemouth when Rolls lost his life, the first fatality among British aviators.

Geoffrey de Havilland was fourteen when his family moved to Crux Easton, a small village near Newbury, just south of the Berkshire/Hampshire border. By 1908, aged twenty-five, he was working as an automobile engineer when news of Wilbur Wright's magnificent flights in France inspired him to build an aeroplane. Like everyone else at the time, his ideas about aeroplane design were entirely guesswork. Nevertheless, his grandfather agreed to loan him £1,000 and he set about the task, assisted by his friend, Frank Hearle.

They began by designing the engine, contracting to have it manufactured for £220. Then, in a small shed in Fulham, they began to build the airframe. In May 1909 Geoffrey married the governess of his young brother and sister and she played a part in their work by sewing the fabric on the wings.

In the summer of 1909, during a visit to Crux Easton, the two friends walked to a nearby historic site, Seven Barrows. There they found some sheds built by John Moore-Brabazon to house his first aeroplane, although he never used them. Geoffrey bought the sheds and transported his half-built aeroplane down from Fulham.

He took rooms for himself and Frank Hearle at the nearby Carnavon Arms public house and, by December, their aeroplane was assembled and ready for testing. However, when Geoffrey tried to get it into the air, it showed a marked reluctance to leave the ground.

Finally, a sloping area was chosen and, with the machine accelerating downhill, he pulled back sharply on the controls. The machine leapt in the air but, immediately, the fragile wings buckled and it crashed back to earth.

Geoffrey was lucky to walk away virtually unscathed from the tangle of metal, wood and fabric. Nothing could be salvaged except the precious engine — and his unshakeable resolve to fly.

Geoffrey de Havilland went 'back to the drawing board' and, the following summer, the two friends were back at Seven Barrows with a completely different design. This time, their careful testing, just a foot or so at a time, higher and higher, proved 'No.2' could actually fly.

Later, Geoffrey sold it for £400 to the Government Balloon Factory at Farnborough, where both he and Frank Hearle went to work. He offered the £400 to his grandfather, but was told he could keep it. For British aviation, the £1,000 had proved to be a good investment.

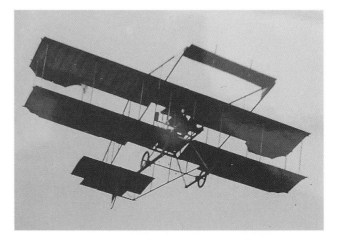

Above: 'No.2' flying at Farnborough in 1910, in the hands of Geoffrey de Havilland.

Below: Geoffrey de Havilland at Farnborough seated in 'No.2'

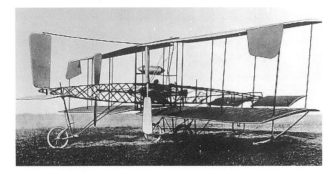

Above: Geoffrey de Havilland's first unsuccessful design.

Painted in oils on canvas. 2003. 500mm x 600mm.

"Look! It's Mr de Havilland's flying machine"

In the summer of 1910, Geoffrey de Havilland, in his first successful aeroplane, taught himself the mysteries of flight in the skies around Newbury. Having fitted a second seat, his friend Frank Hearle, who had helped him build this pioneering craft, was his first passenger. Then it was his wife's turn, clutching their baby son, Geoffrey, in her arms.

Despite the ever growing number of successful aeroplanes, many influential people could not see a really practical use for them. Certainly the British military were not interested and, perhaps half-heartedly, continued to develop airships. The first — 'Nulli Secundus' — flew in September 1907, Samuel Cody having played the major part in its design and construction, with Patrick Alexander as an advisor.

In France and England, ballooning had become a popular sport by 1906 – if you were wealthy enough to take part. Meetings usually included a 'race' that entailed landing as close as possible to a target area, pre-determined by studying the weather conditions. The first in England, organised by the Aero Club, was in early July 1906 and Charles Rolls competed in his balloon 'Enchantress'. Later that month, he brought it to an Aero Club meeting at Reading gasworks, where he took part in a 'Hare and Hounds' race.

The first 'international' balloon race in England took place in May 1908 from the Hurlingham Club, Fulham, with the 'winning post' at Burchett's Green near Maidenhead. The winner was Patrick Alexander's old friend and collaborator, Griffith Brewer, who perhaps had 'insider knowledge' as he then actually lived at Burchett's Green. Brewer remained involved with aviation and, in the 1940s, was the Royal Aeronautical Society's president.

Later in 1908, a resident of Maidenhead, Violet Kavanagh, made her first balloon flight from the town's cricket ground. Following in the footsteps of Garnerin, she became a professional balloonist and parachutist, making more than three-hundred flights, as well as being the first woman to pilot an aeroplane. Sadly, her career was short-lived, for she was fatally injured when her aeroplane crashed at Coventry in July 1910.

As more and more of the 'sporting balloonists' took up flying aeroplanes, the popularity of 'lighter than air' aviation began to wane. The First World War halted any non-military ballooning and although, in post-war years, a few enthusiasts continued flying, the first era of ballooning had effectively ended. The last flight of a balloon from Reading gasworks was in February 1929.

It would be another forty years before the modern era of 'hot air' ballooning began, following the introduction of the propane gas burner. Hot-air balloons could be said to be based upon the ideas of the Montgolfier brothers, back in 1783. In fact, they more truly reflect the ideas of the Reverend John Bacon, which he demonstrated with his balloons at Newbury in 1902 and 1903. Fittingly perhaps, from the beginning of the modern era in the early 1970s, Newbury has remained one of the UK's most important centres for ballooning.

Back in the first decade of the 20th century, as the interest in sporting ballooning waned, the construction of airships in the UK gathered pace. With one notable exception, this was all in the hands of the Army and the Navy.

The exception was Ernest Willows, the son of a Cardiff dentist who, in 1905, when he was just nineteen, built his first small airship. Over the next four years he designed and built a larger version, which first flew in 1909. However, it was his night-time flight from Cardiff to Crystal Palace in August 1910 that brought him to the attention of the public, in particular to the citizens of Berkshire. Navigating by the stars and also the lights of the towns, he steered a course crossing Hungerford, Newbury, Reading, Wokingham and Bracknell.

A useful piece of equipment Willows carried was a megaphone and when he was unsure of his whereabouts, as it seems he frequently was, he descended to a few hundred feet and asked the local populace for directions. After dark, it must have been an unnerving experience for many of Berkshire's late-night revellers.

King George V, who came to the throne in 1910, showed great interest in the many exciting developments in aviation and, in February 1911, invited the twenty-two-year-old Tommy Sopwith to demonstrate his latest aircraft at Windsor Castle. Sopwith had often flown to his sister's house at nearby Datchet and landed there first before going on to land on the lawns at the castle, where he met the King and Princes John, Henry and George, who all showed great interest in the aircraft.

An extract from Gertrude Bacon's book 'Memories of Land and Sky', published in 1928, writing about her first flight in an aeroplane with R Sommer in 1909.

"The ground was very rough and hard, and as we tore along, at an increasing pace that was very soon greater than any motor I had yet been in, I expected to be jerked and jolted.
But the motion was wonderfully smooth – smoother yet - and then - !

"Suddenly there had come into it a new indescribable quality - a lift - a lightness - a life!

Very many there are now who know that feeling: that glorious, gliding sense that the sea-bird has known this million years, and which man so long and so vainly envied and which, even now, familiarity can never rob of its charm.

"But picture if you can, what it meant for the first time; when all the world of aviation was young and fresh and untried: when to rise at all was a glorious adventure, and to find oneself flying swiftly in the air, the too-good-to-be-true realisation of a life-long dream.

"You wonderful aerial record breakers of today and of the years to come, whose exploits I may only marvel at and envy, I have experienced something that can never be yours and can never be taken away from me – the rapture, the glory and the glamour of 'the very beginning'."

Gertrude Bacon, with her father, about 1903

At Datchet the large crowd that gathered to watch Sopwith that day included an eighteen-year-old from Windsor, Sidney Camm. He was the eldest of twelve children of a local carpenter, the family living in Alma Road. Passionate about aircraft design, Sidney had already founded the Windsor Model Aeroplane and Gliding Club. It is interesting to note that, when the club found itself in financial difficulties, there is evidence to suggest that it was Patrick Alexander who came to its rescue.

Just over ten years later, while working for the Martinsyde aircraft company, Sidney Camm came to the attention of Tommy Sopwith, by then chairman of Hawker Aircraft. Sopwith hired Camm as a draughtsman and, just a few years later, appointed him chief designer, a position he held for thirty-four years. He became chief engineer in 1959 and, eventually, managing director. In 1953, Sidney Camm was knighted for his services to aviation and so, very belatedly, was Tommy Sopwith.

Below: Tommy Sopwith's aircraft on the lawns at Windsor Castle in 1911. The Howard Wright biplane was a British design and had no direct connection with the better-known Wright brothers' designs.

Sidney Camm has been described as tall, hook-nosed, hard-swearing, explosive and demanding. Tommy Sopwith once said "I can't imagine why his men put up with him". But he also said "he was the finest designer of aircraft there has ever been".

As early as 1925, Sopwith asked Camm to design aircraft in metal instead of wood and so the unique Hawker method of fabric-covered, jointed tubular structures came about, a construction that proved its worth from the pre-war Hart/Fury biplane family to the legendary 'Battle of Britain' Hurricane.

Camm was sometimes regarded as too traditional in his design approach and perhaps he was in much of his time as Hawker's chief designer. However, that argument can certainly not be applied to his last great masterpiece – the unique Hawker Harrier. Sadly, he never saw the Harrier enter operational service with the RAF. He died in March 1966, at the age of just seventy-two.

Today, a blue plaque marks the house in Alma Road, Windsor, where Sidney Camm was born.

Above: Sidney Camm, founder of the Windsor Model Aeroplane and Gliding Club, photographed about the time Tommy Sopwith landed at Windsor Castle.

Interviewed in the late 1980s, as he approached his 100th birthday, Tommy Sopwith spoke of his pioneering days.

"Crashing did not seem to hurt because we did it so nicely and slowly. Even spectacular crashes often used to have happy endings. But bless you – it was fun."

In 1911, a few months after Tommy Sopwith had been invited to land at Windsor Castle, it was announced that, as part of the celebrations to mark the coronation of King George V, it was planned to carry mail between London and Windsor by air, only the second time in the world such a service had been offered. Earlier in the year, also organised by Captain Sir Walter Windham, a similar service associated with the United Provinces Industrial Agricultural Exhibition at Allahabad, India, had actually been the world's first aerial post.

Mail comprised pre-stamped souvenir envelopes and postcards, in different colours, sold in advance through principal London stores where special pillar-boxes were installed. For return flights, mail was collected from the 'Windsor Chronicle' offices.

Flying arrangements were in the hands of the Grahame-White company, operators of Hendon aerodrome, who had hired four pilots. Two were flying Bleriot monoplanes and two were flying Farman biplanes. The service had been planned to start on Saturday 9th September but difficult weather conditions caused it to be postponed and it was nearly 5pm on the following day before Gustav Hamel was able to make the first flight. It took just fifteen minutes and one bag was carried containing about one-thousand items of mail.

The following day the team of pilots was reduced to three, when one of the Farmans crashed soon after take-off, the pilot, Charles Hubert, unfortunately breaking both legs. Despite this, thirty-seven bags of mail, containing over one-hundred-thousand items, were carried from Hendon to Windsor on sixteen flights on ten different days between the 10th and 26th September.

On 17th and 18th September four mail-carrying flights, with some ten-thousand items, were made from Windsor to Hendon.

Right:: This contemporary publicity postcard of Gustav Hamel is in the personal collection of the author.

Below left: An obviously staged photograph by the publicity-conscious Grahame-White company.

Below right: This original souvenir postcard from 1911 is in the personal collection of the author. The message on the reverse from 'Arnold' explains how he was unable to send it on the first day and sent it the following day. In the event, it is difficult to determine exactly what would have been a 'first day cover'. On that very first flight, the one-thousand items carried by Gustav Hamel were all 'violet' coloured letters and cards, specifically for the Organisers and special 'privileged persons'. 'Arnold' also claims that Warwick Lendon, the artist who drew the picture on the front of the card, is a friend.

(Address only to be written here.)

Mrs Snowden
Hill Cottage
Little Baddow
nr Chelmsford

Painted in oils on canvas. 1999. 450mm x 600mm. Selected for the 1999 Aviation Paintings of the Year Exhibition. Original painting in the collection of HM The Queen at Windsor Castle.

'Postman Gustav'

Gustav Hamel, in his Bleriot monoplane, approaches Windsor carrying the first ever UK airmail. It is just after 5pm on Sunday 10th September 1911.

Geoffrey de Havilland and Sidney Camm turned their youthful enthusiasm into careers that, even today, resonate through aviation history. However, in those pioneering days, there were many others who, in their own way, were trying to develop flying machines. Among those 'forgotten pioneers' were three men from the Maidenhead area – George Davidson, Donald Stevenson and John Benton.

George Davidson and Donald Stevenson were aviation 'visionaries', as many of their writings and sketches show. They could perhaps be likened to Jules Verne or HG Wells, although both attempted to turn their 'visions' into reality. As early as 1889, Davidson actually patented an 'Aerial Machine' which was included in Alexander and Brewer's 1893 book 'Aeronautics'.

By 1898, he was working on his first 'gyrocopter' design and engaged a consulting engineer, William Walker, to carry out experiments on the design of 'lifting propellers'. Walker was a colleague of Patrick Alexander and, later that year, the two of them decided to carry out their own extensive investigation into the 'laws' of propeller design covering thrust, speed, horsepower and blade angle. Funded by Alexander, their work became an aviation 'standard' and was widely quoted in Europe for many years.

By 1906, now in America, Davidson was continuing with his ever more ambitious steam-powered 'gyrocopter' projects, which combined both wings and two 'lifting propellers'. By 1910 he returned to the UK, to build his third design, coming to reside at Taplow, near Maidenhead. He employed, full time, as many as twelve skilled craftsmen and, since he failed to find any financial backing, was reported to have spent over £7,000 of his own money. A contemporary photograph shows a structure of such weight and complexity that its chances of eventually flying were, to say the least, remote. Among Patrick Alexander's books of press-cuttings there are reports from 1910 and 1913 of visits to Davidson by officials of the War Office and the Services, but there is no record of his 'gyrocopter' ever being completed.

Donald Stevenson backed up his more fantastic visions of aviation's future with the practical design and construction of flying models and, although he was working in the first decade of the new century, some of these designs would not have looked out of place in the aviation world of fifty or sixty years later. Starting from the idea of a 'delta-shaped' wing, he developed this to a twin-fuselage design that, as one of his drawings suggests, could even be powered by rockets. Although details of his employment are not known, sometime in the years before World War I, he worked for Claude Graham White at Hendon aerodrome. However, by 1913, he began to build up a very successful motor dealership in Maidenhead and, until late in the 1920s, played no further part in aviation.

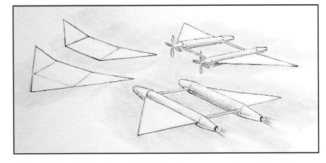

Above: This sketch by the author is based upon a number of Donald Stevenson's drawings. It shows the progression of his design ideas from a simple 'delta-wing' concept, through to a remarkably advanced-looking twin-rocket design. Looking back, this is most probably a visionary's lucky guess. 'Swept-back' wings were subsequently tried at various times, but the mystery of their aerodynamics remained just that until well into the second half of the 20th Century.

Below: 'Johnny' Benton's B6 at Chalvey, awaiting its fabric covering.

'Johnny' Benton was born in Australia, of German parents, who eventually moved to England. He became an electrical engineer, working for Marconi, and his first 'brush with aviation' involved the construction of man-carrying kites, originating from his idea to use them as radio aerials. These also led to the first of many patents he was to file over the coming years.

At Maidenhead, he teamed up with a local man, Will Allen, to build his first aircraft, the B1, in a shed at Bray Road. It looked something like French designs of five years earlier, but with both wings and tailplane of a biplane configuration. Just after Easter in 1911 he managed a few hops in B1. He then rented a larger field and shed near Chalvey, on the way to Slough, where he and Allen built B2.

In a fit of enthusiasm the B2 was entered for the 1911 Daily Mail 'Round Britain Air Race', but never did take part. However, with B3, he managed some genuine short flights near Maidenhead. Then, in 1914, Will Allen was fatally injured by the propeller when starting an engine, but his widow insisted Benton continue with his work and became his new partner. His B6 appeared in 1915, but he failed to interest either the War Office or the Admiralty in his work and became convinced 'the authorities' had stolen many of his patents. His contribution to the war effort came instead with the Benton Munitions company.

There is one last twist to Johnny Benton's various 'brushes with aviation'. Although his final design, B7, never flew, it did incorporate what eventually became known as 'variable geometry wings', a concept similar to that proposed fifty years or so later by Barnes Wallis in his 'swing wing' designs, used with great success on the modern day F111 and Tornado.

'Johnny' Benton in B6

In 1909, when Louis Bleriot had set out to conquer the Channel, he was just one of a number of pilots attempting to win the prize of £1,000 offered by the 'Daily Mail'. The newspaper continued to sponsor aviation and, in 1912 and 1913, Henri Salmet became "the intrepid Daily Mail airman" for a 13-week tour of England and Wales "to prove the practicability and reliability of the modern aeroplane".

In May 1912, Henri Salmet gave demonstrations in his Bleriot monoplane somewhere in the Reading area, before departing for Bath. The following year, during a similar tour, it is known he stayed at the Queen's Hotel in Friar Street, Reading for a few days, while he flew from Woodley Farm, close to the railway at Sonning Cutting, giving two-guinea 'joyrides'. The local newspaper announced a special 'Ladies Day' when there would be a 'lucky dip' for free flights.

Desperate to fly, but without the necessary two guineas, eleven-year-old Winifred Antell from Reading, as she said eighty years later, "made herself really helpful all day around Henri Salmet". Eventually, at the end of the day, she got her free flight, as she vividly recalled when, at the age of ninety-one, she was a guest of honour at the opening of the museum, just a mile or so from where she flew in 1913.

Above: In 1914, Gustav Hamel loops his Bleriot above Windsor Castle.

Also in 1913, Gustav Hamel came to Woodley Farm in his Bleriot, giving demonstration flights and 'joyrides'. Early in 1914, he was invited by the King and Queen to demonstrate 'the loop', a daring new manoeuvre being perfected by leading airmen of the day. Hamel no doubt greatly impressed their Majesties when, on 2nd February, he looped his Bleriot fourteen times consecutively above Windsor Castle.

Sadly, he lost his life just three months later when, flying back from Paris in a new aircraft, he disappeared over the Channel.

Left: Henri Salmet, the "intrepid Daily Mail airman".

Right: In 1913, during Army manoeuvres near Wantage, the Royal Flying Corps flew their Bleriot monoplanes

Within a few weeks of his death, World War I began. Days of flying just for fun were over. It is known that Henri Salmet flew with the French Air Force during the War but, it is thought, he did not survive the conflict.

The Army and Navy had both continued to build airships and, in the Spring of 1913, Berkshire had witnessed a number of military 'lighter than air' flights. However, the future of military aviation had been signalled the year before by the establishment of the Royal Flying Corp and, in the Autumn of 1913, their newly purchased Bleriots took part in Army manoeuvres near Wantage.

When the War began in August 1914, the RFC had a total of seven squadrons of aircraft. Many were of French origin, such as the Bleriots, Moranes and Farmans. Even the few British-built aircraft were powered by French engines.

However, in their different ways, British aviation pioneers such as Geoffrey de Havilland, Tommy Sopwith, the Short brothers, Frederick Handley Page and AV Roe, as well as the Vickers and Bristol companies, were all to play a part in the rapid development of a British aviation industry.

Motor car manufacturers too, such as Alvis, Napier and, of course, Rolls Royce, with Ernest Hives in a leading role, all developed aero engines and, within a short time, thousands of people around the country were learning the new skills demanded by the manufacture of aircraft.

In Reading, for instance, Herbert Engineering, in Wolsey Road, Caversham, became experts in the rebuilding of the French Clerget and Le Rhone rotary aero engines, salvaged from crashed aircraft.

With the rapid expansion of the Royal Flying Corps, the training of its own personnel took on a vital importance and soon Reading was to play a leading part. In 1915, the RFC established a school for flying instructors at Reading, taking over buildings and playing fields owned by the University, including Wantage Hall which still exists today. The following year it was renamed the No.1 School of Military Aeronautics and, about the same time, the Co-op Jam Factory, in Elgar Road, was requisitioned for the No.1 School of Technical Training (Men). Yeomanry House in Castle Hill, now the Register Office, was used as the headquarters for both schools.

At the time, RFC flying activities in the UK were mainly centred at Upavon in Wiltshire and few flights would have been made as far as Reading. However, in August 1915, two 'incidents' involving service aircraft were reported in Reading's weekly newspapers.

The first was the landing of a two-seat aircraft in a field just south of the Basingstoke Road, supposedly "out of fuel". It left later in the day. The second, more serious, incident involved an RFC pilot attempting to land in Coley Park, close by Elgar Road. The newspapers reported "The pilot had lost his way in the misty conditions and was landing to seek directions." Unfortunately he overshot the main part of the field and, realising he could not stop in time, jumped out just before the aircraft ran through a hedge and overturned in a lane. He was lucky to escape without serious injury.

Later in the year, an RFC airfield, known as Coley Park, was indeed established behind the jam factory, in low-lying fields now crossed by the South Reading Relief Road. So perhaps that pilot had known more about the soon-to-be new airfield than the local newspapers.

To modern eyes, training methods at the No.1 School of Military Aeronautics, may seem quite bizarre. However, the lack of purpose-built two-seat training aircraft and, initially at least, the very real shortage of experienced flying instructors, certainly stretched the imagination of the school's senior staff.

With this in mind, it can be seen that using wingless aircraft to teach pupil-pilots was probably quite effective, both in terms of time and also manpower. Potentially dangerous activities such as swinging propellers and removing wheel-chocks could be demonstrated and practised. In the cockpit, pupils could gain familiarisation with all the controls. They could even taxi around the field. It is probable that few pupils had ever had to read a constantly moving compass, as they would when flying. How better to demonstrate this than on a turntable?

Above: These two sketches are based upon photographs taken at the No.1 School of Military Aeronautics in Reading during World War I. They were seen by the author at the RAF Museum in the early 1990s. Sadly, by 2005, re-organisation of the museum's Photographic Section meant that the original photographs could not be found.

Left: In attempting to land in misty conditions in what would later be Coley Park airfield, the pilot of this 'Shorthorn' was lucky to avoid serious injury. The railway bridge in Southcote Farm Lane looks much the same ninety years later.

As far as pupil-observers were concerned, how did you demonstrate what you saw when flying over the enemy trenches? The answer was to put them in an 'aircraft' fifty-feet up in a tree, above a quarter-scale model of a trench system, complete with drifting smoke. It was just like flying over the real thing at two-hundred-feet – without the enemy shooting at you of course!

Compared to the training of the officers destined to be pilots or observers, the training of 'other ranks' at the No.1 School of Technical Training (Men), was very conventional. Hundreds of engine fitters, airframe fitters and riggers were trained in the old jam factory, going on to service the ever growing range of aircraft being introduced into the RFC.

However, in 1917, the decision was taken to relocate Reading and similar technical schools around the country to Halton in Buckinghamshire. By the following year, when the RFC changed its name to the Royal Air Force, the Halton school was growing into what eventually became the famous apprentices school where all RAF engineering staff were trained.

Above: Although almost certainly 'staged' for the camera, this photograph taken on the playing fields in Reading used by the No.1 School of Military Aeronautics, illustrates the use of aircraft without wings, in which students were taught familiarisation with the controls, 'swinging' propellers, 'revving' engines and, perhaps, 'taxiing'.

Below: The first two photographs, taken at Coley Park around 1918, show an Avro 504, which had proved to be an effective training aircraft. In the bottom photograph, a visitor to Coley Park shows off his single-seat Sopwith Pup.

Painted in oils on canvas. 2000. 500mm x 400mm.

'Close Encounter at Coley Park'

It was the photograph on Page 50 and a visit to the railway bridge that can be seen, that inspired this somewhat 'lighthearted' painting. In any case, for a predominantly aviation artist, it was another chance to paint a train! The aircraft shown is a Geoffrey de Havilland design, the DH 1, which was, apparently, not a particularly successful one. For trainspotters' benefit, the engine is an 0-4-2

Not surprisingly, aircraft design and construction developed considerably during the war years. The British aircraft and engines in production when the war ended were far better than those available to the RFC when hostilities began. In fact, these aircraft and engines were to set the standards for aircraft design for very nearly the next twenty years.

It was, of course, the age of the biplane. For not very clear reasons the monoplane, such as the original Bleriot and some wartime German designs, was not trusted by the 'authorities'. Biplanes ruled supreme!

Just one pre-war design — the Avro 504 — which first flew in 1913, was developed and improved to such a degree that various versions of it continued in RAF service until well into the 1930s. And it was the Avro 504K that played the vital role in Berkshire's next 'brushes with aviation' when, immediately after the war, the exciting days of 'barnstorming' began.

Fred and John Holmes were brothers whose home was in the small village of East Hanney, near Wantage, in West Berkshire. Before the war, they were at school in Hampstead and being "mad on flying", spent most of their leisure time at Grahame-White's Hendon airfield.

Fred left school in 1912, aged fifteen, and joined the Avro company as an engineering apprentice. At the outbreak of hostilities, he joined the Royal Naval Air Service.

In 1916, when John was eighteen, he obtained a commission in the RFC and learned to fly at Upavon. With just over three hours' experience flying solo, he decided to undertake the somewhat daring cross-country flight to East Hanney, in a BE2 – Geoffrey de Havilland's last design at the Farnborough factory.

'Berkshire's Barnstormers'

One of the most mysterious things about Berkshire's famous White Horse at Uffington is that it can only be seen effectively from the air. Even the nearest hill only offers a limited view of this evocative tribal symbol or whatever our ancestors intended it to be when they first dug it out of the grass around three thousand years ago. Probably the very first to enjoy this now very well known aerial view were Fred and John Holmes and their partner in the Berkshire Aviation Company, Alan Cobham, when they flew their Avro 504K from nearby East Hanney in 1919.

Painted in oils on canvas. 2007. 600mm x 430mm.

Above: John Holmes' BE2 at East Hanney in October 1916. It was John's father, a keen photographer, who recorded his arrival.

In 1917, when serving in France, engine trouble caused John Holmes to land behind enemy lines and he spent the rest of the war as a prisoner, returning home early in 1919.

Fred and John were keen to build on their aviation experience and pooled their resources with the idea of starting some sort of 'joy riding' activity. In a kind of 'Aviation Exchange & Mart' of the time they advertised for another pilot to join the venture and received a reply from Alan Cobham, an ex-RFC pilot. Thus, in May 1919, the Berkshire Aviation Company came into being.

Cobham went to the Aircraft Disposals Board at Waddon and purchased an Avro 504K – the very first aircraft the Board sold – then flew it to Avro at Hamble for a quick conversion to a three-seater, before flying it to Thatcham where, as Cobham wrote later, there were twelve passengers already waiting for him, with their £1 notes. In a particularly fine summer they also flew in other parts of Berkshire, from Reading (in the fields south of the Basingstoke Road), Abingdon, Faringdon and Wantage, as well as further afield at Aylesbury, Oxford, Bedford and Leighton Buzzard.

However, to quote Cobham's own words, "No sooner were we started than we came up against bureaucracy and 'the rules'.

"Since civil aviation was only just beginning, nobody quite knew what the rules were. I managed to convince the Air Ministry that I was entitled to a pilot's 'B' or commercial licence and Fred Holmes was able to secure his twofold ground engineer's licence, the 'A' licence for the airframe and the 'C' licence for the engine.

"The aircraft itself had to be officially inspected and granted its Certificate of Airworthiness. Then we found that every field from which we proposed to take passengers would need to be inspected and licensed in advance. We intended to visit a great many places, staying from two to five days in each. Countless fields were to be involved and we and the Air Ministry were going to drown in paperwork. But by pleading the cause of civil aviation we managed to secure a 'working arrangement'."

Despite these frustrations, the company carried ten thousand passengers in its first year. On the August Bank Holiday Monday of 1919, for the first time, they also demonstrated 'wing walking', the classic 'barnstormers stunt'. Both Fred and John Holmes carried out the stunt, and continued to do so many times over the following years.

To continue in Alan Cobham's own words, "We were very much like a theatrical touring company and even made it our practice to stay in theatrical lodgings. And we soon learned all the arts of promotion and ballyhoo. We would plaster a town in advance with posters, we would drive around it with banners; we would contact the local press and anyone else who might be influential, promising free flights in return for publicity. We found it useful to enlist the aid of other people in show business and the consequent publicity was very good for business.

"Had we but known it, the small operation which we then had was just about the most substantial thing in the whole of civil aviation. But we were not content with it. Promises of financial support came rolling in and we decided to double our operation, running two shows at once in the summer season and establishing permanent bases in eight seaside resorts. It meant that we needed to engage several more pilots and mechanics."

It was at this time that Oscar Jones, a young ex-RFC friend of Cobham, joined the Berkshire Aviation Company. Always known as OP Jones, he was another who, like Alan Cobham, would become a 'legend' in civil aviation.

Below left to right: Alan Cobham, John Holmes and Fred Holmes, with their first Avro 504K in April 1919.

In Cobham's own words again, "Things started to get difficult. Councils and landowners were increasingly reluctant to allow us to use their fields. And we now carried the burden of a weekly wage bill which came to nearly £100.

"Then, to our alarm, the promises of financial backing started to fade away. We decided to carry on in the hope that the Easter holiday season and the fine weather of springtime would surely put us on our feet. Easter came and it rained solidly for three weeks. We sat idle and watched our scanty resources running down the drain."

Cobham was despondent, nearly broke and suffering ill health. "I took my share of the assets and my share of the debts, and pulled out."

Exactly what happened over the next few years is now unclear. It is known that the Berkshire Aviation Company was officially wound up in 1921. Yet it was claimed that, after carrying ten thousand passengers in its first year, by the spring of 1922, passengers had risen dramatically, to nearly thirty-four thousand.

John Holmes gave up flying in 1923, when he joined British Petroleum. He remained on the Officers Reserve of the RAF, however, and retained an involvement with his brother at East Hanney where, it appears, some sort of 'barnstorming' activity must have continued.

In 1925, Fred Holmes and OP Jones formed Berkshire Aviation Tours which became a limited company the following year when, as seen on the aircraft, FJV Holmes was the 'sole proprietor'. A move to Witney saw the addition of six extra aircraft and, three years later, the company merged with Northern Air Transport at Manchester.

Fred Holmes formed Air Travel Limited in 1929 and, although little is known about its activities, it continued until 1936. That year Fred Holmes joined Airports Limited as works and service manager of the new Gatwick Airport. He remained there until 1947, receiving an MBE for his wartime services. In 1948, he joined a new aviation company called Tiltman Langley, as works manager, eventually retiring in 1963, but continuing as a consultant until his death in 1969.

John Holmes, like all Reservists, was called into the RAF at the start of World War II. He became a squadron leader and served as an operations

Top: Fred Holmes (left) and OP Jones, with local children at East Hanney. 'Holmes' can be seen painted on the aircraft, indicating that the photograph was taken some time during the 'in between' years before Berkshire Aviation Tours was established.

Centre: The Berkshire Aviation Tours' fleet of Avro 504Ks in 1925.

Right: A publicity postcard of the company's Avro 504K about 1927, when Fred Holmes was the 'sole proprietor'. It includes the photograph of the pilot, C S Kent, as well as his signature.

controller in Fighter Command, first at Biggin Hill and Hornchurch during the Battle of Britain and then at Tangmere during the run-up to D-Day. Little is known about his post-war activities.

It was, of course, Alan Cobham who went on to become one of the best-known names in British aviation. On leaving Berkshire, he first went for a few months to the Airco company, where Geoffrey de Havilland had been chief designer before setting up his own company. Then, in January 1921, Cobham was hired as the first pilot of the newly formed de Havilland Aeroplane Hire Service. He undertook photographic work, as well as air-taxi and charter flying that included long-distance flights throughout Europe and the Middle East.

He also began test-flying new types of de Havilland aircraft and flying in competitions such as the King's Cup Air Race, which he won in 1924 in the prototype DH50. That year he also flew the director of Civil Aviation, Sir Sefton Brancker, on a tour to explore possible airship routes to the Far East.

Over the next two years, Cobham flew other pioneering flights in de Havilland aircraft, to South Africa and Australia. In 1926, on his return from Australia, he landed his seaplane on the Thames, in front of the Houses of Parliament, watched by an estimated crowd of one million people. Soon after, by now an international celebrity, he was knighted for his 'services to aviation'.

Leaving de Havilland the following year, he set up his own company and, between 1929 and 1935, toured the UK with what became popularly known as 'Cobham's Flying Circus', with his team of aerobatic pilots, 'wing walkers' and parachutists, as well as giving the public opportunities for 'joy rides'.

Although perhaps still associated with his 'Circus', it was Alan Cobham's work begun in the late 1930s that is his real 'aviation legacy'.

Flight Refuelling was the company he started then and its equipment and methods developed before World War II, still provide the basis for techniques used today by airforces throughout the world.

OP Jones' career is more difficult to trace. Somehow, he graduated from flying single-engine, 3-seat 'joy-riders', to four-engine, 28-seat airliners and, by the mid-1930s, was a captain on Imperial Airways' fleet of giant biplane Handley Page HP42s. And he was a well known captain too, who often featured in the company's publicity. Perhaps it was his 'sea-captain's beard' that gave added assurance in the still youthful world of air travel.

World War II brought a halt to his career as an airline pilot and he joined the Air Transport Auxiliary. In the post-war years, with the creation of BOAC, he became the company's senior captain, continuing in the role through to the introduction of jet-airliners.

Left: Sir Alan Cobham at Reading Aerodrome, in the early 1930s.
Below right: OP Jones (right) near the end of his long airline career.

While the Holmes brothers were 'barnstorming' their way around the country, in Sussex another young man was taking his first uncertain steps in a career that would eventually bring him to Berkshire and the leading role in the county's aviation history.

Frederick George Miles was the eldest son of the owner of the Star Laundry in Portslade, a small town between Brighton and Shoreham. In 1916, while his father had been serving in France and his mother struggling to keep the laundry going, he had decided to leave school. He was just thirteen. With the little money he had, he bought an ancient motorcycle, which he hired out to other boys at sixpence an hour. Problems with such things as licences and insurance were 'overlooked' and the enterprise proved so successful that he obtained a second machine.

He then bought an equally ancient Ford Model T van and set up a delivery service for small businesses, including the family laundry. Hauling big laundry baskets about was incredibly hard physical work for a young lad, but it helped him develop a strong physique. Inevitably, the ancient van eventually disintegrated around him. He had to seek more gainful employment and, eventually, he became the projectionist at the local cinema.

Although originally known as Fred within his family, he was gradually called 'FG' or just 'Miles' by his friends and colleagues and it was thus that the young entrepreneur would become known as his career blossomed.

In 1925, when FG was twenty-two, he flew for the first time — a five-shilling joy-ride. Suddenly, aviation became his passion and, from the very beginning, he wanted to design and build aeroplanes.

He had been building a small sports car but, with the aid of one of his brothers and a few friends, its wooden bodywork was transformed into the framework of a small biplane, to be called the Gnat. All this was going on in the laundry premises at Portslade and it should be remembered that 'behind the scenes' was FG's father. He seems to have given his eldest son unstinting support as the young man pursued his dreams and this was never more in evidence than when, with the Gnat's construction well underway, FG decided he must learn to fly. Typically for him, this idea was soon developed into a much more exciting and ambitious project.

FG had been told of a local man, Cecil Pashley, who had learned to fly in 1908 and, before the war, had run a flying school at Shoreham with his brother. In total he had amassed an astonishing six thousand hours in the air. Although he owned an Avro 504K which was in store at Croydon, he had retired from flying and worked in London.

FG went to see him and, surprisingly perhaps, the brash twenty-two-year-old persuaded the vastly more experienced Pashley, fifteen or so years his senior, to join him in a new aviation venture. The idea was to start a flying school, a joy-riding concern and eventually to design and build aircraft. Pashley was to receive a reasonable wage, financed by FG's father, of course, while FG would just have his expenses covered.

In this way, the Gnat Aero Company was born.

In fact, the Gnat itself was never completed. Perhaps Cecil Pashley, the one real aviator among them, didn't think it looked right. Perhaps, as a single-seater, it was realised it would not be of much use. Instead, it was Pashley's Avro 504K that replaced the Gnat in the Portslade laundry, being dismantled and refurbished by Miles and his friends, no doubt under Pashley's close supervision.

Over the following months, the new company's activities expanded. First, a small field and barn near Shoreham were rented, but the application for use as an airfield was refused by the Air Ministry. Nevertheless, the refurbished Avro was transported there and 'Pash', as he was better known, began flying lessons for FG and four other pupils.

With a few hours' dual-instruction behind him, FG thought he was ready to go solo, but the more cautious 'Pash', probably thinking of his precious Avro, the company's one and only asset, advised against it. Early the next morning, FG went to the airfield alone, started the aircraft himself and went solo. In the afternoon, he began to give two other people lessons.

The next few years saw a whirlwind of activities as the company expanded. Cecil Pashley obtained his 'B' licence – an absolute necessity if you were flying 'for hire or reward'.

The youngest Miles brother, George, then in his mid-teens, joined the enterprise and, with FG, gained much valuable experience for their later careers as designers by carrying out maintenance and repairs on the Avro.

Below: The 'Gnat', taking shape in the Star Laundry at Portslade.

Within a short time, thanks to yet more help from FG's father, the fledgling company bought the first of a number of 'antique' aircraft, plus spare engines and other equipment. Then, when this expansion required the acquisition of a real hangar, a World War I vintage Bessoneaux type, was found.

Early in 1926, they were able to lease a more suitable field nearby, to which they transferred their operations. The Gnat Aero Company became Southern Aircraft Limited and the Southern Aero Club was formed. To gain publicity and attract potential members, it was decided to give a flying display. However, hardly had advertisements appeared, when a letter arrived from the Civil Aviation Authority telling them to cease all operations and to expect a visit from no less a person than the director, Sir Sefton Brancker.

Don Brown, a friend of Miles and one of the team of 'local volunteers', recounted the story of Brancker's visit many years later in his excellent book. He told how Miles, having heard nothing further from the Authority, decided to carry on with the flying display. He felt he couldn't let the public down and hoped that he could, at least, repay some of his father's money.

Then, an hour or so before the actual display, Brancker arrived, piloting himself in a Bristol fighter and landing successfully on the small field — no mean feat in a heavy machine without brakes. "So this is the headquarters of the Independent Air Force," he greeted Miles. However, he accepted a beer in the new clubhouse.

Later, as he looked around the makeshift workshop, he remarked "No licences, no certificates of airworthiness and no proper inspection, eh?" But he listened as Miles told him of his hopes and plans for the future. Then, as he prepared to leave and Miles waited for the final blow, Brancker said, "Really you chaps, you know this sort of thing mustn't go on indefinitely".

Sadly, four years after he 'turned a blind eye' and gave Miles his chance to succeed in his chosen career, Sir Sefton Brancker lost his life when the airship R101 crashed on its way to India.

Right: At Shoreham in 1925. FG Miles is on the extreme right. Cecil Pashley is in the centre. It is thought Lionel Bellairs is on his right.

True to his promise to Brancker, Fred Miles and his team at Southern Aircraft did mend their ways. Fred himself gained his 'B' licence and could then, legitimately, fly with pupils and fare-paying passengers.

Later, he also gained four different categories of licence as a ground engineer. He was the first to acknowledge the debt he owed to his friend, Don Brown, who boosted Fred's curtailed schooling by coaching him in mathematics.

It was a real blow to the company's future when 'Pash' suffered an engine failure when taking off in the Avro. Luckily, he and his two passengers escaped serious injury, but the aircraft was a write-off. None of their other 'antiques' could earn money like the Avro and, once again, it was Fred's father who came to the rescue. The replacement Avro 504K had previously been owned by John Cobb, the famous racing motorist, and it can still be seen today in the RAF Museum at Hendon.

Right: The ex-John Cobb / Southern Aircraft Avro 504K. sketched by the author at the RAF Museum in 1998.

Luck was on their side when, through the closure of the Avro factory at Hamble, they were able to buy a lot of equipment, including airframes and engines. Before long they were able to build a second Avro 504K and had enough spares and other equipment to ensure both machines could be kept flying.

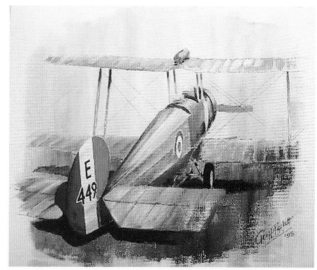

So began a period that Don Brown described as "the best in our career" -- 'barnstorming' around Sussex in much the same way as Alan Cobham, the Holmes brothers and OP Jones had 'barnstormed' around Berkshire.

'Pash' led one joy-riding team and FG Miles led another. Flying lessons back at Shoreham were in the hands of a new flying instructor, just one new member of staff employed as the little airfield and its clubhouse grew in popularity.

They continued to buy and sell secondhand aircraft, some interesting but otherwise of doubtful use like a troublesome 1918 Martinsyde fighter. Some were more practical, such as two Desoutter 3-seaters and other Avros, all used for joy-riding.

The cost of the most successful 'club aeroplane' of that time, the de Havilland 'Moth,' was beyond their means. However, when a visitor badly damaged his Moth trying to land in the small field, they bought the wreckage and rebuilt what became known as 'Jemimah'.

While all this was going on, FG Miles hadn't forgotten his dream of being an aircraft designer. Among the aircraft bought from Avro was a small low-powered biplane known as the 'Baby'. Pioneer aviator Bert Hinkler had flown it non-stop to Turin a few years earlier.

Miles decided to fit it with a more powerful engine and, although his 'unscientific' approach to the re-design caused Don Brown some concern, the refurbished aircraft flew well. It seems Miles had an instinctive feel for aircraft design.

FG's next design project was more ambitious – an even more extensive re-design of the Avro Baby – and it resulted from the desire of one of the Southern Aero Club members, Lionel Bellairs, to have his own aerobatic aircraft. Bellairs had been involved with Miles since the days of building the Gnat and had been one of the five original pupils taught by Pash. Wealthy enough to buy his own aircraft and also generous enough to pay frequent progress payments, Bellairs was even willing to allow the fledgling aircraft manufacturing company to use the first aircraft for demonstrations while he waited for the second to be built.

'Well travelled Martlet'

Lionel Bellairs originally took delivery of G-AAYX, the fourth Martlet to be built. During 1934 it was owned by the Reading Aero Club but, after a crash, was rebuilt at Gatwick. In use until the outbreak of the War, it was then stored in a barn until 1947 when it was restored at Woodley and flown again by FG and George Miles and Don Brown. By then it had been bought by Billy Butlin for demonstrations at his holiday camps.
It still exists today, owned by the Shuttleworth Trust.

Painted in watercolours. 2005.
150mm x 200mm.

The more complex design work involved in the construction of a virtually complete new aircraft led to the employment of an experienced aviation draughtsman, Horace Miles (no relation).

Writing much later about those days, Don Brown said "Design work proceeded concurrently with construction and there were occasions when there was some doubt as to which came first! Miles, in particular, was prone to go ahead with the manufacture of welded metal fittings, leaving the drawings and calculations to follow after and, as he was the only one of the team who could weld, it was difficult to stop him."

FG Miles first flew the new aircraft in the early summer of 1929 and it proved to be an instant success. It was named the 'Martlet', after the heraldic bird of the county of Sussex. Although it was designed to be a two-seater if required, the six aircraft that were eventually built between 1929 and 1931 were all single-seaters, fitted with five different types of engine. While the second and third Martlets were being constructed, FG was somehow persuaded to undertake the design of a 'more modern' variation which became known as the 'Metal Martlet.

Financed again by Lionel Bellairs, it had a fuselage constructed in square-section metal tubes covered by detachable wood and fabric fairings. The wooden wings were conventional but, unlike the original Martlet, were designed to fold. Its handling was just as good as the original Martlet, but its more powerful engine gave it a much higher speed.

It was then decided that the purchase of a large field next to their airfield would result in the ideal regional airfield for the future. Thanks to their growing success and supported by the stature in the local community of FG's father, the bank lent them the considerable sum of money involved.
The gamble eventually paid off and, for many years, Shoreham Airport has been one of the busiest in the south of England.

Success seemed assured for FG Miles. He was already an aircraft designer and manufacturer, as well as being a director of a successful flying club with its own airfield.

Then, in the summer of 1931, to the amazement of his friends and work colleagues, he threw it all away and emigrated to South Africa.

A year earlier, among the new members of the Southern Aero Club were Maxine Freeman-Thomas and her husband, Viscount Ratendone. Better known to her friends as 'Blossom', she came from a well known acting family. Her father was Sir Johnston Forbes-Robertson, one of the foremost actor/ managers of the day, and her mother was the actress, Gertrude Elliott. Her aunt, Maxine Elliott, after whom Blossom was named, was another popular actress who also played a big part in London 'high society'.

Despite the privileges of her upbringing, Blossom had suffered a handicap since childhood when, following an illness, she had lost an eye. The fact that she had overcome this handicap — and, in later life, many people did not even realise she had a glass eye — says much for her character and personality.

She had inherited talents in all the arts and languages and, although her formal education almost certainly didn't include higher mathematics, she had demonstrated various practical skills.

In 1924, she had married the Hon. Inigo Freeman-Thomas, Viscount Ratendone and, in the opinion of her Aunt Maxine, was lucky to have made such a match. However, for Blossom, it had proved to be an unhappy and empty life.

In 1930, by joining the Southern Aero Club and learning to fly, perhaps Blossom thought it would be an outlet for the energies and intellect she had been unable to satisfy in her married life. In the months to come, flying was certainly to change her life, but not in the way she had expected, because she fell in love with her flying instructor, FG Miles.

With the passage of time, it is now difficult to trace the course of their love affair. Blossom went solo in July 1930, after just fifteen hours' tuition. Shortly after, her husband bought her the de Havilland Moth 'Jemimah' which had, of course, been rebuilt by Southern Aircraft. Later in the year, he became a director of the company.

Early in 1931, Blossom ordered a Martlet, the sixth and last to be built, which first flew in May. Blossom's log book showed that she and FG visited Reading Aerodrome in her Moth in June 1931. Exactly what happened next is impossible to know but, in August, in what looks like panic, FG sold everything he had and emigrated to South Africa, taking with him a small Simmonds Spartan biplane. However, it seems his love for Blossom was just too strong and, in September, he sold the Spartan for just enough for his return fare to England. Miles, as she always called him, and Blossom started a life together very different from the life she had known. They 'barnstormed' around the country with friends, living in a caravan, then rented a small office above a shop in Sevenoaks, where they began to design their first aeroplane together.

In the meantime, Blossom was going through divorce and, in March 1932, she and Miles married.

Painted in oils on canvas. 1997. 500mm x 600mm. Original painting in the collection of Mrs V Beckett

'Time to head home'

As storm clouds gather in the North, FG Miles banks the new 'Metal Martlet' above Beachy Head and decides it would be wise to head back to his base at Shoreham.

The scene is set in 1930, when the twenty-seven-year-old Miles had been involved in aviation for five years and already had one successful design to his credit. It seems that he was persuaded by some of his RAF friends that metal construction would be required in the future, particularly for service aircraft. Quickly adapted from his first design, the Metal Martlet proved to be another success. However, fate was soon to take a hand in his life and it would be another ten years before metal construction was again used on a Miles design.

Nothing is really known about their financial situation in those early years together. Miles had lost what little he may have had and his potential for earning must have been limited. Did Blossom have a personal income? Or was her divorce settlement particularly generous? Certainly, their relative affluence in just a few years would seem to have depended on Blossom.

Under the guidance of her new husband, Blossom's natural talents quickly made her a more than competent aviation draughtswoman and she played a major part in the design of their first aircraft. It was a tiny single-seat sporting biplane known as the 'Satyr' and it was built for them by Parnall Aircraft at Yate, near Bristol, for whom Miles had previously carried out test-flying.

The Satyr first flew in the early summer of 1932, but it was a few months later, in August, when Miles was flying it from Yate to Shoreham that he decided to call in at Reading Aerodrome for lunch.

It was a decision that would change his life.

Above and below:
Miles with the Satyr, clearly showing the aircraft's small size.

'Fateful day'
Miles, in the Satyr, arrives at Reading Aerodrome in August 1932.

Painted in watercolours. 2005. 300mm x 200mm

Reading Aerodrome can be traced back, indirectly, to World War I, when Herbert Engineering in Caversham began by rebuilding aero engines. Among the apprentices, joining the company soon after the war, were Charles Powis and Jack Phillips. Perhaps it was then that the seeds of an interest in aviation were planted in Charles Powis. However, the main engineering experience of the two boys was gained in the post-war years when the company began to build the HE range of motor cars. Well made, but rather expensive, the cars were originally a success and the company prospered. By 1924, however, falling sales resulted in the company going into receivership for the first time, and their apprentices were made redundant.

Although they were still in their very early twenties, Jack Phillips and Charles Powis decided to go into business together, setting up a small motorcycle repair and sales centre, the 'Reading Motor Exchange'. The business prospered to such an extent that they quickly outgrew their original premises and bought land in the Oxford Road, where they constructed purpose-built showrooms and workshops. Over the next ten years or so, Phillips & Powis diversified into sales of bicycles, wireless sets and, eventually, motor cars, operating from shops, showrooms and workshops in different parts of Reading.

However, it was in 1928, just four years after they first set up in business, that Charles Powis persuaded Jack Phillips their company should expand into a new and exciting activity — aviation. His enthusiasm began when, for their summer holiday in France, he and his wife decided, in his own words, "to be very brave and fly". On their return, Powis began flying lessons at Brooklands. His instructor was OE Simmonds, designer of the Simmonds Spartan aircraft. Powis gained his pilot's licence in October.

Although Phillips & Powis Aircraft (Reading) Limited was not registered until March 1929, Charles Powis had wasted no time. Even before he gained his pilot's licence, he had acquired the sales agency for two types of aircraft, not only the Simmonds Spartan, but also the very popular de Havilland Moth. By mid-September 1928, a Moth was displayed in P&P's Oxford Road showroom.

Before the end of the year, not only had P&P purchased a Moth and an Avro 504, but they had also 'borrowed' (and later purchased) an area known as 'One Hundred Acre Field' in the then scattered little village of Woodley, near Reading.

Local interest in aviation had already been demonstrated in July 1928, when the Berks, Bucks & Oxon Flying Club (BBO) was formed in Reading. The club's aims were 'the training of pilots and the furtherance of civil aviation'. But the enthusiastic members lacked both aircraft and an aerodrome! In September, the club first offered flying lessons, by an arrangement with the London Aero Club at Hanworth. In October 1928, it organised Reading's first 'Air Pageant' at Swallowfield Park. Among the visitors were Charles Powis and FG Miles, who was representing the Southern Aero Club. It was perhaps, the first time the two met. One of the first BBO members was Winifred Spooner, who had recently moved to Wokingham. She did have her own aircraft and was already very well known in aviation circles, having learned to fly in 1927 and quickly gained her 'B' or commercial licence. She was a very successful racing pilot, coming third in the 1928 King's Cup and fourth in the 1930 Circuit of Italy. In December 1930 she made national headlines when, during an attempt on the Croydon to Cape Town record, her aircraft 'ditched' in the sea about two miles from the Italian coast. Her co-pilot was injured and, leaving him floating on a wing, she

Above: Winifred Spooner

swam ashore to organise his rescue. For this heroic deed, early in 1931, she was given the 'Freedom' of Wokingham, cheered by the crowds as she travelled to and from the Town Hall in the town's largest fire engine. Meanwhile, P&P had continued their perhaps more 'commercially focussed' aviation activities. In September 1928 a P&P advertisement in the local newspaper mentioned a new aerodrome and flying club and, later, the newspaper claimed that Air Ministry approval had already been obtained.

In the spring of 1929, the aerodrome began to take shape, the level, grassed, well-drained field offering a landing run of some seven hundred yards in most directions. Several lock-up garages were erected to house aircraft with folding wings and there was a single fairly large hangar, probably the World War I 'Bessoneau' type. At Easter, flying displays and joy-riding were planned by the Thames at Caversham, promoting the new Reading Aerodrome.

P&P had recruited two ex-RAF officers to be flying instructors and, for two afternoons, they gave flying demonstrations and took several hundred people for flights over Reading in the company's Moth and Avro 504. But, on Easter Monday, disaster struck. As the Avro was being brought in to land at Caversham, a strong gust of wind caught the aircraft and it crashed. Luckily the occupants were unhurt, but the aircraft was severely damaged. As if that wasn't enough, within hours, a gale developed at Woodley, blowing down the hangar and damaging the Moth. Fortunately, the aircraft was quickly repaired and, within a few days, eight pupils had received instruction.

A replacement hangar was acquired, supposedly part of a large Handley Page shed sited near Stonehenge. It was to serve the company for many years. A replacement Avro 504 was bought from Southern Aircraft and was delivered to Woodley by FG Miles in early May.

Before the end of the month, Sir Alan Cobham brought his 'Flying Circus' to Reading Aerodrome for the first time, an event that attracted thousands of spectators. Among the many hundreds of 'joy-riders' who flew during the two days were one hundred and twenty local children, their flights being among the ten thousand sponsored by Sir Charles Wakefield, during Cobham's national tour.

Despite the setbacks at Easter, P&P's activities at Woodley prospered, particularly aircraft sales. The flying school turned out a stream of qualified pilots and Charles Powis and his wife, Pauline, decided to start a club for the ex-pupils. Thus the Reading Aero Club came into being. By contrast, the fortunes of BBO declined until National Flying Services (NFS), with ambitious plans to set up a chain of flying clubs and airfields across the country, took it 'under its wing'.

'The Circus comes to Town'

Sir Alan Cobham brought his 'Flying Circus' to Reading Aerodrome three times between 1929 and 1932, with the aim of making Berkshire people 'air-minded'. He was, of course, no stranger to the Reading area, having flown from the fields near the Basingstoke Road in his 'barnstorming' days with the Berkshire Aviation Company.

Painted in oils on canvas. 2000. 750mm x 600mm

62

NFS reached an agreement with P&P to lease some land in the north-east corner of the airfield where, with Government funding, they built a clubhouse and a hangar for twelve aircraft.

For the next few years, P&P's aircraft sales and service activities and the work of the two flying schools ensured the airfield was a busy place. Indeed, the P&P flying school alone boasted eight assorted Moths, all painted in their distinctive yellow and cream colour scheme. P&P also bought a Desoutter cabin monoplane for air-taxi work.

Special events, such as the visits of Cobham's 'Flying Circus', always attracted huge crowds. There were three such visits between 1929 and 1932. However, all records were broken in June 1930 when, in perfect weather, twenty thousand people came to a BBO 'Air Fete', being treated to a four-hour flying display.

On 16th May 1931, despite heavy rain in the morning, some forty visiting aircraft flew into Reading Aerodrome for the official opening of Reading Aero Club's new clubhouse. As part of an afternoon flying programme, a Ladies' Handicap Race was held, with two heats and a final, over a triangular course starting and finishing at the airfield. The spire of St Paul's Church in Wokingham and Twyford Railway Station were 'marker beacons'.

Below: Seven of the nine competitors who took part in the Ladies Handicap Race. The winner, Miss GE Aitkin, unfortunately cannot be identified here. However, in second place was Pauline Gower, seen in the centre, who would eventually be head of the women's section of the Air Transport Auxiliary in World War II. In third place was Amy Johnson, seen here on the extreme left, who had shot to international fame the year before when she flew from England to Australia. Winifred Spooner who, at 106mph, flew the fastest lap that day, is second from the right. Sadly, in January 1933, she died of pneumonia, aged just thirty-two.

Left: A typical Sunday morning scene at Reading Aerodrome in 1930. The sign above their first wooden hangar reads Phillips & Powis Aero Garage. All the aircraft appear to be variations of the de Havilland Moth.

Left: The clubhouse of the Reading Aero Club was opened at Woodley in May 1931.

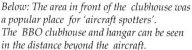

Below: The area in front of the clubhouse was a popular place for 'aircraft spotters'. The BBO clubhouse and hangar can be seen in the distance beyond the aircraft.

Painted in oils on canvas. 1997. 600mm x 700mm. Original painting donated to the Museum of Berkshire Aviation. 2006.

'Ladies Race'

In the afternoon of 16th May 1931, four ladies 'battle it out' around the 'marker beacon' of Twyford railway station, before heading back to the finish line at Reading Aerodrome

The Reading Aero Club's new clubhouse had proved an attraction for both members and visitors to the airfield. Such was the case on the morning of 14th December 1931, when Jack Phillips' brother, a flight lieutenant in the RAF, flew in for a visit. With him were two colleagues from No.23 Squadron, based at RAF Kenley, their Bristol Bulldog fighters no doubt causing great interest among the pupil pilots present on that Monday morning.

One of the pilots also caused great interest because, not only was he one of the RAF's leading aerobatic pilots, but he was also a celebrated rugby player, who many expected would be playing for England against the touring South Africans in a couple of weeks. Twenty-one-year-old Pilot Officer Douglas Bader was, indeed, a first-class sportsman. At Cranwell, he had gained his 'blues' in cricket, rugby, hockey and boxing. He had represented the RAF at rugby and cricket and had recently played rugby for the Combined Services against the South African 'Springboks'.

More importantly perhaps to the trainee pilots, a few months before, Bader had flown with his flight commander, Harry Day, in a breathtaking two-man synchronised aerobatic display at the RAF's famous Hendon Air Display. Bader had often been disciplined by Day for his habit of 'bending the rules', in particular where low-level aerobatics were concerned. Nevertheless, Day usually tolerated what he saw as the young man's high spirits and 'devil may care' attitude, recognising Bader was an exceptional pilot.

In the Hendon display they had flown Gamecock fighters, a lighter and more manoeuvrable machine than the more powerful Bulldogs. Nevertheless, Bader had flown more than thirty two hours on Bulldogs and was cleared to be fully aerobatic.

Paul Brickhill recounts in his book 'Reach for the Sky' that, when the RAF pilots were about to return to Kenley, Bader was asked to 'put on a show'. Bearing in mind Harry Day's many warnings, Brickhill says he declined, but an injudicious remark by one of the trainee pilots angered him.

Others who knew him have suggested, Bader just couldn't resist 'putting on a show' and would have made a small gesture of thanks for a pleasant visit without being asked. Whatever the truth of the matter, as the three Bulldogs were climbing away, Bader banked his aircraft sharply to the left and headed back to perform a low-level, slow roll across the airfield.

Perhaps he had failed to gain enough speed or perhaps he just misjudged his height but, as he rolled out of the inverted position, the aircraft sank lower and the wing tip touched the grass, tipping it forward into the ground. The engine broke clear and the remainder of the airframe somersaulted over and over. When the small group from the clubhouse reached the wreckage, they found a semi-conscious Bader, still strapped in, trapped by his legs.

If it was, indeed, an injudicious remark by a trainee pilot that, indirectly, caused Bader to crash, it was quick thinking by of one of the other trainees that saved his life. An Australian trainee, Jack Cruttendon, was one of the first to reach the tangle of wreckage and saw that Bader was bleeding profusely from his badly injured right leg.

He managed to staunch the flow of blood by pressing on the femoral artery and continued to do so while they freed Bader from the wreckage, waited for the ambulance to arrive from Reading and then made the return journey with him to the Royal Berkshire Hospital.

Luckily, one of the best local surgeons, Leonard Joyce, had been operating at the hospital that day and was detained just as he was leaving. Despite Bader being in deep shock, Joyce decided to amputate his right leg just above the knee. It was only Bader's superb physical condition that kept him alive. Two days later, Joyce had to amputate his left leg below the knee. Slipping in and out of consciousness, with morphine masking the pain, Bader's life hung by a thread for more than a week.

As he got stronger, further operations followed and, in early February, his left leg was fitted with a pylon, or 'peg-leg'. With the aid of crutches, he began to move around the hospital and its surroundings. He even went down into Reading to the cinema, accompanied by two of his nurses.

Right: Douglas Bader (right) and Harry Day with one of their Gamecock fighters in which they performed their synchronised aerobatic display at the 1931 Hendon Air Display.

'Bader's Bad Show'

When he returned to RAF duties, Douglas Bader completed his flying log book for Monday 14th December 1931. He wrote "Cross country to Reading. Crashed slow rolling near ground. Bad Show".

Painted in oils on canvas. 1998. 600mm x 500mm.
Selected for the 1998 'Aviation Paintings of the Year' Exhibition.
Original painting donated to the Royal Berkshire Hospital 2006.

The wreckage of Douglas Bader's Bristol Bulldog at Reading Aerodrome on 14th December 1931.

Dorothy Brace was the closest of all the nurses who tended him and, eventually, she became matron at Battle Hospital, Reading. Many years later she recalled that Bader once said wryly to her "never do anything in a temper", perhaps confirming his reason for attempting that fateful slow roll.

An RAF Court of Enquiry was held at the hospital and, somehow, avoided the question of blame, perhaps thinking Bader had been punished enough. It was the middle of April before he left the Royal Berkshire Hospital and transferred to the RAF hospital at Uxbridge.

There he was fitted with artificial limbs, ironically perhaps, made by the Desoutter brothers who had previously made aeroplanes. Bader's remaining 'brushes with aviation' do not generally relate directly to Berkshire and, in any case, his inspiring story has been well documented many times.

In the post-war years, when working for Shell, his personal aircraft was a Miles Gemini. He visited Woodley on a number of occasions and, in 1956, opened the Coronation Hall there. He was eventually knighted for his charitable work for disabled people.

Above and left: The Douglas Bader that most people remember, the World War II 'hero' with his Hurricane at the time of the Battle of Britain. In the larger photograph he is seen with some of his pilots from 242 Squadron.

Below: Douglas Bader in the post-war years, seen at Woodley in his twin-engine Miles Gemini.

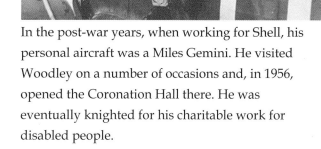

The RAF returned to Berkshire for the first time since World War I, when the new airfield at Abingdon was opened in 1932.

No.15 Squadron were the first residents, flying Fairey Gordon bombers.

Soon after, No.40 Squadron also took up residence, with their new Hawker Hart bombers.

A few years later Abingdon became the long-term home of the Oxford University Air Squadron.

Fairey Gordon

During the early 1930s, civil airfields in Berkshire experienced mixed fortunes. Just a few months after Charles Powis opened Reading Aerodrome, the pioneer, Donald Stevenson, having built up his successful motor dealership, decided to create an airfield and club at Bray, near Maidenhead.

It opened with a fanfare of local publicity but, just eight weeks later, without any clear reason for doing so, it ceased to function. The airfield was used when Sir Alan Cobham brought his 'Flying Circus' to Maidenhead in 1932 and continued to be used intermittently for many years.

A few years after Bray first opened, an airfield with the grandiose title of Cookham International Airport was opened a few miles away. It appears that an adjacent hotel hoped to cash-in on Maidenhead's then reputation for being the place for 'naughty weekends'. Photographs showed that the airfield attracted a few flyers from France and Germany but the generally poor ground conditions counted against it, as well as the local council and some nearby residents. The 'international airport' did not survive long.

In 1935, what was to be by far the most successful of East Berkshire's airfields came into being when the de Havilland company opened White Waltham as a Reserve Flying School for the RAF.

'White Waltham Tigers'

Below: De Havilland Flying School Tiger Moths, with their distinctive red and silver livery, were a familiar sight in the Maidenhead area until the outbreak of World War II.

Painted in watercolours. 2005. 150mm x 200mm

Below: The de Havilland Flying School at White Waltham in 1935

At Reading Aerodrome, there were also mixed fortunes. While Reading Aero Club prospered, in 1933 the parent company of BBO, National Flying Services, was forced into receivership. Many of the club's members and, indeed, a flying instructor transferred to the Reading Aero Club. P&P took over the large BBO hangar at the opposite end of the airfield, which became their new Repair and Service Department. Charles Powis and his wife, Pauline, took over the old BBO clubhouse as their new home.

However, by then, the whole character of Reading Aerodrome was about to change. It all began on 25th August 1932 when FG Miles arrived for lunch in his Satyr. It was the day when he and Charles Powis exchanged ideas about the ideal training aircraft. Details of the business arrangement Powis reached with Miles and Blossom are not known but, soon after, they brought their caravan to Woodley and began work on the design of a new two-seat low-wing monoplane. It was agreed that they would build the aircraft in one of the P&P hangars, with Blossom funding at least part of the costs. The selling rights would belong to P&P.

Soon after, Harry Hull, a veteran carpenter who had worked for Miles at Shoreham, joined the company. He built the Hawk, as the new aircraft became known, with just the help of a young lad and went on to become manager of the Wood Shop as the company grew — becoming one of the real 'characters' of Woodley.

About the same time, Charles Powis and Jack Phillips decided to go their separate ways, Powis taking the aircraft business and Phillips taking the remainder of their activities.

FG Miles first became an employee of P&P Aircraft as technical manager then, when it became a 'quoted company', he became technical director, with Charles Powis as managing director.

Top right: The P&P Christmas card for 1932 – three months before the Hawk flew. A photograph of a model of the Hawk was superimposed on a photograph of the airfield, to promote the company's move into aircraft manufacturing.

Right: A rare photograph taken inside the first wooden P&P hangar showing the Satyr dwarfed by de Havilland Moths.

The 'Hawk' was a very different aircraft from the Martlets and the Satyr. Indeed, in many ways it was unlike any other aircraft flying at that time. It is therefore worth looking in some detail at its 'design pedigree'.

By the late 1920s, the little airfield at Shoreham had become a 'Mecca' for local people interested in aviation, including others, like FG Miles, interested in aircraft design. Among them were Horace Miles, who FG employed for design work on the Martlet, as well as the Henderson brothers, Basil and Winfred, trading as Hendy Aircraft Ltd. When Miles designed the Metal Martlet, Basil Henderson joined Horace Miles in some of its detail design.

Although every aircraft manufacturer in the UK was producing biplane designs—actively encouraged by the Air Ministry—various monoplane designs had appeared in Germany, France, Russia and the USA. Almost certainly the various designers at Shoreham knew of at least some of these from the aviation press and would have discussed the merits of monoplanes with cantilever wings and the problems of their construction. Indeed, in 1929, Horace Miles and the Henderson brothers applied for a patent covering the design of cantilever monoplane wings.

By the time Miles and Blossom were designing the Hawk, Basil Henderson had completed his first aircraft using his patented monoplane wing, the Hendy 302. His wing design was again used when he worked on the Percival Gull, which first flew early in 1933. Then, later, Hendy Aircraft amalgamated with Parnall Aircraft and, in the mid-1930s, produced the Hendy Heck designs.

Going back to the Shoreham days, it is perhaps interesting to wonder whose idea it was to form the leading edge of the Martlet wing with a skin of plywood. Techniques of veneering and laminating wood have been used for centuries. However, the mass production of plywood is a 20th century American innovation and it was not until 1935 that an exterior grade was produced using waterproof glue. By 1932, when design work began on the Hawk, plywood had been little used in the aircraft industry and generally not for exterior skinning. Notable exceptions were Fokker airliners from the 1920s, the first monoplane designs using thick cantilever wings skinned in plywood.

In 1932, Miles designed what now appears to be the first aircraft in the world to have its entire wings and fuselage skinned in plywood. Since the plywood was glued to the ribs and frames, it added considerable strength to the structures, becoming what later became known as a 'stressed skin'.

A critical factor in the Hawk's design was the paint required to waterproof the plywood. Made by Titanine, the standard paint colour was described in the first P&P brochure as "aluminium" with a "satin finish" which could be polished "comparable to a high-class motor car".

Miles always maintained that Charles Powis was equally responsible for the idea of building a cheap, robust, two-seat low-wing monoplane. In one respect at least Powis also contributed to its construction when he came up with the idea of using a stapling machine to hold the plywood skin in place while the glue dried. More importantly perhaps, it was Charles Powis who found a batch of 95hp Cirrus engines which he bought very cheaply, making a major contribution to the exceptionally low price of £395 at which the Hawk was introduced.

Plans of the Hawk, discovered some fifty years later, suggest Miles and Blossom actually produced a bare minimum of detail design before construction began. Aided by the highly skilled and experienced Harry Hull, it seems much of the Hawk's design—and, indeed, the Hawk Major's that followed—was carried out with rough sketches.

This is also borne out by the fact that many of the drawings the author catalogued for Julian Temple in 1985 were actually produced by a young draughtsman, Tommy Botting, as late as 1935 — long after the original Hawks had been completed.

Miles made the very first flight in the Hawk late in the day on 29th March 1933. It was a flight of only a few minutes and, after landing, he declared the aircraft fine and invited Charles Powis to fly it. The next day, with only a small adjustment to the engine cowling, it was flown for a total of six hours by various pilots. Within a week, the Hawk had been flown by more than fifty pilots of varying skills and experience, a testimony to its robust construction and easy handling. Within a month, the number of pilots who had flown the Hawk had risen to eighty, among them Sir Geoffrey de Havilland, his son and other pilots from their company – the Hawk was a serious competitor to their recently introduced Tiger Moth, at about half the cost and some 40mph faster.

A Press Day on 2nd October had resulted in many positive comments about the Hawk. The Daily Mirror quoted Miles as saying that orders for three had already been received and construction of six aircraft would begin the following day. In fact, orders continued to pour in and, in just fifteen months, forty-seven Hawks were sold in the UK alone. Various special models were built, including five three-seaters for the joy-riding market and, by July 1934, a total of fifty-five Hawks had been completed.

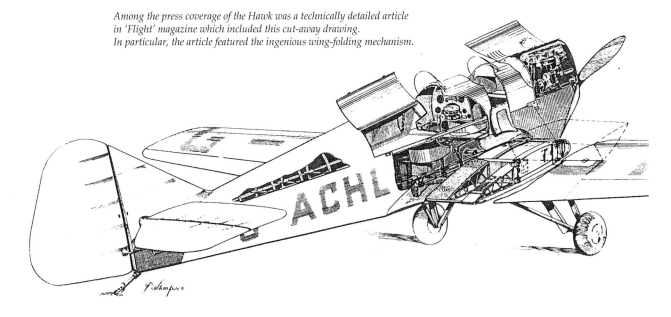

Among the press coverage of the Hawk was a technically detailed article in 'Flight' magazine which included this cut-away drawing. In particular, the article featured the ingenious wing-folding mechanism.

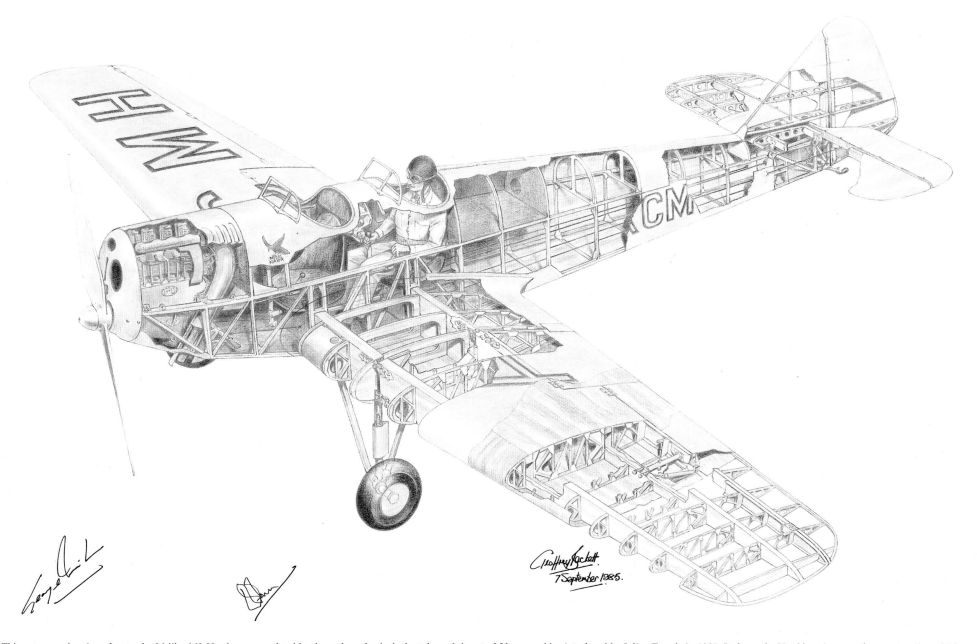

This cut-away drawing of a standard Miles M2 Hawk was completed by the author after he had catalogued the set of fifty-year-old prints found by Julian Temple in 1985. It shows the Hawk's unique wooden construction which became the basis of all Miles designs that followed.

Spruce members were joined by 'fillets' of plywood to form the fuselage framework and wing ribs and the box-section main wingspars had top and bottom spruce laminates with plywood sides. The plywood skin, attached directly to these structures, ensured tremendous rigidity and, unlike fabric-covered designs, no internal bracing was required. Only the tail unit on the 'Hawk' used fabric instead of plywood and the internal bracing wires can be seen.

This drawing shows the additional fabric skin on the wings which was included on the 'Colonial' model at additional cost. It also shows a colour different from the standard 'aluminium' finish, which would have cost an additional £10. The M2 Hawk had wooden engine mountings. The enclosed exhaust system shown here was introduced later, by which time the price for the standard model had been increased from £395 to £450.

Among the fifty-year-old prints was a full set of manufacturing drawings of the Cirrus engine, lending strength to the belief that Charles Powis had obtained an agreement to build the engines under licence. However, it was the Blackburn company that eventually built Cirrus engines.

Painted in oils on canvas.1999. 600mm x 850mm. Original painting donated to The Museum of Berkshire Aviation 2008.

'Woodley's first'

Late in the afternoon of 29th March 1933, construction of the Hawk was complete, apart from its final coat of paint. Miles said he would first test it by taxiing around the airfield. However, when he reached the far side, the few watchers heard him open the throttle and, seconds later, he was airborne. After a circuit of the airfield, he landed and handed the Hawk over to Charles Powis to try. The first air-to-air photographs of the Hawk show it as seen in the painting, with its white primer paint, and just the aluminium engine cowling in the eventual red finish of the fuselage. It is thought that the wings and tailplane were eventually finished in the 'aluminium' colour standard to later Hawks, emulating the red and silver colours commonly used for training aircraft at the time.

Right: The happy P&P team at Woodley in October 1933 (left to right) Charles Powis, FG Miles, Blossom Miles and Harry Hull with the prototype Hawk

Charles Powis had many times demonstrated that he knew the power of what we now call 'public relations' and he and Miles were happy to promote and, perhaps, even overplay Blossom's role as an 'aircraft designer'. But, of course, the Press loved it! Perhaps it also helped them to move on beyond her 'fifteen minutes of notoriety' when she "ran off with a pilot", as a contemporary society figure, the novelist Barbara Cartland, later said.

Blossom certainly revelled in her new life and, by 1934, having moved into a brand new house close to the airfield, for which she almost certainly provided the money, with a baby son to care for as well, she still played a pivotal part in the company. She continued to work with Miles on the design of new aircraft and, increasingly, took the leading part in the welfare, education and social life of the ever growing numbers of employees of the company. When the Hawk went into production in 1933, there were around forty employees. In just five years, there would be more than one thousand.

When Miles and Blossom began to work together, they called themselves the Miles Aeroplane Company. The Satyr was designated the Miles M1.

The Hawk therefore became the Miles M2 and, for the various versions that followed, a suffix letter was added. For example, the three-seat version was the M2D. It was the M2F, known as the Hawk Major, that really established the 'character' of future Miles designs and laid the foundation for P&P to become one of the world's foremost manufacturers of light aircraft — second only to Geoffrey de Havilland's long established company.

Below: Blossom the 'aircraft designer' with FG Miles. A P&P publicity photograph from 1933.

'Tribute to Charles Powis'

Painted in oils on canvas. 1997. 600mm x 750mm.

In 1934, the Reading Aero Club purchased its own Miles Hawk, affectionately known as 'Ruddy Duck'. It was allowed the registration letters COP, the initials of Charles Powis, and was one of the earliest known examples of this now common practice. Later, G-ACOP also played a part in aviation history when Miles fitted it with experimental trailing-edge flaps. The success of this experiment led to the fitting of flaps of this type to all subsequent Miles aircraft and, indeed, to most aircraft subsequently designed worldwide. Sadly, in 1935, due to a ground-handling error, G-ACOP was destroyed in an accident at Woodley, which tragically cost the life of the chief flying instructor, John Lawn, and his pupil.

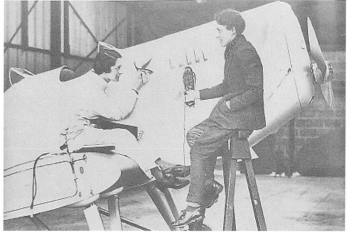

Above: When it was decided to include a 'Hawk' motif on all Miles-designed aircraft, a national newspaper printed this photograph of Blossom 'painting' the motif onto an aircraft, while her sister Jean, a well-known actress, holds the 'model'. In fact, the motif was always applied by a transfer.

Below: Blossom 'christened' Reading Aero Club's new Hawk G-ACOP at Woodley in 1934. Here she is seen with flying instructors John Lawn (right) and Bob Milne.

It created aviation history in November 1934 when it became the first aircraft in the world to be fitted with trailing-edge flaps as standard — an advance subsequently followed by every other aircraft manufacturer. Miles did not invent this type of flap, indeed various 'experts' had discussed the idea and declared it useless! Ever the practical man, Miles made some flaps from bent aluminium, which he screwed to the wings of 'Ruddy Duck'. The results were so dramatic that he immediately designed manually-operated flaps for the Hawk Major — and every one of his designs that followed.

Indeed, the 'rightness' of the original 1933 Hawk design was proved again and again as various developments kept the workforce at full stretch. From 1934, design after design appeared with astonishing regularity from the ever-expanding factory at Woodley. These included single-seat racers, cabin monoplanes and training aircraft. In particular, successes in the field of air-racing brought ever growing recognition of Miles and the P&P company.

Above: Miles M2 Hawks, under construction in the third P&P hangar at Reading Aerodrome in 1933.

A few years earlier, de Havilland had begun to manufacture 'Gypsy' 4-cylinder inverted engines which proved very successful and popular, fitted to their own aircraft, such as the new Tiger Moth and, also, the new Percival Gulls. Much more expensive than the Hawk, the Gulls were cabin monoplanes intended for the 'luxury touring' market.

At Woodley, the stock of Cirrus engines was running low and, it appears, when attempts to convert one to an inverted layout proved unsuccessful, Charles Powis' ideas of manufacturing engines were postponed. Instead, the new M2F Hawk Major was fitted with a Gypsy Major engine and, unlike the original M2 Hawk, it had metal engine mountings. A new 'trousered' cantilever undercarriage added to its streamlining. First flown by Miles in July 1934, it took the original Hawk design to a completely new level.

Right: In 1935 P&P built a large hangar across the front of their original three hangars, specifically for the assembly of new aircraft. Towards the end of that year, as the photograph shows, Hawks, Hawk Majors, Falcons and Merlins were all under construction.

"Last one home buys the tea"

This painting of two Hawk Majors sets out to capture the spirit of club flying in the mid-1930s. The sport of air racing had long attracted the public and the competitively-priced Hawk Major brought the chance of taking part in such events to a much wider range of pilots.

Painted in oils on canvas. 1999. 360mm x 260mm.

75

'Record Breaker'

Hugh Brook may have been unlucky in the England-Australia Race, but he was determined to prove himself and his aircraft on the return journey. He had additional long-range fuel tanks fitted and, clearly aiming to create a new record, he managed to obtain commercial sponsorship, primarily, it seems, from the Ovaltine company, although other company logos can also be seen in contemporary photographs. The original colour of the Falcon was cream but, for the return flight, the fuselage was repainted red to give a red/cream colour scheme to suit Ovaltine's image.

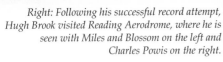

Right: Following his successful record attempt, Hugh Brook visited Reading Aerodrome, where he is seen with Miles and Blossom on the left and Charles Powis on the right.

'Perfect Day'

A Hawk Major climbs lazily into the summer sky from a small country airfield, in a painting aimed at capturing the carefree, less regulated days of the mid-1930s.

With the Hawk of 1933 and the Hawk Major of 1934, P&P played a big part in making light aircraft more affordable, safer and easier to fly.

Flying for sport and flying just for pleasure were growing in popularity among many young men and women of the time.

Original painting owned by Miss P Taylor.

The owner of the first production M2 Hawk had flown it in the 1933 King's Cup Air Race, although an engine problem caused him to retire. However, just two weeks later, he won the Wakefield Cup Air Race in the Hawk, at an average speed of 116mph. The following year, the well-known sporting pilot, Tommy Rose, flew the prototype Hawk Major into second place in the prestigious King's Cup at an average speed of 148mph. These were the first of many racing honours for the Woodley team.

Although a number of Hawks had been fitted with covered cockpits, Miles and Blossom's first real cabin design was the four-seat Falcon, designed at the same time as the Hawk Major. It was built specifically for Hugh Brook to fly in the England to Australia Air Race in October 1934. This race was eventually won by one of the three ultra-streamlined de Havilland Comets entered, which were a dramatic departure from that company's traditional designs.

P&P were represented, not only by Hugh Brook's Falcon, but also by a Hawk Major, flown by L MacGregor and M Walker, which came fifth in the handicap section of the race and established a new record for a single-engine aircraft.

Hugh Brook had provided the engine for the Falcon, taken from his own Puss Moth which, when owned by Jim Mollison, had been flown across the Atlantic. Sadly, in the race, the engine let him down, although he did eventually reach Australia. He flew back five months later, leaving Darwin on 23rd March 1935 and, in seven days, nineteen hours, fifteen minutes reached Croydon, breaking the record for a solo flight in a single-engine aircraft.

1935 had begun with a flurry of further developments of the Hawk Major and the Falcon. Among these was a Hawk Major incorporating full dual controls and wider cockpits, allowing both pilots to wear parachutes. This became known as the Hawk Trainer and, eventually, thirteen were authorised by the Air Ministry to be used at the new Reserve Flying School operated by P&P.

This period also saw the first flight of the largest of all the aircraft based on the original Hawk — the M4 Merlin, powered by a de Havilland Gypsy Six engine. It provided comfortable accommodation for the pilot and four passengers at a cruising speed of 140mph, over long distances.

Painted in oils on canvas. 1997. 450mm x 600mm.

'International Taxi'

The prototype Merlin was built in the spring of 1935 to the requirements of Birkett Air Services of Heston. Three others were eventually built, seeing service in India and Australia. Among many long- distance flights by the prototype, G-ADFE, was a charter to Addis Ababa during the Abyssinian War.

Miles next began to design a more powerful version of the Falcon, fitted with a 200hp Gypsy Six engine. The prototype, G-ADLC, first flown by Miles on 20th July, was a three-seater and the first aircraft to feature the distinctive forward-raked windscreen.

By then, Powis and Miles had decided that the forthcoming King's Cup Air Race would provide an excellent 'showcase' for their company and no less than thirteen aircraft were being prepared – out of a total entry of thirty-six. One of them was Blossom's one and only solo design.

With just two months to go, Miles had announced he wanted to fly in the race himself. With his 'hands on' approach, Miles was already fully committed with all the other aircraft, so Blossom undertook the design and, as Don Brown later wrote, she also undertook the vital role of 'progress chaser' — not an easy task at that hectic time for the workshops. Adapting standard Hawk components, Blossom shortened the wingspan and the fuselage, lowered the overall height and evolved a superb little racing machine, the Sparrowhawk — certainly one of the 'prettiest' aircraft ever produced by the company.

On the 6th and 7th September 1935, the King's Cup Air Race weekend began with an elimination race of almost one thousand miles, starting and finishing at Hatfield, with compulsory stops at Glasgow, Belfast and Cardiff.

Successful aircraft would then compete in the next day's final— a seven-lap handicap race over a triangular course of approximately fifty miles.

The elimination race soon developed into a duel between the two designer-pilots, Miles in the Sparrowhawk and Edgar Percival in his more powerful and faster Mew Gull. However, Percival 'nursed' his engine, flying at some 75% full power, 'protecting' his handicap for the next day's final, while Miles threw caution to the wind and flew at 95% full power over the whole course.

For the final stage, Percival left Cardiff just three minutes ahead of Miles, confident of winning in his faster aircraft. However, he made a mistake in course-keeping in the last few minutes and handed victory to Miles.

However, the Sparrowhawk's unexpected win resulted in it being heavily handicapped for the next day's final, putting it well out of contention.

On 7th September, the day of the final, in the public enclosure at Hatfield, around two hundred P&P employees, wore red and cream rosettes, matching the livery of most of the Miles-designed aircraft entered in the race. Coaches had brought them from Woodley and their anticipation was high following the unexpected success of Miles in the elimination race the previous day.

Tommy Rose, P&P's recently appointed sales manager, was flying the prototype Falcon Six, G-ADLC and, by accurate course-keeping and immaculate cornering, coaxed some 20mph above the aircraft's 'handicap speed'. In just over four laps, he moved up from thirteenth place to first and went on to win by some six minutes.

Having landed, Tommy Rose taxied the Falcon Six over to the public enclosure to salute the wildly cheering P&P employees. However, their cheers were soon ringing even louder when Hawk Trainers finished second and third, giving their company a never-equalled 'clean sweep' in this prestigious event. Indeed, when another Falcon gained fifth place, it capped an outstanding achievement for the still fledgling Berkshire aircraft manufacturer.

Below: Miles-designed aircraft lined up at Reading Aerodrome, prior to the 1935 King's Cup. In the foreground is the Sparrowhawk. Beyond that is a Hawk Speed Six which was unplaced (perhaps because it was flown by a Miss Slow). Beyond that are the two Hawk Trainers which finished second and third in the final.

Painted in oils on canvas. 1999. 450mm x 650mm. Original painting donated to the Museum of Berkshire Aviation. 2008.

'On course to win!'

As Miles, in the Sparrowhawk, dived towards the finishing line at Hatfield, he must have thought he was still in second place in the 1935 King's Cup elimination race. However, to his surprise, Edgar Percival's Mew Gull suddenly appeared ahead of him, flashing towards the finish from the wrong direction. Somehow, in the final few minutes, Percival had failed to see the airfield and had flown past some miles to the north before realising his mistake. In the next day's final, the Sparrowhawk carried a handicap that put it well out of contention.

'Into the lead!'

The final of the 1935 King's Cup Air Race was a seven-lap handicap race over a triangular course of approximately fifty miles. At the beginning of the fifth lap, the prototype Falcon Six, G-ADLC, swept past the two earliest starters, to take the lead and go on to win by some six minutes. By accurate course-keeping and immaculate cornering, Tommy Rose coaxed some 20mph above the Falcon's 'handicap speed' and, in just over four laps, moved up from thirteenth place to first.

Painted in oils on canvas. 1998. 60mm x 500mm

Production of Hawk Major developments continued well into 1936 and around eighty were built at Woodley, as well as others built under licence in India and Spain. At the same time, more than thirty-five Falcons were built. Miles also began to work closely with the Royal Aircraft Establishment at Farnborough and, over the next decade, many research aircraft were built for full-scale test flying, based upon the Falcon, Sparrowhawk and, later, the Whitney Straight design.

Whitney Straight was a millionaire racing driver who was trying to popularise aviation by establishing a number of flying clubs around the country. Following P&P's success in the King's Cup, he approached Miles and, in much the same way that the original Hawk had been evolved with Charles Powis three years before, they discussed ideas for the ideal aircraft for both club flying and the private owner.

Their thoughts coincided and the two-seat Miles Whitney Straight was quickly designed and put into production. With side-by-side seating and dual controls, in a roomy and comfortable cabin, it was reasonably fast, easy and safe to fly, as well as being economical to operate and maintain. The Straight Corporation had sole selling rights and many overseas customers were included for the fifty or so aircraft that were built in just two years.

Right: Whitney Straight at the controls of the Miles-designed aircraft that bore his name. In 1985, it was discovered that this was just one of a series of promotional photographs taken by Norman Parkinson. Probably taken early in his career, 'Parks', as he became better known in post-war years, became famous for his fashion photography and portraits of the Royal family.

"That's the way to learn to fly"

The Miles Whitney Straight was the first aircraft specifically designed for flying training where the instructor and pupil sat side-by-side in a comfortable covered cabin, with advanced features such as trailing-edge flaps and brakes. At the time it first flew most flying training was still undertaken in the old fashioned de Havilland Moth and pilots who had learned to fly in them must have appreciated the considerable advance that the new Miles design represented.

Painted in oils. 2003. 660mm x 400mm

Painted in oils. 2003. 660mm x 400mm

'Tough Competitor'

Today, most aviation enthusiasts view the de Havilland biplane airliners of the mid-1930s with nostalgic affection. In their time, they were very successful yet, even when first built, they were already outdated. In America, Douglas, Boeing and Lockheed were producing far more advanced monoplane airliners. In Britain, Airspeed, Avro and Percival were working on monoplane airliner designs. In 1936, P&P entered this market with the Peregrine. In both performance and cost it far outclassed the de Havilland Dragon Rapide and compared very favourably with the other British monoplane designs. It is interesting to consider what the fortunes of the various British companies might have been in the civil airliner market, if the expansion of the RAF hadn't changed the future of all the aircraft concerned. Despite winning provisional orders, the Peregrine had to be abandoned when the demands on the P&P factory dramatically increased with the award of an Air Ministry contract for the RAF's first monoplane trainer – the Magister. In 1938, a second Peregrine was built specially for the RAE at Farnborough for research work.

In 1936, another new design was going through the P&P factory, the Miles M12 Mohawk. It had been ordered by Charles Lindbergh who, some ten years earlier, had become world famous when he was the first man to fly solo across the Atlantic. In 1935, Lindbergh had been asked by Pan American Airways to find possible air routes in Europe and Asia and, the following year, he visited Woodley to discuss with Miles his requirements for a suitable aircraft.

He flew the prototype Whitney Straight, but decided he needed a faster, more powerful aircraft, with a range of over one thousand miles and capable of flying at high altitude. That was when Miles offered him a one-off design with an American-built Menasco supercharged engine.

Left: Charles Lindbergh (in the helmet) is seen at Woodley in 1936, discussing his Menasco-engined M12 Mohawk with the youngest Miles brother, George (left), who had recently joined P&P to manage the Menasco project.

Painted in oils on canvas. 1999. 450mm x 600mm.

For some time, both Miles and Powis had felt that the British manufacturers were failing to develop engines for light aircraft beyond the, by then, rather old-fashioned Cirrus and Gypsy models.

Early in 1936, Charles Powis had opened negotiations with Menasco for the manufacture under licence of their engines in the UK. Various Menasco engines were tested in different aircraft and the youngest Miles brother, George, joined P&P to manage the project.

Detailed negotiations continued with Menasco for well over a year. Various problems were overcome, including getting the necessary certificates from the Air Ministry. Then, after a considerable amount of money and effort had been spent, the whole engine project was abandoned.

'Lindbergh over Moscow'

During 1937, Charles Lindbergh and his wife made many long distance flights in the Mohawk, even as far as Moscow and India.
The distinctive colour scheme of the aircraft was specifically ordered by Lindbergh, to show up in the event of a forced landing no matter where it happened – desert, jungle, snow, water or any other surroundings.

Towards the end of 1936 the success of the Hawk Trainers at the Reserve Flying School at Reading Aerodrome helped to persuade the Air Ministry that the RAF needed a monoplane initial trainer and a contract had been placed with Phillips & Powis for the Magister. It was the final development of the original Hawk design and became probably the best remembered aircraft of all those built at Woodley. In placing the contract, the Ministry also reversed a decision not to order any more wooden aircraft.

The first Magister contract was for just ninety aircraft and P&P were told there would be no further orders. Therefore the construction of jigs and tools and the allocation of factory space reflected this. The failure of other aircraft designed to a later specification from the Air Ministry resulted in more and more orders for Magisters until, by early 1941, some twelve hundred had been supplied to the RAF. Over one hundred were also supplied to foreign air forces.

However, these subsequent orders were for just fifty to two hundred aircraft and never allowed the company to benefit from mass-production methods. Indeed, the last Magister built cost virtually the same as the first. It badly affected the company's pre-war profitability and this would become a major problem during the war years when the Government, as they had in WWI, again introduced an Excess Profits Tax.

Throughout 1936, the factory had been working at full stretch on the Whitney Straight and other projects, such as the Peregrine, the Mohawk and the prototype Magister. By this time, the Drawing Office had a staff of nearly seventy.

However, FG had built up a small team of experienced designers and project engineers who worked closely with him and, over many years, the range of projects that flowed from them was unequalled in the aircraft industry.

By the summer of 1936, FG Miles was convinced that another European war was inevitable and he began work on a new project. New aircraft, such as the Fairey Battle and Bristol Blenheim were already in service with the RAF. More importantly perhaps, the Hurricane and Spitfire were on order. These were all high performance monoplanes equipped with features such as retractable undercarriages, flaps and variable-pitch propellers.

A line-up of Magisters, seen at Woodley in 1938. The award of the Magister contract called for further extensions at the factory and led to a considerable increase in the workforce. It also led directly to the abandonment of the Peregrine and played a part in the cancellation of the Menasco project. In this photograph, the re-designed rudder of the Magister can clearly be seen. The earliest Magisters retained the triangular fin and rudder of the original Hawks, but spinning problems caused by the wider cockpits led to the re-design.

To FG, one of the most experienced designer/ pilots in the industry, it was totally inconceivable that pilots for these monoplanes could be adequately trained on the old-fashioned biplane trainers still used by the RAF.

He set out to design a powerful advanced trainer, equipped with all the latest features, to mirror the performance of the new service aircraft.

Developed around a 750hp Rolls Royce Kestrel engine, then still in full production for aircraft such as the Hawker Fury and Hart biplanes, FG drew up the plans and specification for an advanced two-seat monoplane trainer.

When he presented his concept to the Air Ministry it was rejected on the grounds that no such aircraft was required. However, encouraged and, indeed, aided by Rolls Royce, Miles decided to go ahead with the Kestrel, as he had decided to name it, as a private venture.

Below: George, the youngest of the Miles brothers, joined P&P in 1936. In 1938, he began his career as an aircraft designer and quickly proved he was every bit as talented as his elder brother.

'Showstopper'

In June 1937, at the RAF Hendon Air
Display, the Kestrel impressed spectators
with its clean monoplane design and a speed
and handling performance approaching that
of the Hurricane, which was soon to enter
squadron service.

Built as a private venture by P&P, with the
invaluable assistance of Rolls Royce, the
Kestrel had been thought 'premature' when
its concept was presented to the Air
Ministry a year or so earlier.

It was another twelve months before it was
ordered, with many Ministry modifications,
as the Master I.

Painted in oils on canvas. 2001. 500mm x 500mm

Whether the approach by Miles finally made the Ministry realise the folly of their ways will never be known. However, shortly after rejecting the Kestrel, they decided an advanced trainer was indeed urgently required and issued a specification. On seeing it, Miles predicted that an aircraft built exactly to that specification would be a failure and carried on with the Kestrel. A design based exactly on the specification was presented by the de Havilland company and, unusually for the time, it was ordered 'off the drawing board'.

Miles first flew the Kestrel on 3rd June 1937 and its performance exceeded everyone's expectations. With a maximum speed of nearly 300mph, it was almost as fast as the first Hurricanes, even though its engine was only three-quarters of their power. More importantly, in its handling characteristics, it accurately reflected those of the Hurricane and the Spitfire.

Even while the de Havilland advanced trainer was being built to the Ministry's own specification, Miles continued to promote the merits of the Kestrel. He even arranged for Bill Skinner, P&P's chief test pilot, to fly from Oxford to Farnborough in a fairly steep dive, with a northerly gale as a tail-wind. Later, Miles sent a telegram to the Air Ministry, "Kestrel has today achieved 504mph". It seems someone at the Ministry had a sense of humour. The reply came back, "Congratulations on meteoric flight".

Nevertheless, the Air Ministry could not have been laughing when, just as Miles had predicted, the de Havilland advanced trainer did indeed prove to be a failure. Now desperate, having lost a valuable twelve months, the Air Ministry turned to P&P to develop the Kestrel into what eventually became known as the Master I.

All of this was played out against a background of dramatic changes in the company's management. Just a month after the Kestrel's first flight, in July 1937, Charles Powis resigned. To the vast majority of the employees, this came as a complete surprise and it must have been a sad day for many at Woodley when he left the company he had created.

As far back as 1935, the need to strengthen the company's financial situation had led to the flotation of P&P as a public company. Just over a year later, following a further issue of shares, Rolls Royce had became a major shareholder, with two representatives on the P&P Board.

Looking back, it is obvious that the Rolls Royce involvement provided much needed working capital for P&P. However, it seems the new members of the Board also saw the need for better financial controls. A 'culture' of building 'cheap' aeroplanes had perhaps continued too long after the very first Hawk and it appears even the Whitney Straight, then virtually in 'mass production', had been priced without any real profit margin.

By then, Rolls Royce had also no doubt recognised the pivotal role in the company that Miles was playing. Perhaps Charles Powis began to feel inadequate in his role as managing director in the new regime. It seems likely that the Rolls Royce board members had been instrumental in the abandonment of the Menasco project, and perhaps Powis had strongly disagreed. Certainly, by then, he was experiencing personal problems. His health was poor, his baby son had died and, eventually, he and his wife were to divorce.

Below: The Hobby at an air display at Woodley in the spring of 1938, with FG and Blossom Miles and their son, Jeremy.

Following Charles Powis's resignation, FG Miles, as he was usually known after George Miles joined P&P, was appointed joint managing director with Lt Col Darby of Rolls Royce. There is no doubt that the Rolls Royce involvement saved P&P from a critical situation, not only in stricter financial controls, but also in virtually every other aspect of the business, from ordering of raw material to various manufacturing methods.

Looking back, it is incredible to think that, while all this was going on, FG and his team found time to design two other aircraft of such a contrast that, although neither of them would appear in a list of P&P's great successes, they are worth looking at in detail. One was a four-engine airliner, the X2, and it appears that FG had long had an ambition to build airliners. The other is the smallest aircraft he ever designed, a diminutive racer called the Hobby.

The M13 Hobby was designed for FG himself to fly in the 1937 King's Cup. It had a retractable undercarriage, built by a specialist sub-contractor and, just one week before the qualifying heats for the race, it was found that the wheel-hole in the wing was too small! Despite a day and night effort to rebuild the wing, it was not finished in time. The following year, the Hobby's wingspan of just over twenty-one feet, was the prime factor in the RAE's decision to purchase it for full-scale research in their twenty-four-foot wind tunnel.

The origin of FG Miles' X2 airliner concept, dates back to 1920 when a Russian called Woyevodsky put forward the idea—it seems blindingly obvious today but not then—that the performance of aircraft would be considerably improved if they were designed as aerodynamically clean, cantilever monoplanes, fitted with a retractable undercarriage. He also suggested that, not only the wings, but also the fuselage, should be of an aerofoil shape. The British Air Ministry became interested when wind-tunnel tests confirmed these theories and they asked Westland to build the twin-engine aircraft suggested by Woyevodsky.

However, when the Westland 'Dreadnought' was completed in 1924, it had only a single engine and a fixed undercarriage and, when it crashed soon after take-off, the project was abandoned.

Twelve years later, having just built his first twin-engine design, the Peregrine, FG Miles was keen to pursue his ambition to build airliners. He thought that Woyevodsky had been right and his ideas were capable of development and he set about designing the 'X2'.

To obtain maximum aerodynamic cleanness, the fuselage was wide and shallow so that it simply 'merged' into the thick wings, in which the four engines were buried, with the propellers driven through extension shafts. An all-metal aircraft of ninety-nine-foot wingspan, it was to be powered by four 900hp Rolls Royce engines.

By 1938, with the rapid expansion of the RAF, the Air Ministry was not really interested in civilian aircraft and, when FG Miles presented his X2 concept, he was only offered a small development contract. It was far too small to allow for any detail design or construction work and the project was dropped. "Gone but not forgotten" was, perhaps, the best epitaph for the X2.

Below: Model of the X2, showing the advanced thinking of FG Miles and his design team well before World War II.

Painted in oils on canvas. 2000. 300mm x 400mm.

'Nightwork'

In 1935, in what was basically a development of the Falcon Six, FG Miles designed the M7 Nighthawk, as a trainer for night-flying, instrument flying, navigation and radio instruction. Although it began as a private venture, it created official interest and a contract was awarded for extended handling trials. Subsequently, this led to a contract for the M16 Mentor, seen here, of which forty-five were built in the years before World War II

Below Right: New developments at Reading Aerodrome. The M17 Monarch, which first flew in 1938, was the first design undertaken by George Miles. In many ways, it can be seen as a three-seater 'up graded' Whitney Straight and would no doubt have been just as successful if the pressures on the factory due to production of Magisters and Masters for the RAF had not restricted the number that could be built to twelve. In the event, most of these were impressed into the wartime RAF and just three survived the hostilities. In the background is the Falcon Hotel, built by Simonds Brewery on the edge of the airfield in 1937. Wartime extensions of the airfield on either side eventually gave it an unusual almost central position. FG Miles' own two-tone-grey Rolls Royce Phantom II, CGK891, complete with 'chauffeur', also plays its part in this 1938 publicity photograph, which is thought to have been taken by Norman Parkinson. Seventy years later, the car is still on the road!

In these years before World War II, the whole character of P&P can be seen to be changing dramatically. But, in other ways it was certainly 'business as usual'.

In February 1936, Tommy Rose had flown the King's Cup-winning Falcon to South Africa and back, breaking records in both directions. Although P&P did not enter as many aircraft in the 1936 King's Cup, Tommy Rose flew a Hawk Speed Six into second place, with a Hawk Major coming fourth. In the 1937 race, Whitney Straights were second and fourth and, in the 1938 race, a Hawk Major finished third.

In September 1936, RAF Abingdon was the unlikely starting point for another record attempt — this time by Beryl Markham, flying a Percival Vega Gull. With a number of record flights already to her credit, she was aiming to fly to New York in under twenty-four hours.

Her attempt might be considered foolhardy since it appears her aircraft carried only enough fuel for twenty-four hours in the air in favourable conditions and, when she set out, conditions were anything but favourable. In fact, for twenty hours, she faced fog, rain, turbulence and headwinds! She had set out with just a flask of coffee, a few nuts and some fruit, but when she tried to take her first drink, she spilt it!

Eventually, her first glimpse of land — Newfoundland — was accompanied by a 'knocking' in the engine. The fuel-gauge showed she should land quickly but, with the fog below, she had no choice but to fly on. In desperation, she headed for Nova Scotia and, soon, through gaps in the fog, she saw what appeared to be an open field. It was open indeed, but also boggy! When local people found her sitting in the wreckage, she was bruised and shaken, but apparently laughing. Beryl Markham was the first woman to fly the Atlantic, from east to west.

A major expansion and re-organisation of the RAF had begun in 1934 and, when Bomber Command was formed in July 1936, RAF Abingdon became a part. By then, construction of a new Berkshire airfield was well underway at nearby Harwell and, in February 1937, this also became operational within Bomber Command. The following year, squadrons at both Abingdon and Harwell were re-equipped with Fairey Battles. In May 1939, RAF Harwell hosted an 'Empire Air Day' with many thousands of visitors.

The expansion of the RAF called for many more pilots to be trained and the five existing training airfields had been deemed inadequate. That was when, in 1935, various commercial companies had been invited to set up a total of thirteen Reserve Flying Schools around the country including, of course, P&P at Woodley and de Havilland at White Waltham.

In the years before World War II, continued expansion under the RAF Volunteer Reserve Scheme saw service types such as Hawker Harts, Fairey Battles and Avro Ansons added to the fleets of training aircraft flown by the schools at Woodley and White Waltham. Indeed, Woodley was to see a build-up of the RAF presence that would last throughout the war years and well into the 1950s.

Among the students at White Waltham who went on to achieve great things in their flying careers were Roland Beaumont and Neville Duke, fighter aces who became well known test pilots in post-war years. Another was Eric Nicolson who, when flying his Hurricane in the Battle of Britain, became the only RAF fighter pilot to be awarded the Victoria Cross.

At Woodley, one of the students at the Reserve Flying School was Leonard Cheshire VC, who led the famous 617 'Dambusters' Squadron after Guy Gibson and, in post-war years, created the Cheshire Homes. Another Woodley student was John Nettleton VC, who, in 1942, led his squadron of Lancasters on the daring low-level, daytime attack on the Augsburg diesel engine factory in Southern Germany.

With the availability of flying training under these new RAF schemes (at least, for men) it is perhaps not surprising that civilian flying clubs were losing members. Reading Aero Club had had an additional problem since 1935 when the expansion of the P&P factory had gradually swallowed up their club house, virtually cutting off its direct access to the airfield. In 1937, the transfer of club activities to the new Falcon Hotel helped to stem the loss of members. Then, in August 1938, the Government launched the Civil Air Guard scheme and Reading Aero Club was invited to take part. The aim of the scheme was to increase quickly the number of qualified civilian pilots, both male and female, by subsidising clubs to enable them to offer flying lessons at exceptionally low rates. In the first week of the scheme some sixteen thousand enquiries were received at Woodley. Blossom Miles was invited to be the Civil Air Guard commissioner for the South of England, responsible for twenty-eight flying clubs.

Left: Beryl Markham's Vega Gull 'The Messenger' in a hangar at RAF Abingdon before her record-breaking flight across the Atlantic.

Right: Blossom Miles (right) is seen in her role as Civil Air Guard Commissioner for the South of England. It is believed she is talking to Joan Hughes who had actually learned to fly when she was just fifteen and, in the Civil Air Guard, became an instructor. A few years after this photograph was taken, she went on to be the youngest and smallest of the first female recruits for the ATA. Despite this 'handicap' she flew even the biggest types of aircraft such as Lancaster and Stirling bombers. In post-war years she continued flying as an instructor at White Waltham and even starred in the film 'Those magnificent men in their flying machines' as the real pilot of the tiny 'Demoiselle' monoplane.

In April 1937, a new Berkshire aircraft manufacturer took to the air, when the Chilton monoplane made its first flight. The Chilton name came from Chilton Foliate, near Hungerford where, at the stately home of one of its designers, the aircraft had been constructed.

The Hon. Andrew Dalrymple, son of the Earl of Stair, who owned Chilton Lodge, and 'Reggie' Ward, son of the Hon. Sir John Ward, had met as students at the de Havilland Technical School and it was there that they designed the aircraft. In May 1936, having completed their course at the school, they persuaded their woodworking instructor to join them and began construction in a wooden building specially erected in the grounds of Chilton Lodge.

The Chilton design can be seen to owe something to the then very popular Miles Hawk Majors, although it was much smaller, with a wingspan of only twenty-four feet. It was a single-seater and, although classed as an 'ultralight', could easily cruise at 100mph. A landing speed of just 35mph was achieved by the use of split trailing edge flaps, as developed by FG Miles for all his designs.

The Chilton's 'clean' design obviously made a contribution to its outstanding performance, but much of its speed - and reliability - resulted from its 32hp engine adapted from the Ford 10 motor car engine. Known as the Carden-Ford engine, it had been developed in 1935 by Sir John Carden who was previously technical director of Vickers Armstrong, primarily as a power plant for the 'Flying Flea'. Sadly, when he was killed in an airliner crash, his company was taken over and, in 1937, was acquired by Chilton Aircraft.

The prototype Chilton made its first flight in the hands of Ranald Porteous, a fellow student of Dalrymple and Ward at the de Havilland Technical School. Porteous was involved in events at Woodley where he became a flying instructor under the Civil Air Guard training scheme and, later, became chief test pilot for Auster Aircraft.

In August 1939, the prototype Chilton was entered for the Folkstone Aero Trophy Race at Lympne and, with Andrew Dalrymple at the controls, romped home to win at an average speed of 126mph. However, with the declaration of war just a month later, this was the very last air race to be held for many years.

The Chilton was too small to be deemed suitable for impressment as a service aircraft and the four aircraft that had been completed were put into storage for the war years.

The Chilton company became a sub-contractor, mainly for other aircraft manufacturers, for small machined metal parts and, from two men and a boy in 1938, the workforce grew to around two hundred and fifty people by the end of the war. Although both Dalrymple and Ward were capable pilots, their eyesight was not up to the standard required for RAF operational flying and their war effort seemed destined to be the management of their small but growing factory.

However, with the formation of the Air Transport Auxiliary and its subsequent expansion programme, 'Reggie' Ward saw the chance to fly again and, from 1941 to 1945 he was an ATA pilot, flying all types of service aircraft.

Opposite page:
'Mitchell's Memory'
A vital cog in the build-up of the RAF in the second half of the 1930s was the Supermarine Spitfire, the brainchild of the talented designer RJ Mitchell. The prototype Spitfire, K5054, first flew at Eastleigh on 11th May 1936. A few days after that first flight, having been given a coat of high-gloss blue/grey paint, it was to be photographed air-to-air for the very first time by John Yoxhall from 'Flight' magazine. 'Mutt' Summers, chief test pilot of Supermarine's parent company, Vickers, was to fly the Spitfire and Jeffrey Quill, later chief test pilot at Supermarine, was to fly the photographer in Vickers' communications aircraft, a Miles Falcon. At the last minute, Mitchell decided that he would also fly in the Falcon. It is believed to be the only time he saw his magnificent creation air-to-air in the element it was to grace with such distinction in the years to come. Already seriously ill with cancer, Mitchell died just over a year later.

'Chilton's challenge'
The Chilton Monoplane, powered by a specially adapted Ford motor car engine, flourished briefly in the pre-war years, but was destined for a surprising revival many years after it was first designed.

Painted in watercolours. 2007. 225mm x 275mm.

Painted in oils on canvas. 2006. 410mm x 510mm.

It was the spring of 1938 before the Air Ministry finally accepted their own specification for an advanced trainer could not be met. P&P were asked to prepare the Kestrel for production. However, the Ministry demanded certain changes to be made, the most notable being the installation of a down-rated 715hp Rolls Royce Kestrel engine. This caused major installation problems and eventually led to the re-positioning of the air intake to a position underneath the fuselage. The rear half of the canopy was changed and the fuselage in front of the tailplane had to be 'thickened'. Nevertheless, even before these modifications could be adequately tested, in June 1938, the Ministry placed a £2 million contract for an initial batch of five hundred Master Is—the largest contract for a training aircraft to that date.

Thanks to all the modifications, the Master I, with a maximum speed of 226mph, was some 70mph slower than the original Kestrel. But this was still a performance better than any other trainer in the world and, as Don Brown wrote many years later, its handling characteristics remained so similar to the Hurricane and Spitfire that the thousands of pilots trained in Master Is felt perfectly at home when they climbed into one of these fighters for the first time. He also wrote that the Woodley team considered the Master I to be the company's major contribution to the war effort.

It was the end of March 1939 before FG Miles made the maiden flight in the first production Master I. Incorporating all the modifications demanded by the Ministry had cost a lot of time. More importantly perhaps, the factory as it was in June 1938 was hopelessly inadequate for the mass production of an aircraft as complex as the Master I.

A massive extension to the factory was begun. The workforce increased dramatically, including senior managers from other industries with experience of mass production methods. The very first moving production line in the aircraft industry was designed and installed and, within two years, one aircraft a day was being completed.

However, as the Duke of Wellington said after Waterloo, "it was a damned close run thing". When the war began in September 1939, just seven Master Is had been delivered to the RAF. By the time of the Battle of Britain, one year later, five hundred were in service.

The design and manufacture of literally hundreds of jigs took time, as did the training of hundreds of new workers. New managers from other industries introduced improved methods in aspects such as materials ordering and stock control. But it all took time and, although the exact numbers are not known, there is no doubt that the first Master Is to leave the factory at the time of the outbreak of World War II were built before the introduction of the moving assembly line.

It was the far-thinking production planning — breaking the aircraft into virtually completed major components before bringing them together on the moving final assembly line — that eventually saw the Master I, and its later variants, being produced at the rate of fifty aircraft per month.

At the beginning of the line, with the fuselage and wing centre section, complete with undercarriage, assembled together, each aircraft was placed on trolleys. These trolleys were linked together by cables attached to a winch at the end of the line. Each assembly stage, including necessary inspection operations, was timed to be completed within four hours, after which the whole line was winched along one stage. On completion, each aircraft was wheeled from its trolleys, which were taken back to the start, and pushed straight into the paint shop.

Opposite page top: The much enlarged P&P factory seen shortly before the outbreak of World War II. In the foreground, air raid shelters are under construction and what is thought to be a compound eventually used by the Home Guard.

Opposite page bottom: N7408, the very first production Master I, which first flew in the hands of FG Miles on 31st March 1939.

Right top: The moving final assembly line at Woodley, probably taken in 1940 when Master Is were in full production. In the foreground, the breakdown of the aircraft into major sub-assemblies is clearly demonstrated by the wing centre sections, complete with the undercarriage, ready to go onto the line.

Right bottom: An evocative scene showing early Master Is being prepared for their test flights outside the flight shed at Woodley.

Painted in oils on canvas. 2006. 200mm x 300mm.

'1939 Masterwork'

This painting is based exactly on a black-and-white photograph taken at P&P in 1939, showing the construction methods used for the Master I. Other photographs in the series can be seen on the following page.
The colour in the painting helps to differentiate between the wooden structure of the fuselage and the metal of the main fuselage jig. This jig assembly was itself a complex structure that was a masterpiece of the company's jig-and-tool design department and allowed a wooden aircraft as sophisticated as the Master to eventually be built at a rate of fifty per month.

Existing P&P workers, with their experience of wooden aircraft, were used to building components by using jigs. So too were many of the new workers who came from other industries such as furniture-making. However, the complexity of the Master, particularly with its additional service equipment, brought new problems. More importantly perhaps, the number of aircraft on order and the speed of production required, meant that all major components had to be interchangeable. This called for jig design and construction far beyond anything experienced before in the factory.

For the fuselages in particular, this called for really 'creative thinking' and it came mainly from a new team of production managers brought in from other industries. Some now unknown person discovered that the poles that had supported the overhead power cables for Reading's recently replaced tramways system were in a local scrapyard. These became the main cantilever 'spindle' of the highly complex fuselage jigs which can be seen on these pages. Presumably from the same source, tramlines were sunk into the floor for what became the world's first moving assembly line for aircraft.

1. *A completed fuselage shell is carefully removed from its jig. In the bottom left corner, note part of the main structure supporting the cantilever spindle.*

2. *More work is carried out on the fuselage shells before they are taken to the main assembly line.*

3. *Construction of the wing centre section spar. Note the top and bottom members in laminated spruce, much heavier than any previous Miles design, with pre-cut plywood sheets on both sides forming a box section.*

4. *Outer wing construction, as well the tailplane, was a conventional FG Miles design. Glue would have been applied to the wing structure before the plywood skin is carefully positioned.*

5. *The pre-formed plywood leading edge is glued in place.*

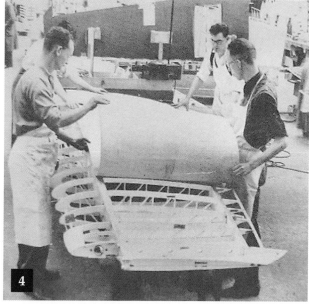

Painted in oils on canvas. 1998. 600mm x 750mm. Selected for the 1998 Aviation Paintings of the Year Exhibition.

'Masterwork I'

In the months leading up to the Battle of Britain, many of the pilots who would fight so valiantly against the Luftwaffe, learned their advanced flying skills in Master Is, before going on to fight in Hurricanes and Spitfires. Here pupils are learning to fly in formation and aviation enthusiasts will note that this is based on the 'vic' formation almost invariably used by the RAF at that time. Note the instructors in the rear seat have it in the raised position to give them a better all-round view.

Right: Even before the Master I was in service, the Master II was ordered, to be fitted with a Bristol Mercury radial engine, and the two types originally carried out the same training function.

Painted in watercolours. 1999. 160mm x 200mm.

Eventually, some nine hundred Master Is were to be built. However, even before the first aircraft had come off the production line, the Air Ministry realised that, with the Kestrel engine no longer in production at Rolls Royce, reserve stocks would be insufficient for their requirements. Therefore P&P were requested to re-design the Master using a Bristol Mercury radial engine and so the Master II was born. Tommy Rose, now P&P's chief test pilot, flew the prototype in late November 1939. Some eighteen hundred Master IIs were eventually to be built, both at Woodley and a new Government - financed 'shadow' factory near Swindon, which was built and managed by P&P.

However, the Air Ministry and, later, the wartime Ministry of Aircraft Production demonstrated what was to become an all too familiar incompetence. Even before production of the Master II had really got underway, in the Summer of 1940, the Ministry informed P&P that there were not enough Mercury engines available. Could they re-design the Master yet again, this time to utilise the American Pratt & Whitney radial engine? Thus the Master III came into being, the prototype first flying in December 1940. Then, even before flight testing of the Master III was completed, the Ministry suddenly discovered that, after all, there were plenty of Mercury engines and decided both types should be built Eventually, in addition to the eighteen hudred Master IIs, some six hundred Master IIIs were built just at Swindon.

Thus, the variations of the Master provided the main output of P&P in the early war years, as the one-thousand-strong workforce, which had built the Magister, expanded to more than six thousand.

Below: Pupil pilots and their instructors receiving a briefing before another day's work in their Master Is. Note the Hawker biplane trainer in the background which the Master I replaced.

Painted in oils on canvas. 1999. 300mm x 400mm.

'Going solo'

Magisters, in their wartime camouflage finish, are seen at one of the hundreds of small airfields in the UK where they were based, in the training role for which they were designed. Instructors watch their pupils start their first solo flights, probably the most challenging event so far in their young lives.

In addition to some four thousand workers at the airfield factory, the rest were to be found in more than twenty dispersed production and storage units scattered around Berkshire and neighbouring counties, later increasing to more than thirty sites. Among the most important were two in Reading— the Serpells Biscuits factory in Liverpool Road and the Berkshire Printing Works in Oxford Road. The Hughendon Furniture Company in High Wycombe and the Princes Risborough Furniture factory also provided large production facilities. Talbot's Garage in Henley was another production facility, as were the Swears & Wells and Eden Fisher factories in Basingstoke Road, Reading. Hewen's Garages in Reading and Maidenhead, Abbey Motors in Reading and the Methodist Chapel in London Street, Reading became storage units, while East Berkshire's Binfield Hall and Newall Hall provided office space.

In a quirk of Berkshire's history, Ernest Hives, the young Reading lad who, in 1903, went off to work for Charles Rolls, returned to the county when, in 1939, he became a Rolls Royce representative on the P&P Board. However the Rolls Royce interest in P&P would not last much longer. In April 1941, the Rolls Royce shares in the company were purchased by the Miles family and P&P became Miles Aircraft Limited. FG Miles became chairman and was joined on the Board by Blossom Miles, George Miles and WH Gatty Saunt. The thirty-year-old George Miles became technical director and chief designer.

'Masterwork III'

Pupil pilots flying in the 'finger four' formation, used by the RAF after the Luftwaffe demonstrated its effectiveness in the Battle of Britain, learn to peel off into the line-ahead attack formation from 'out of the sun'.

The squadrons from Abingdon and Harwell were among the first in the RAF to learn that the Germans were going to be very tough opponents. Sent to France the day before war was declared, they were soon to find their Fairey Battles hopelessly outclassed by the Luftwaffe fighters.

Back in the UK, the Air Ministry decided that the Berkshire airfields were too far from the east coast to be operational airfields and they were designated Operational Training Units (OTUs). Their task was to weld together whole crews—pilots, navigators, wireless operators and gunners— giving them the experience to perform effectively when they eventually went on operations. At Abingdon and Harwell, the aircraft assigned for the task were Whitleys and Ansons. Various nearby sites were chosen as satellite airfields and 'reserve landing grounds', as Berkshire's training role for the RAF expanded dramatically. Hampstead Norris, Watchfield and Greenham Common were all planned around this time, but all went on to play different roles in the years to come

At Woodley and White Waltham, the flying schools came under full RAF control at the outbreak of war, although they were still managed respectively by P&P and de Havilland. Their 'reserve landing grounds' at Theale, which went on to be a training school in its own right, and Crazies Hill, near Wargrave, which was to play a dramatic part in Berkshire's aviation history, were both operational in the early years of the war.

These first months of the war subsequently became known as 'The Phoney War', but it gave P&P the chance to deliver many hundreds of Master Is to the RAF and, without them, the proper training of 'The Few' in their Hurricanes and Spitfires may well have resulted in a very different outcome to the Battle of Britain.

In that summer of 1940, the threat of invasion was very real and desperate times called for desperate measures. At Woodley, a number of Magisters were fitted with bomb-racks and twenty-four Masters Is were authorised to be converted to single-seat fighters. The new Ministry of Aircraft Production feared that Hurricanes and Spitfires would be lost quicker than they could be replaced. Then FG Miles offered them a possible solution.

Painted in oils on canvas.1998. 400mm x 500mm.

'Just 65 days!'

A main feature of the M20 was its fixed spatted undercarriage which required no hydraulics. Another was its 'bubble' canopy — the first fighter in the world to be designed with this later commonly used feature.

His idea was to build a fighter entirely in wood, to be constructed very quickly and cheaply both in the UK and Canada. Using the well-proven Merlin engine, it would have as many Master components as possible and no hydraulics would be employed, saving weight, space, cost and construction time. When the contract for a prototype was received, FG and his team designed, built and flew the M20 in the remarkably short time of sixty-five days. However, by October, when it first flew, 'The Few', without losing as many Hurricanes and Spitfires as feared, were on the verge of defeating the Luftwaffe.

The M20 never went into full production but, had it done so, how would it have compared with its legendary companions? It was faster than the Hurricane, but slower than the Spitfire. The extra space in the wings meant it could carry twelve machine guns, instead of the eight of the other two, plus twice the ammunition. Furthermore, it could carry approximately twice the fuel load, allowing it to stay in combat much longer.

In 1984, Lettice Curtis, one of the most experienced ATA pilots and a contemporary of pilots who actually flew the M20, told the author "it landed like a brick". With its short wingspan and a fairly high landing speed, it was perhaps inevitable. However, in most ways FG Miles had produced yet another winner, at a time when winners were badly needed.

Painted in oils on canvas. 1999. 600mm x 750mm. Selected for the 1999 Aviation Paintings of the Year Exhibition.

'Squadron Hacks'

Both the Miles Magister and the Miles Master were, of course, originally designed for the RAF as training aircraft and served in this role throughout the war years. However, both types were also widely used by the RAF as 'squadron hacks', transporting personnel between airfields. In June 1940, at the time of the Dunkirk evacuation, one squadron even sent its Master 'hack' across to Calais to pick up a downed pilot, but he and his rescuer had to hide in a ditch while their escorting Spitfires fought off a group of ME109s before they could take off and 'wave hop' back home. Within a few months during the Battle of Britain, when the RAF fighter squadrons were stretched to the limit to continue the fight against almost overwhelming odds, the role of 'squadron hack' became a vital one. When pilots were forced to bale out or to crash-land, probably many miles from their home base, it was essential they were quickly returned to rejoin the fight. Every frontline fighter squadron in the Battle of Britain had a Magister or a Master – and sometimes both types - in this vital role.

Although the RAF eventually inflicted the first defeat ever suffered by the Luftwaffe and ended the threat of invasion, the enemy's bombers were still a force to be reckoned with. The daylight attacks of August and September 1940, with massed squadrons of bombers and fighter escorts, were largely broken up by the RAF over South and East England, but smaller bomber groups managed to break through as far as the Midlands where, on August 13th, the massive new Spitfire factory at Castle Bromwich received its first, relatively unsuccessful, attack. This factory, which had produced its very first Spitfire in June was vital to Britain's war effort. The two Supermarine factories at Southampton and the final assembly hangars at nearby Eastleigh airfield, were all dangerously close to the Luftwaffe's newly captured airfields in France.

Berkshire's RAF airfields also came under attack around this time. On 16th August, Harwell and its satellite at Stanton Harcourt were bombed with some loss of life, but little real damage. However, that same day, nearby Brize Norton in Oxfordshire, a maintenance unit absolutely packed with aircraft, suffered badly in one of the worst raids on any RAF station. More than forty aircraft were destroyed but, thankfully, there were relatively few casualties. Woodley was also bombed that day, with very little damage. White Waltham had been bombed the previous month, with some casualties and aircraft destroyed. There were further attacks on these same Berkshire airfields in the following weeks, usually by single bombers and with very little real damage.

However, on 28th September, around sixty Luftwaffe Heinkel 111s carried out devastating attacks on the Supermarine works in Southampton, which were completely destroyed, although many of the Spitfire production jigs and machine tools were salvaged. Surprisingly, the hangars at Eastleigh airfield were untouched.

In an inspired piece of planning, in just over six weeks, Vickers management, with the help of the Ministry of Aircraft Production, diversified Spitfire production to a total of thirty-six premises such as garages, laundries and bus stations around four main centres in the southern counties. A dramatic new chapter in Berkshire's aviation history was about to be written.

Above: Vincents Garage in Station Square, Reading, became an important location for Spitfire production from November 1940. Complete fuselages were manufactured there before being transported to Henley airfield for final assembly and test flying.

Below: Great Western Motors in Vastern Road, Reading, was another important location from November 1940. Here, Spitfire wings were assembled.

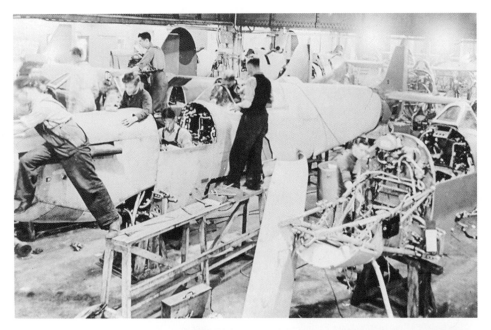

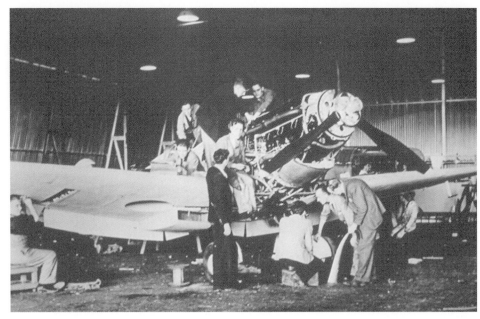

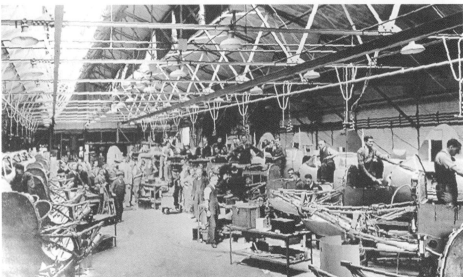

Left top: Spitfire fuselages under construction at Vincent's Garage, Reading.

Left centre: Spitfire fuselages being assembled at the Star Road factory in Caversham.

Left bottom: The Star Road factory.

Above top: Final assembly of a Spitfire in the Robins hangar at Henley aerodrome.

Above bottom: Spitfires outside the Robins hangar awaiting test flying.

Painted in oils on canvas.1998. 400mm x 500mm.

'First flight'

A Spitfire IX destined for an RAF Photo Reconnaissance Squadron, but as yet without its Squadron recognition letters, climbs away from Henley airfield on its test flight. The airfield was at Culham Farm, Crazies Hill, above Wargrave, on the Berkshire side of the Thames, but it was always known as Henley airfield. The town of Henley-on-Thames, with its easily recognised church and bridge, can be seen in the background. Major components of hundreds of Spitfires were manufactured in Reading and then transported to Henley airfield on low-loader lorries, known as 'Queen Marys', for final assembly. Factories at Newbury and Hungerford were also used in the production of Spitfire parts and, by 1945, when Aldermaston airfield became available for final assembly and test flying, for manufacture of major components. Final assembly of components built in Reading also transferred to Aldermaston at that time.

Why were you twice as likely to see a Spitfire take off from Woodley airfield in the war years as you would be to see one land?

A

Because Spitfires arriving for the first time at Woodley had been damaged in some way and many of them were 'landed' from 'Queen Mary' low-loader lorries.

Spitfires also played a part in another of Berkshire's unusual 'brushes with aviation'. Late in 1940, FG Miles had won for P&P a contract to repair damaged Spitfires, perhaps surprisingly for a company that had only built wooden aircraft.

Two new hangars were constructed close to the existing repair & service hangars at the eastern end of the airfield and a dedicated team of metalworkers was recruited.

Over the following five years it is thought that well over one thousand Spitfires were repaired and returned to squadron service — another important contribution to the war effort by the workforce at Woodley.

From 1942 until 1945, the main factory's contribution was building the final development of the 1937 Kestrel design — the Martinet. Similar to the Master II in being fitted with a Bristol Mercury air-cooled radial engine, the Martinet was the RAF's first purpose-built target-towing aircraft. More than seventeen hundred were built at Woodley, including sixty-five radio-controlled, pilotless, target versions known as the Queen Martinet which, for some reason, was kept on the 'secret list' until well after the war's end.

Air Transport Auxiliary

"From small beginnings the ATA grew into a national organisation which figured in a big way towards the sum of our victory in the air. I saw much of the ATA work. Many of its members were my friends. I salute in reverence and sorrow those who laid down their lives in the course of duty. We fly with them on missions of delivery to a multitude of RAF bases, often under conditions which would keep most of us thankfully earth-bound. I marvel how, with the very limited air and ground aids of those days, these men and women managed to get through and to deliver safely and on time the aircraft vitally needed by the RAF. These ATA pilots were combat pilots in the full sense. They did not fight the enemy with guns but they fought and beat an enemy which can kill just as effectively as the bullet. Snow, fog, ice and storm were faced daily and only triumphed over through skill and courage."

Extract from the forward by Lord Balfour of Inchrye to Lettice Curtis's book, 'The Forgotten Pilots'.

From a wartime airfield somewhere in the UK, a Spitfire is about to be flown to an operational squadron of the RAF. The scene might be at Woodley, where the aircraft had been repaired. It might be at Henley, where the brand new aircraft had been assembled. It might be at White Waltham, where an overnight stop had been made on its delivery from the massive Spitfire factory at Castle Bromwich. In fact, little is known about this particular Spitfire, which was just one of over fifty thousand flown by pilots of the Air Transport Auxiliary.

About the pilot, however, a great deal is known. She is First Officer Lettice Curtis, a resident of Berkshire for over fifty years, an early member of the Berkshire Aviation Group and a generous supporter of the Group's Museum project. She joined the ATA in July 1940 and remained on active service until its disbandment in November 1945. More than one hundred and sixty Spitfires were among the total of nearly fifteen hundred aircraft she flew in that period. Much of the information about the ATA that appears in the following pages are extracts from her book 'The Forgotten Pilots' which was first published in 1971 and subsequently formed the basis for a TV documentary.

In the months before the outbreak of war, in anticipation of immediate air attacks by the enemy, various executives within the Air Ministry and the main British airline companies were considering the formation of some sort of 'reserve' for civilian pilots who were not eligible for RAF flying duties. They would fly aircraft that had been impressed by the Ministry and carry out such duties as the transport of civil authorities personnel, despatches, mail, medical supplies and personnel. It was envisaged it would be a specially recruited branch of the recently formed British Overseas Airways Corporation, which would provide advanced training when required.

The question of ferrying military aircraft was apparently discussed but the Air Ministry felt that the RAF could handle this themselves. Indeed, from the spring of 1939 the RAF set up an organisation of ferry pilots and 'taxi' aircraft for the collection and distribution of aircraft from various manufacturers.

On 3rd September 1939, the 'reserve' scheme was given official approval and the Air Transport Auxiliary was born, under the command of Gerard d'Erlanger, a former director of British Airways Ltd. A number of pilots were recruited and evaluated at the RAF's Central Flying School at Upavon, before being attached to the RAF Ferry Pools. For some months then, the ferrying of service aircraft depended on a somewhat uneasy relationship between the RAF and the forty or so civilian ATA pilots, who were based at their Ferry Pools.

By January 1940, a women's section of the ATA was formed, under Pauline Gower, its first eight recruits based at the de Havilland factory at Hatfield specifically to fly out Tiger Moths to RAF units.

This was still the time of the 'phoney war' and in 'official circles' it only slowly dawned that the RAF would benefit by the release of trained pilots from ferry duties and that the ATA, as an independent civilian organisation, could be quite capable of ferrying all types of service aircraft.

At the time the Air Ministry's director-general of civil aviation was still nominally responsible for the ATA and, under a new arrangement to allow further expansion, BOAC, through d'Erlanger, became responsible for all financial matters and No.41 Group RAF Maintenance Command took over operations from the Air Ministry.

Looking back, it hardly seems the most efficient structure in which d'Erlanger could manage the growth and development of the ATA. However, when rationalisation of the RAF ferry pools led to the handing over to the ATA of the Avro Ansons used as 'taxis', it might just have seemed a step in the right direction.

In the meantime, d'Erlanger had agreed with de Havillands to use their airfield at White Waltham in Berkshire as the ATA headquarters and, in time, their No.1 Ferry Pool. This came into effect in February 1940 and, in the first three weeks there, with forty-three pilots, some two hundred and sixty aircraft movements were logged. However, it soon became apparent that the more work they were able to do, the more they were being offered.

Above: Four of the original ATA pilots at White Waltham who, generally, flew the Anson taxi aircraft. Their wide experience qualified them to fly passengers and, for some of them at least, their 'wide' build was easier to get into an Anson than many other aircraft. On the left is Ronnie Malcolm, whose company eventually became ML Aviation, one of the most innovative companies to be based at White Waltham.

Below right: A typical morning scene at the ATA's No.1 Ferry Pool at White Waltham. Pilots wait for their ferry chits or stand ready to be called to a taxi aircraft.

Below left: Tea on the terrace at White Waltham for some of the original ATA pilots. Commodore Gerard d'Erlanger, the founder and commanding officer of the ATA is second from the right.

Painted in oils on canvas. 2006. 450mm x 600mm.

'Taxi to Langley'

This painting is set in the early 1940s and a group of Air Transport Auxiliary pilots are arriving at Langley, near Slough, in modern Berkshire, the main Hawker production plant for the Hurricane fighter. Awaiting them is what would probably have been, in the peak war years, just one day's production of this vital RAF fighter, ready to be ferried directly to operational squadrons or to dispersal units around the country. The headquarters of the ATA was at White Waltham, near Maidenhead and it was also home of the No.1 Ferry Pool. Between early 1940 and late 1945, a total of over thirteen hundred pilots, as well as a number of flight engineers and radio officers flew with the ATA. Mostly, pilots flew alone, using eye, compass, maps and stopwatch, without any modern navigation aids or even radio. They had to contend with all weather conditions, as well as other hazards such as barrage balloon defences around the factory airfields from which they flew. They flew brand new aircraft that had received just the minimum testing. And they flew obsolete aircraft that were past their useful service life. A total of one hundred and fifty three ATA aircrew lost their lives, including sixteen women. Every type of aircraft was flown by the ATA, from single-engine trainers to four-engine bombers, a total of over three hundred thousand in just over five years. Their taxi-aircraft alone, such as the Avro Anson shown here, flew a total of one hundred and eighty thousand hours. At present, there is no adequate commemoration anywhere in the UK of the vital wartime role carried out by these civilian pilots. This painting, in its own small way, aims to be a commemoration of those gallant pilots and aircrew.

The first stage of expansion took place in May 1940, when two new Ferry Pools were established at Whitchurch, near Bristol and Hawarden, near Chester, their nucleus of pilots and taxi aircraft being transferred from White Waltham. The following month, more female pilots were recruited, including Lettice Curtis and the internationally renowned Amy Johnson. Like all new pilots they were still being cleared to fly by the RAF Central Flying School. However, it was decided that female pilots would be allowed to ferry all types of service aircraft except operational fighters and bombers.

That month, around the time of the Dunkirk evacuation, the new prime minister, Winston Churchill, created the Ministry of Aircraft Production, under the leadership of the dynamic Lord Beaverbrook. The RAF still had a great number of pilots involved with ferrying aircraft from the various manufacturers' airfields and sought to have the ATA take over this work. However, there were still some in the RAF who wanted ATA pilots to have temporary commissions and be subject to service discipline. Nevertheless, when the new Ministry gained control of the ATA it became apparent it would remain a civilian organisation.

This was a time of continuing growth for the ATA and, by the end of 1940, its staff had grown to more than six hundred, comprising some two hundred and twenty male and twenty-six female pilots, more than two hundred ground engineers and around one hundred and fifty other staff. The number of Ferry Pools had grown to twelve (later sixteen), plus a Central Flying Control Unit and two Flying Schools.

An ATA classification scheme for different aircraft was introduced for training and ferrying purposes, with certain 'more complicated' aircraft being placed in sub-categories. Pilots Notes were also introduced, setting out the information required to fly a particular aircraft. Surprisingly, for the majority of types, this information was able to be condensed to fit on one 'postcard-sized' page, cards eventually being contained in a pocket-size ring binder covering all types of aircraft the pilot was qualified to fly. In July 1941, the restriction on female ATA pilots ferrying operational fighters and bombers was lifted, although many months passed before they got their hands on flying virtually all of them.

The first of them to fly a bomber was Lettice Curtis, who learned to fly a Halifax in September 1942. She went on to ferry more than 200 Halifax bombers and some 150 other heavy bombers such as the Lancaster, Stirling and Liberator. Also in 1942, Joan Hughes learned to fly Stirling bombers and went on to be the only female pilot qualified to instruct in all five of the land-based classes of aircraft.

Many different nationalities were to serve in the ATA, among the first being Poles who escaped their country when it was overrun by the Germans in 1939. One of them, a founder member of the Polish national airline LOT, had been flying for twenty years. There were more than twenty of his fellow-countrymen who eventually served in the ATA, including two female pilots. Another early 'recruit' was a Danish airline pilot who arrived with his German-built Focke Wolfe 'Condor', which was used for a time for four-engine training at White Waltham.

Americans also played a major part and, between August 1940 and September 1941, some 200 male pilots signed up. Sadly, fourteen others didn't survive the hazardous sea crossing to get to the UK. Many returned to America to serve after December 1941, when the Japanese attack on Pearl Harbour brought their country into the war. However, around twenty continued to serve with the ATA until 1945. From April 1942, American female pilots also began to arrive and, eventually, around twenty-five served with the ATA. There were also pilots and flight engineers from Canada, Australia, New Zealand, South Africa, Ceylon, Austria, Belgium, Chile, Czechoslovakia, Eire, France and Russia.

Above: Faith Bennett, who joined the ATA in 1941, signs the required form, before ferrying a Hudson bomber. The Hudson was classified as 'Advanced twin engine', but had the additional requirement for a 'pilot's assistant' to be carried. Hudsons, as well as Liberator bombers destined for the RAF, were ferried to the UK across the Atlantic by a separate Atlantic Ferry Organisation, set up in 1941 by Lord Beaverbrook, which employed both British and American pilots and aircrew. Lettice Curtis, who flew this type of aircraft twelve times, wrote "the Hudson was never one of my favourite aircraft."

ATA Aircraft Classifications

Class 1. Light. Single engine
(types such as Tiger Moths and Magisters)

Class 2. Advanced. Single engine.
(types such as Spitfires and Hurricanes)

Class 3. Light. Twin engine.
(types such as Ansons and Oxfords).

Class 4. Advanced twin engine.
(types such as Beaufighters and Mosquitos)

Class 5. Four engine.
(types such as Lancasters and Stirlings).

Class 6. Flying boats and seaplanes.
(types such as Sunderlands and Catalinas).

The ATA continued to grow steadily from 1941 through to 1944, when it employed an average of six hundred and fifty pilots, around one hundred of them being female, with eleven qualified to fly four-engine aircraft.

Aircraft deliveries eventually totalled well over three hundred and eight thousand, rising from over twenty thousand in 1941 to well over seventy eight thousand in 1944.

Over the four years of war, the ATA employed a total of around thirteen hundred pilots, of whom one hundred and sixty six were female. In addition there were some one hundred and fifty flight engineers. Sadly, more than one hundred and fifty pilots and aircrew lost their lives during service, fifteen of them being female, including Amy Johnson, who died in 1941 in somewhat mysterious circumstances.

Above: Joan Hughes stands dwarfed by the Short Stirling bomber she first learned to fly in the autumn of 1942. The smallest of the original eight female pilots recruited by the ATA, she was the only female pilot to qualify as an instructor in all five land-based aircraft classifications. She served with the ATA until its disbandment in 1945 and, after the war, returned to White Waltham as a flying instructor.

" A job well done"

Letters of congratulations from the MAP to the ATA followed the exceptional performance on 7th–8th November 1943, when eight hundred and seventy six aircraft movements were recorded over the two days. However, the ultimate record came on 21st February 1945 when five hundred and seventy aircraft movements were achieved in just one day.

To illustrate what this might entail for just one pilot, here is an extract from the log book of Lettice Curtis for just one day, sometime in 1942.

Taxi Anson	White Waltham—Brooklands
Wellington	Brooklands—Little Rissington
Spitfire	Little Rissington—Llandow
Mosquito	St Athan—Ford
Mustang*	Ford—Lichfield (* first flight in type)
Taxi Puss Moth	Lichfield—Castle Bromwich
Wellington	Castle Bromwich—W. Waltham

Departure White Waltham 10-45. Return 18-05.
4hrs 5mins total flying time.
Longest time on ground 1hr 15mins waiting at Ford for daily inspection of Mustang.

"Looking back I never cease to marvel at the number of days on which ATA pilots managed to get around without any form of navigation or landing aids whatsoever. Now, as I stare from my window on seemingly endless days of damp winter greyness or misty summer haze, wondering whether to take to the air in a small light aircraft equipped with radio and beacon navigation, I am appalled by those minimum flight conditions of 2,000 yards visibility and 800 feet cloud-base, and the thought that in these conditions we flew (to say happily would be an exaggeration) the Mosquito, for example, or the Wellington, the four-engine bombers, let alone the single-engine fighters with their poor forward view.

"The fact was that the old hands of ATA were getting very expert indeed at their job of moving aircraft from one site to another. When we frightened ourselves now it was more likely to be as a result of a calculated over-estimation of our ability rather than, as in the early days, by simply letting matters get inadvertently out of hand. New types of aircraft came up less frequently and when they did they tended to differ little from types we were currently flying. As to navigation, we were now familiar with just about every landmark on the main route between airfields—the roads, the woods and even the houses—and we knew the exact form at the various airfields and Maintenance Units we visited. To a large extent, therefore, fear of the unknown had died. Nevertheless it would be very far from the truth to suggest that over-confidence in the ATA was widespread."

An extract from Lettice Curtis's book, 'The Forgotten Pilots', looking back to the last year or two of the war.

The main aircraft types ferried by the ATA during the war years

Aircraft type	1940 / 1941	1941 / 1942	1942 / 1943	1943 / 1944	1944 / 1945	1945 (Feb-Nov)	Totals
Spitfire/Seafire	2,279	5,815	12,567	12,907	16,802	6,916	57,286
Hurricane	4,049	7,703	8,269	7,035	2,036	309	29,401
Master/Martinet	843	1,675	1,913	2,681	1,808	612	9,532
Wellington	1,433	3,871	6,158	6,921	5,845	1,948	26,176
Oxford	936	2,436	4,122	3,789	2,505	579	14,367
Beaufighter	153	1,363	3,649	4,245	3,468	725	13,603
Mosquito	—	3	789	2,717	5,377	3,594	12,480
Blenheim	2,006	3,512	1,770	988	277	16	8,569
Anson	639	783	1,714	2,107	2,247	1,038	8,528
Lancaster	—	5	858	2,665	4,473	1,804	9,805
Halifax	6	208	1,158	3,147	3,376	1,431	9,326

It is interesting to note that the total number of ATA flights made in most types far exceeds the total number that were built. For instance, the total number of Spitfires built was in the region of twenty-three-thousand and Mosquitos some seven thousand. It seems that the ATA must have flown many individual aircraft on at least two or more separate occasions.

Total annual deliveries by the ATA during the war years

Aircraft type	1940 /1941	1941 / 1942	1942 / 1943	1943 / 1944	1944 / 1945	1945 (Feb-Nov)	Totals
Single-engine	13,243	25,555	32,621	35,907	44,402	20,206	**171,934**
Twin-engine	7,392	18,506	24,971	26,293	23,873	9,601	**110,636**
Four-engine	19	319	2,848	7,366	9,865	4,613	**25,030**
Flying boats	–	–	39	416	311	201	**967**
Totals	**20,654**	**44,380**	**60,479**	**69,982**	**78,451**	**34,621**	**308,567**

Painted in oils on canvas. 2007. 500mm x 600mm.

'All in a day's work'

By the Spring of 1942, production of the various types of Master had been completed and, in its place, for the next three years, the factory at Woodley produced a target-towing development of the Master, known as the Martinet. In all nearly eighteen hundred Martinets were built, including sixty-five pilot-less radio-controlled versions known as the Queen Martinet. In the painting, a Martinet is seen, about to be flown out for delivery to the RAF by a female ATA pilot. She had probably been flown in to Woodley by a 'taxi' aircraft from White Waltham and the Martinet's delivery would perhaps be just one of five or six such flights she would make that day around the country. Already taking off is a re-furbished Spitfire, perhaps flown by another ATA pilot. Over the war years, it is thought that well over one thousand Spitfires were repaired and returned to service, making another important contribution to the war effort by the Woodley factory. In the background, two Tiger Moths from Woodley's RAF Flying Training School can be seen on a circuit of the airfield.

By 1941, the wartime roles of the Woodley and White Waltham airfields were well established but, what of Berkshire's other airfields?

The pre-war RAF stations at Abingdon and Harwell would generally retain their roles as OTUs and would soon be joined by many other new airfields, mainly in the same role. This would eventually change dramatically after America came into the war and, particularly in West Berkshire, nearly all the airfields would play a major part in the build-up to D-Day and the assault by both British and American airborne forces on Normandy.

Abingdon

By 1941, the OTU squadrons operating from Abingdon were mainly equipped with Whitleys, supported by some Ansons and Lysanders and later, Martinets and then Hurricanes for gunnery training.

Although the squadrons' role was primarily a training one, a number of operational bombing missions were mounted from Abingdon, particularly when Bomber Command, mainly for 'propaganda' purposes, mounted one-thousand-bomber raids. The squadrons also carried out many leaflet-dropping operations over France through to 1944.

Until 1943, Abingdon was a wholly grass airfield but, in March of that year, two concrete runways were installed. It was in October 1944 that the last Whitley left Abingdon, being replaced by Wellingtons. Its role as an OTU continued until the end of the war after which, in a number of different roles, it was to play its part in the RAF for another forty years.

Aldermaston

In 1941, the site on the hill above Aldermaston village was chosen to be yet another of Berkshire's OTUs and, by July 1942, it was completed with a standard three-runway layout, extensive dispersal areas and a large bomb dump. However, the intended Wellingtons never arrived because Aldermaston was handed over to the Americans and became USAAC Station No.467. The 60th Troop Carrier Group moved in with four squadrons of C47 transports, better known to the British as DC3 Dakotas.

First used for cargo flights, the C47s were soon employed in the training of paratroopers. Indeed, the very first practice jumps by the Americans in the UK were made at Aldermaston in September 1942.

Through to March 1943, many changes to the organisation of the American squadrons took place, as the build up of their forces for the eventual invasion of mainland Europe gathered strength.

C47s from Aldermaston did see action in October 1942 when the Allies landed in North Africa and they carried hundreds of American troops there. Again, in May 1943, a detachment of C47s was despatched to Algeria to back up the forces invading Sicily.

A few months earlier, in February 1943, the only RAF aircraft to use Aldermaston took up residence for a month, when their airfield was out of action. These were Miles Master IIs with Hotspur gliders, which were being used to train pilots for the new British Glider Pilot Regiment.

July 1943 saw a completely new development at Aldermaston, when Vickers took over a hangar for the assembly of Spitfires which were, by then, being built in Newbury as well as in Reading.

In February 1944, another short-term resident of Aldermaston was a USAAC group flying Lockheed Lightning fighters.

It was the following month when the American 434th Troop Carrier Group moved into Aldermaston with its four squadrons and began intensive training with the 101st Airborne Division which, by then, had turned virtually the whole of West Berkshire into one enormous army camp.

'Masterwork II'

When the decision was taken to create a British glider-borne force, the General Aircraft Hotspur was designed as the standard training glider. Initially, a number of virtually obsolete – and totally unsuitable – aircraft were employed to tow them but it soon became apparent that a purpose-built 'tug' was required. That is when Miles Aircraft were asked to adapt the Master II, proving to be an ideal aircraft for the task.

Painted in oils on canvas. 2000. 500mm x 600mm.

Bray

This short-lived, pre-war civil airfield was little used during the war years. A gliding school, mainly used by the Air Training Corps, operated there for a number of years and, for a few months, it also served as a relief landing ground for the RAF Elementary Flying School at White Waltham.

Bush Barn

This small airfield, which the Admiralty took over in 1944, was originally a 'production satellite' operated by the Ministry of Aircraft Production. Thereafter, Fleet Air Arm aircraft from Worthy Down (HMS Kestrel) were stored there. Another Fleet Air Arm airfield at Culham, known as HMS Hornbill, just a few miles away across the river in Oxfordshire, also opened in 1944 as an aircraft receipt and despatch unit.

Great Shefford

Laid down as a scatter-field for Woodley airfield, the idea was that, if Woodley appeared to be under direct threat of being bombed, as many aircraft as possible would be flown out to Great Shefford. Later, it became an emergency landing ground for the many airfields in the area.

Greenham Common

Originally planned in 1941 as a satellite for the proposed Bomber OTU at Aldermaston, Greenham Common was nearing completion in the summer of 1942 when it became one of the many airfields in West Berkshire earmarked for the USAAC. Before the Americans really got themselves organised a variety of aircraft could be seen at Greenham Common. For almost a year, the RAF moved in with Airspeed Oxfords being used for pilot training. In October 1943 a USAAC Fighter Group was there for just a week while they collected their brand new Merlin-powered Mustangs, the first to enter service in Europe. Then, for about a month, another fighter group 'worked up' on their Thunderbolt fighters and actually carried out one offensive operation along the French coast. Finally, when the 438th Troop Carrier Group moved in with their C47s, Greenham Common was set for its major contribution to the D-Day airborne operations.

Grove

Originally planned as a well equipped, three-runway bomber airfield, Grove suffered a confused early existence and its final completion dragged on well into 1943, although it was in use from the summer of 1942. That year, when nearby Brize Norton became a glider pilot training unit, Grove came under its control. However, there were soon plans for it to take over from Hampstead Norris as Harwell's satellite and Wellingtons of No.15 Bomber OTU flew from there in August 1942. Then the nearby gliding activity caused complications and Grove was transferred to Flying Training Command.

For a few months early in 1943 it was used by Whitleys and Horsa gliders from Brize Norton and even Typhoon fighters flew from Grove for a few days during an exercise.

It seems likely it had already been earmarked for the Americans but, before they took over, the RAF flew Oxfords at Grove for three months for advanced flying training.

From July 1943 until the end of hostilities, Grove came under the control of the US 9th AAF Support Command and it was primarily used as a repair and maintenance base for C47s and, later, C46s. The following year, communications aircraft of the 9th AAF were also based at Grove. It also became a delivery base for small aircraft, such as Piper Cubs, which were shipped over the Atlantic in crates. Over the next two years, hundreds were assembled at Grove and flown out to airfields and camps all over Southern England.

Left: Piper Cubs assembled at Grove airfield could often be seen flying low along the river at Reading.

Hampstead Norris

Opened in the summer of 1940, as a satellite for Harwell, Hampstead Norris was the first airfield in Berkshire to have runways constructed. They are believed to have been of the steel-mesh type. Although it was frequently used as an OTU throughout the war years, it was as a departure point for the overseas ferrying of Wellington bombers that Hampstead Norris is best remembered. Between May and December 1941, more than two hundred Wellingtons, carrying some thirteen hundred airman, made the long and hazardous flight to Gibralter, before going on to Egypt. A few even flew direct to Malta, which entailed crossing occupied France. Inevitably there were some losses and a number of the Gibralter-bound crews found themselves interned in Portugal.

Hampstead Norris was sometimes a convenient airfield for the diversion of aircraft returning from operations and, notably, in January 1942, when eleven of 214 Squadron's Wellingtons arrived following a raid on Brest in northern France, it stretched the relatively small airfield's resources to the limit, providing food for the crews, as well as the usual debriefing, plus refuelling for the aircraft.

During 1942, a total of four-hundred-and-fifty Wellingtons flew overseas from Hampstead Norris and Harwell but, by early 1943, most ferry flights were starting from Harwell. Throughout this time Hampstead Norris continued in its role as an OTU but, from March 1944 to February 1945, it was raised in status to a self-accounting station giving refresher courses for glider pilots who had originally trained for the airborne assault on Sicily and were now being prepared for the Normandy invasion. Tiger Moths, Whitleys, Albermarles and Horsa gliders were all used in the training.

In March 1945 it again became a satellite of Harwell and the refresher-course aircraft gradually left to be replaced by Mosquitos of No.13 OTU. However, the war years—and Hampstead Norris's time on active service—soon ended. Its final role was as an accommodation centre for men of the Glider Pilot Regiment and redundant RAF glider pilots.

Harwell

With the outbreak of war, Harwell's Battle squadrons departed for France and the airfield took on its role as an OTU equipped with Wellingtons and Ansons. Like at Abingdon, some crews and aircraft undertook leaflet-dropping operations over France.

Harwell was involved in offensive operations when, in 1940, Whitley squadrons from Yorkshire used it as a departure and return point for a long haul to bomb northern Italy.

In July 1941, the airfield was virtually closed down for four months while three concrete runways were constructed. In April of that year, Harwell had begun training crews to ferry Wellingtons to the Middle East. The main departure point was nearby Hampstead Norris but, in the summer of 1943, around eighty of these ferry trips set out from Harwell.

Twice in 1942 Wellingtons from Harwell took part in one-thousand-bomber raids and, in 1943, they undertook operations to lay mines. Occasionally, they also carried out air-sea-rescue searches.

It was in March 1944 that Harwell's OTU closed and, a month later, the airfield became one of the most important bases for the training of Britain's rapidly growing airborne forces and, three months later, played a major part in the D-Day operations.

Below: Martin Baker, who were based at Denham, first flew their remarkable prototype MB 5 fighter on May 23rd 1944 from Harwell's concrete runway. It impressed many in the RAF with its maximum speed of 460mph speed, its excellent handling and its four-cannon armament. Powered by a Rolls Royce 2,340hp Griffon engine with contra-rotating propellers, it was, in fact, very similar to the final marks of Griffon-powered Spitfires. There could be a number of reasons why the MB 5 was never put into production. Perhaps the well proven production record of the Spitfire gave it the edge. In any case, the first jet fighters were soon to be built. Within a few years Martin Baker pioneered the design and manufacture of aircraft ejection seats and, ever since, has led the world in this important technology.

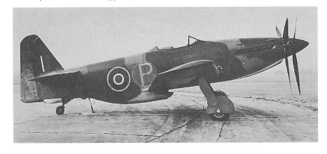

Painted in watercolours. 2007. 220mm x 300mm.

Henley

It may have had a humble beginning as a relief landing ground for the flying schools at White Waltham and Woodley, but Henley went on to play a unique part in UK aviation history. Assembly and test flying of Reading-built Spitfires transferred to Aldermaston in July 1943 and, although little is known about events at Henley over the following year, August 1944 saw dramatic developments.

The Air Ministry had first bought six C30 autogiros in 1935. The RAF's very first rotary-wing aircraft, they were built by Avro under licence from the Spanish Cierva company and given the collective name Rota. In 1939, the RAF gained five of the more powerful C40 models and they were soon at work helping to calibrate the ground units of the new, highly secret Radar system being developed at that time. The work, carried out by Flight 1448 from RAF Halton and Duxford, generally entailed flying off the east coast at specific points while the radar units 'focussed' their equipment. In June 1944, Flight 1448 became Squadron No.529 and, in August 1944, moved to Henley where calibration work continued until the end of hostilities.

'Henley's pioneering Rotas'

Cierva C30 autogiro, manufactured under licence by Avro and known as the Rota by the RAF were first based at Henley airfield.

The RAF's very first helicopter, known as the Hoverfly, was an American Sikorsky YR-4, which entered service in 1944. The more powerful R-6 model followed and, in May 1945, 529 Squadron at Henley became the very first to receive helicopters for operational use. By then, of course, the war in Europe was ending and, with it, Henley's pioneering days of rotary flying were soon over. 529 Squadron was disbanded in October 1945.

An interesting footnote is a story that surfaced around 1990 which suggested that Henley autogiro pilots were used as 'airborne dispatch-riders' in the intelligence war against the enemy. With Henley close to RAF Medmenham, the home of the Allied Central Intelligence Unit where photographic images were interpreted, Bletchley Park, the home of the Enigma codebreakers and RAF Benson, the leading photo reconnaissance airfield, the story sounds plausible enough but it doesn't appear to have been verified since.

Kingston Bagpuise

Kingston Bagpuise opened in January 1942 and was briefly used as a reserve landing ground for Shellingford. Eventually it was to become USAAC Station 403 and was equipped with two steel-matting runways. Nothing is currently known about the American squadrons and aircraft that flew there.

Membury

Construction of Membury was authorised in May 1941 and it was designed to be an OTU. However, as it neared completion, it was earmarked for the Americans and, in August 1942, now designated Station 466, headquarters staff of the VIIIth Ground Air Support Command arrived.

Early in September, the 3rd Photographic Group, and the 67th Observation Group, both nominally with four squadrons, as well as the 153rd Liaison Squadron moved in. It might sound impressive, but the aircraft involved were just six B17 camera ships and a few Piper Cubs. Nine PR versions of the P38 Lightning arrived later but only stayed a few weeks. The North African operations prevented Membury's further build-up. By the end of the year, the 67th Group had thirty-six Spitfire Vbs, spread among the four squadrons and, early in 1943, a number of target-towing A20 Havocs arrived.

Although, initially, the 67th was little more than a training unit for Spitfire pilots who promptly moved on when qualified, it gradually developed as a tactical training unit with Spitfires being used for observation, photography and artillery spotting.

During the summer of 1943, a number of offensive operations were undertaken by Membury aircraft, usually in conjunction with the RAF. By the end of the year, P47 Thunderbolts and P51 Mustangs could be seen there, as their pilots 'worked up' before moving on to other airfields.

However, Membury's role was to change again, when it was chosen as a base for a Troop Carrier Group of the American IXth Air Force, requiring the lengthening of one of its runways. Now, like so many airfields in West Berkshire, Membury became home to C47 troop and cargo aircraft, together with Hadrian and Horsa gliders, as intensive training with the 101st Airborne preceded the D-Day landings.

Painted in oils on canvas. 2007. 400mm x 300mm.

'Ridgeway rivals'

For a few days in 1943, Spitfires Vbs from American and British PR Units both flew from Membury in an exercise with the Canadian and British land forces. The painting suggests that a certain amount of friendly rivalry would have been expected.

Shellingford

In the summer of 1940, with the need to move RAF elementary flying training schools away from the 'aerial battleground' that the South Coast had become, the pressure was on to find suitable sites in areas such as north Berkshire.

No.3 EFTS which had originated at Hamble as far back as 1931, became a 'lodger' at a number of small airfields in the Faringdon area until, in September 1941, it took up residence at Shellingford, a new site which had first interested them some months earlier. Although they were quickly instructed to begin night-flying instruction and a flare-path was installed, it was December before all the buildings were completed and they were able to fully move in with their fifty-six Tiger Moths.

In July 1942, Army pilots joined No.3 EFTS for pre-glider flying training and they remained a part of Shellingford's activities until well into 1943.

Smith's Lawn

A pre-war landing strip in Windsor Great Park, this was occasionally used by members of the Royal family. In the war years it became a relief landing ground for the Tiger Moths of No.18 EFTS based at Fairoaks in Surrey. However, its most important wartime use was as a production facility for Vickers Armstrong. In 1940, the company built a large hangar and began a production line for the special high-altitude version of the Wellington bomber. Later, a number of Vickers Warwick bombers were stored there. The Americans also made limited use of the airfield.

Theale

Originally known as Sheffield Farm, Theale was requisitioned in 1940 as a relief landing ground for No.8 EFTS at Woodley, which was managed by P&P. In July 1941 it became No.26 EFTS, with a complement of twenty-four Tiger Moths, still managed by P&P ground services and maintenance carried out by civilian staff. Other aircraft that could be seen at Theale for communication duties included DH Puss Moths, Hawker Hinds and Miles Mentors. Later in the war, it was also used as an ATC gliding school. No.26 EFTS was one of the first schools to close after the war in Europe ended in May 1945.

Watchfield

Although Watchfield would eventually play a unique and important part in RAF history, its actual beginnings are confused. It was available as a landing ground in July 1940 when No.3 EFTS from Hamble were desperately seeking a new home for their Tiger Moths and, soon after, Ansons from two displaced Air Observer Navigation Schools also moved in.

At the time the intention was that No.1 Blind Approach School would be formed at Watchfield but lack of suitable equipment delayed this until the end of October. Blind Approach training in the RAF had actually commenced in March 1939 but the units involved and their specially adapted aircraft had been 'bounced around' various stations and, indeed, completely diverted into a Wireless Intelligence Development Unit investigating the Germans' use of radio beams for navigation.

In the meantime, the urgent need for a Blind Approach School had at last been recognised and, in October 1940, Watchfield finally began its vital work. Four specially equipped Ansons were allotted to the School and any need for secrecy was easily disguised by the many other Ansons flying from Watchfield.

The Dutch manufacturer, Philips, was the leader in the necessary ground equipment and had installed an advanced unit at Schiphol airport but, just before the Germans overran the Netherlands, this was shipped to Britain and installed at Watchfield. One of the most advanced control towers was also built there, with an instructor from the Blind Approach School able to give landing priority to their aircraft.

By May 1941, a Blind Approach Calibration Unit was formed at Watchfield, to liaise with RAF units around Britain where Blind Approach equipment was being installed. The Calibration Unit was soon to operate with six Airspeed Oxfords. By August, an expansion to bring about the training of more than one thousand pilots each year brought yet more Oxfords to Watchfield, which gradually replaced the Ansons previously used. In fact, Ansons disappeared altogether when the two AON Schools moved on. Expansion continued and, in September 1941, training at night started, following the installation of a flarepath. The following month, the school was renamed No.1 Beam Approach School.

In December, No.3 EFTS, with their Tiger Moths, moved to Shellingford, allowing Bomber Command's Regional Control School to move in from Oxford, changing its name to the School of Flying Control. A new 'trade' was now recognised in the RAF—airfield controller. In February 1942, students at the SFC were given flying experience in de Havilland Dominies which were allocated to the BAS. More Oxfords also arrived when the number of pilots to be trained each year was increased to fourteen-hundred-and-fifty.

In early 1944, training was often disrupted when the skies around Watchfield were crowded with transport aircraft and gliders and it would not be until after D-Day that 'normal service' was resumed.

Welford

Originally authorised in October 1941 as a second satellite for Membury, Welford was still under construction when it became one of the many airfields in West Berkshire allocated to the Americans. In fact, the first operational aircraft did not arrive until November 1943 and training with C47s, gliders and airborne troops began a month later. As with many of the airfields, the reshuffling of units continued for some months and it was February 1944 before control of Welford came under the US IXth Air Force and the 435th Transport Group began a concentrated training programme with the 101st Airborne Division.

Winston Churchill and General Eisenhower visited Welford to watch a highlight of the training programme when ninety-seven gliders were towed off in formation for a cross-country flight. Released at a specified place they all glided back to the airfield exactly as planned. It was a convincing display of the group's efficiency and would ensure they were in the vanguard of the D-Day assault.

Winkfield

Like Smith's Lawn, Winkfield was a relief landing ground for No.18 EFTS from Fairoaks in Surrey. Few details of the airfield are recorded and it is probable that only Tiger Moths ever flew there.

Woodley - the RAF ....

At Woodley, the RAF maintained a presence throughout the war years. No.8 EFTS had become a fully fledged RAF unit soon after the outbreak of war. However, in July 1942, it closed and was immediately replaced by a new unit, No.10 Flying Instructors School. Tiger Moths and Magisters were still in use, but six Masters and an Anson were added to the school's fleet for advanced instruction. No.10 FIS continued at Woodley throughout the remaining war years.

In 1940, RAF Flying Training Command moved its headquarters to Shinfield Park, just a few miles from Woodley. Soon after, the command set up a communications flight, based at Woodley, to act as a 'taxi service' for staff to visit flying schools around the country. Aircraft used by the flight included Magisters and Masters, as well as a Proctor, Lysander, Oxford and Anson.

.... and Miles Aircraft

From the spring of 1942, through almost to the end of the war in Europe, the main factory at Woodley was fully occupied in building specialised fast target-towing aircraft. Nearly eighteen hundred Martinets were completed at a rate of more than ten each week. Then, another production line was set up for a new design, the twin-engine Monitor.

The Miles production workers may have had to be 'single minded' in their wartime efforts, but their colleagues in the design offices, particularly those who worked closely with the Miles brothers, showed a remarkable versatility and a 'work rate' that proved to be unequalled in British aviation.

The M20 'utility fighter' of 1940 included a number of progressive features and was, of course, designed, built and flown in just a few weeks. But it wasn't the only fighter they had conceived. Their first was designed as far back as 1938 and could be seen in the background of a very rare photograph taken in the Experimental Department at Woodley. This fighter, surprisingly, was clearly marked as the M20. Back in 1938, with the pressure on to produce the Master I, this first M20 was taken no further than the wooden mock-up. It is therefore puzzling to consider why, two years later, at the time of the Battle of Britain, the designation M20 was also given to the 'utility fighter'.

While all this was going on, Britain's four-engine bombers, the Halifax, Stirling and Lancaster, were going into production and all were to carry a crew of perhaps seven, including navigator, observer, wireless operator and gunners. The only existing training aircraft for aircrews were the near-obsolete Anson and Oxford and FG Miles foresaw the need for replacement specialised trainers. Under the general designation M21, the Miles team produced a number of alternative project designs, ranging from a relatively small aircraft similar in size to the obsolete types, with a crew of four, to a large aircraft powered by two Merlin XX engines, capable of carrying two full bomber crews. When submitted to the Ministry, the concepts were rejected on the grounds that only operational types were to be built.

The Miles designers were not finished with fighter aircraft however and, during 1941, when the powerful Rolls Royce Griffon engine was becoming available, the M22 twin-engine concept was produced which would have carried an impressive ten machine guns at a speed approaching 500mph. Earlier, the Ministry had issued a different specification for a high-altitude day or night fighter to use an advanced Merlin engine and the Miles project to compete for this was the twin-engine, two-seat M22A design. Also in 1941, the M23 high-speed, single-seat fighter was proposed, followed by the M23A high-altitude version. All these designs incorporated many progressive features, but only the 1940 M20 actually took to the air.

The M25 was the Martinet, built under a Ministry specification in greater numbers than any other Miles design. The M28, however, although another very successful aircraft, had a very different background and life story. It had really begun life in 1939, when George Miles began work on a replacement for his brother's Whitney Straight of 1936 and his own Monarch of 1938. However, when the war began, the project was shelved.

By 1941, the design team, now led by George Miles, felt there was a need for a training and communications aircraft more efficient than anything so far produced in that class. It should include features such as a retractable undercarriage, flaps, constant speed propeller and full instrumentation, to reflect the characteristics of operational aircraft. It was also foreseen that it could fulfil the roles of Army co-operation work, radio and navigation training and light ambulance. The company decided to build a prototype as a private venture and it first flew in the hands of George Miles in July 1941.

Owing to the factory's heavy commitment, the M28 never went into production and only four were built in the war years. However, it was evaluated by the Services and it appears to have been the catalyst that persuaded the RAF of the need for side-by-side training in a cabin rather than in tandem open cockpits. It also appears to have inspired certain Army officers towards some 'lateral thinking', but that story has to wait until June 1942 and the M38.

'Wartime private venture'

In 1941, Miles Aircraft designed and built the M28 as an 'all-rounder' that could undertake many different roles, from training to Army co-operation work.
It included all the advanced features to be found in the latest service aircraft. Although just four were eventually built, it played a part in persuading the RAF that training aircraft should be built to a similar format.

The M29 design began life in 1941 as a high-performance trainer to replace the Master, the Miles team's thinking being that the heavier and more powerful fighters then coming into service would require a trainer providing similar handling characteristics. It was intended that the M29 should bear the same relationship to the Hawker Typhoon as the Master had to the Spitfire and Hurricane.

Soon after work began on the M29, the Ministry asked Miles to consider the design of a high speed single-engine target tug to replace the Martinet. Thus the M29 became the basis for the new target tug concept. However, calculations soon showed that a single-engine aircraft could never meet the performance required by the Ministry. This was eventually accepted and, in 1942, a new specification for a twin-engine target tug was issued and, in time, this led to the M33 Monitor.

In between these two projects, the M30 and M32 concepts could not have been more different. The M30 was actually built and flown but it can be seen to be perhaps one of the most questionable decisions made by the company. The pre-war 'X2' project for an airliner had, indeed, "not been forgotten" and, by 1941, the Woodley design team had worked up a number of designs based on the principles developed in 1938 by FG Miles. The M30 'X minor' was designed to test these principles in the air. However, in an aircraft of just thirty-three-feet wingspan, although the principle that the fuselage shape based on an 'aerofoil' section was adhered to, the wings could not be fully faired into the fuselage and neither could the engines be buried in the wings. It is doubtful any really useful data was obtained.

By contrast, the M32 project design was for a very large aircraft—a glider to carry a variety of troops and their vehicles and guns. Alternatively, engines could be attached which, after the aircraft had been towed into the air, would be used to fly it to its destination. In presenting the concept to the Ministry, FG Miles actually suggested the idea would be used by the enemy and, not long afterwards, similar designs from Gotha and Messerschmitt were used operationally. Later the Americans carried out experiments along the same line and, belatedly, a British Hamilcar glider was converted to a powered format. The Miles M32, however, never went beyond the drawing board.

Special demands by the Ministry of Aircraft Production delayed final design of the M33 Monitor and, never being the sort to 'twiddle their thumbs', Miles designers began work on the M34. This was to be a long-range, heavily-armoured, low-attack fighter carrying four 40mm cannons, a formidable opponent for enemy tanks or submarines. Another role could have been as a high-speed target tug the same as the M33. It was presented to the Ministry but the proposed use of Merlin engines, for which there was already enormous demands, counted against it.

It had taken a long time for Miles to convince the Ministry that two engines would be required for the new target-tug, but eventually two American Wright Cyclone radial engines were specified. A request to incorporate Beaufighter wings and undercarriage caused additional problems for the Miles designers. Eventually it proved impracticable to use the Beaufighter wings and Miles-designed wooden wings were fitted. Installation of the Beaufighter undercarriage did prove possible, although it caused problems later. The fuselage was constructed in metal and it was the first Miles design to include a large proportion of metal. Yet more problems arose when a Mark II Monitor destined for the Navy and incorporating many design changes was suddenly given precedence over the RAF's Mark I version.

The initial order, placed in March 1943, was for two hundred aircraft, but Miles was requested to tool up for an eventual two thousand. Further orders were placed and soon cancelled. Eventually, the total was two-hundred-and-sixty, far too few to justify full mass-production techniques, pushing costs even higher. Nevertheless, with major changes to the factory to accommodate the new Monitor assembly line and the recruitment of skilled metalworkers, it must have been a testing time for the factory's production workers at Woodley.

Right: The Monitor assembly line at Woodley in 1944.

However, for George Miles and his project designers, these middle war years were among the most productive in the company's history and a stream of inventive projects have fascinated aviation enthusiasts ever since.

The Miles M35, as a 'flying machine', could be said to have been a near disaster. Nevertheless it was the forerunner of a range of unique and unorthodox tandem-wing designs produced by Miles Aircraft under the Libellula name, the generic name for the dragonfly family.

Late in 1941, George Miles had been thinking about the many accidents involving Seafires and Sea-Hurricanes, aircraft that were not originally designed for operation from aircraft carriers. They were extremely difficult to land on carriers because of the poor forward view and they also required extensive modifications to enable their wings to fold for storage below deck.

Eventually he began to consider the possibility of an aircraft with two wings in tandem, both of which would provide aerodynamic lift and support the weight of the aircraft, as well both including control surfaces such as ailerons and flaps. The wingspan could be smaller than a conventional aircraft, eliminating the need for the wings to fold. The vital 'centre of gravity' position would have a particularly wide fore and aft range between the two wings. With a 'pusher' engine at the rear, the pilot could be right in the nose, giving him an exceptional view.

With typical Miles enthusiasm, George decided to design and build a simple flying mock-up, to give full-scale data without the need for time-consuming wind-tunnel tests, presumably accepting the increased risk for the first pilot. Under George Miles's direction, the M35 was designed at the company's Liverpool Road factory by Ray Bournon and built there secretly in just six weeks, using existing Magister components and scrap wood.

At the end of April 1942, the M35, with its wingspan of just twenty feet, was towed the two miles or so out to Woodley in the early morning where George Miles elected to make the first flight himself. The first problem exhibited by the M35 was a remarkable reluctance to leave the ground and it took a number of attempts to actually get it airborne. It was then that George Miles discovered it was wildly unstable and it took all his skill to complete a circuit of the airfield at a height of about twenty feet. Modifications improved its stability and also the rear-mounted engine's tendency to overheat. Many successful flights were completed but the M35 was never a really successful 'flying machine'.

Despite this, the M35 did enough to convince George Miles of the benefits of a tandem-wing layout and he submitted his proposal for the Libellula fighter to both the Ministry of Aircraft Production and the Admiralty. Sadly, neither was convinced that there was a need to improve on the accident rate of the current carrier-borne fighters and Miles received a reprimand from the MAP for building an aircraft without permission.

Don Brown, the colleague of the Miles brothers from their earliest years in Sussex, had worked for the MAP for a year. In 1941, he had joined Miles Aircraft as assistant to George Miles and played an important part in the Libellula story. Using his 'insider' knowledge, he was responsible for the proposal for a Libellula heavy bomber submitted to the MAP at the same time as the carrier-borne fighter.

Soon after, he was instrumental in the company's proposal to meet the official specification for a high-altitude, lightly-armed, high-speed bomber. This became the M39 and a flying five-eighth scale model of it, the M39B, was the only Libellula design, other than the M35, to fly and, unlike its 'notorious' predecessor, this it did extremely well.

Needless to say the MAP reprimanded Miles for building the M39B, even though the company's proposal clearly stated a flying scale model would be built. However, when flying trials began, the Ministry became very interested and purchased the aircraft for further testing at the RAE. Miles was also instructed to allow the Americans access to all drawings and test data. The Libellula story didn't quite end there. A different heavy bomber proposal was prepared, two more fighters were proposed and an attractive mailplane proposal was met with enthusiasm by its potential customers, but not by the MAP who, once again, frustrated Miles's ambitions.

"What's that?"

The Miles M39B 'Libellula' often flew over Reading in the latter war years and its highly unusual shape created great interest. Over those years, the Libellula concept was used for many design projects, although the M39B, shown here - a five-eighths scale version of a high speed, lightly armed, high altitude bomber - was the only one to actually be built and flown. In the late 1980s, aged 70+, when he was still involved with various aviation projects and reluctant to talk about the past, George Miles did tell the author he regretted never having the chance to build his Libellula bomber, which he felt could have rivalled the magnificent de Havilland Mosquito.

Above: The M35 Libellula after modifications had been carried out, including a large cooling-air scoop under the engine and an extra wheel.

Below: A company sketch of the proposed Libellula naval fighter.

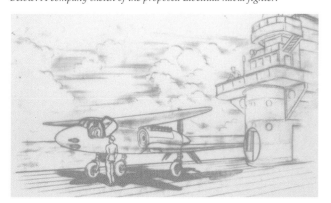

At Miles Aircraft in 1942, at the same time as the Libellula story was unfolding, George Miles was approached by a group of Army officers who had been impressed by the performance of the M28 when it had been evaluated by the Services. They asked if he could design a similar aircraft to be used as an 'Air Observation Post'. This direct approach was highly irregular and George suggested they contact the Ministry of Aircraft Production. However, when the delegation said they needed to get on and win the war, he relented and agreed to build a prototype, stressing that any production aircraft would have to be ordered officially by the Ministry.

The specification of the aircraft was a very tough one. It must fly from small areas of rough ground, often surrounded by trees, and would require a very short take-off run, an exceptional angle of climb, a steep approach and a short landing run. It must carry two crew, radio, armour and assorted military equipment. It must allow for pilots of very limited experience, have a very good view in all directions, operate under all weather conditions and allow for field-maintenance with the minimum of skilled staff.

Utilising the fuselage of the prototype M28 with a new one-piece wing, crucial features of the M38, as it was designated, were large, non-retractable, external flaps and a robust undercarriage providing a high 'ground angle'. Once again built secretly at Liverpool Road, George Miles first flew it on 12th September 1942 and, just three months after the Army's initial contact, it was delivered to one of their squadrons for testing. Everyone flew it, from senior instructors to newest pupils and the message that came back to Miles was "how soon can we have a hundred?"

This, Don Brown wrote, started a war between the War Office and the MAP of such bitterness that the real war paled into insignificance. The Ministry was outraged that, once again, Miles had built an aeroplane without permission. The final outcome of this particular war was the instigator of this AOP idea was posted overseas although, twelve years later, he did receive an award of £1,000 for having had the idea. His Army units were told firmly that they could not have the aircraft that so perfectly suited their requirements, although a contract for a small number of Messengers, as the M38 became known, was issued as a 'communications aircraft' for certain VIPs, including General Montgomery.

Soon after the Messenger first flew, another idea occurred to George Miles. From the early days of the war, enemy U-boats had caused heavy losses among the shipping bringing vital supplies to the UK. The convoy system offered some protection from U-boats by the accompanying destroyers and frigates, but air cover could only be provided by the RAF Coastal Command within a few hundred miles of our coasts. George Miles thought that if some of the merchant ships were fitted with a platform in the stern, about sixty-foot-square, small slow-flying aircraft, carrying depth-charges, could maintain virtually continuous air cover for the convoy during daylight hours. A simple arrester-hook could be fitted to the aircraft but, as an additional safety measure, a large net, with a gap in the middle for the aircraft's propeller, could be stretched across the platform.

With his typical enthusiasm, George Miles had a sixty-foot square area marked out at Woodley, complete with a simple arrestor mechanism and a large net, into which he flew the Messenger, sometimes even before the wheels had touched down. Don Brown told of a bizarre test when the Messenger, piloted by Hugh Kennedy, with George, himself and three others as 'ballast', proved it could carry the weight of the depth charges.

Above: George Miles flying the prototype Messenger into the safety net.

Demonstrations to the MAP, the Admiralty and other officials followed, but the idea was never taken up, the claim being made that helicopters would do the job better. In 1943, it was a little premature to make such claims, helicopters being in their infancy. However, what George did not know and it is likely that very few of the 'officials' knew either, U-boats were gradually being defeated anyway, by new weaponry and, more importantly, the skills of the 'boffins' at Bletchley Park who had broken the tough 'Enigma' code used by the German Navy.

By 1943, neither was the German Air Force, the Luftwaffe, the potent force it had been two years earlier. It could no longer mount the massed bomber raids that had caused such devastation in many British cities. Instead, small numbers or even single aircraft were targeting different towns and it was from just such an attack that Berkshire suffered its most cruel blow of the war.

It was the afternoon of 10th February 1943 when two Luftwaffe Dornier 217s approached the county, one heading for Newbury and the other for Reading. Whether by chance or design, both towns were hit at exactly 4.35 pm, eight bombs hitting Newbury and four hitting Reading. As each aircraft flew low over the town centres, their gunners were randomly firing at anything or anyone they could see below.

In Newbury, the bombs destroyed a church, a school, a row of almshouses and ten other houses. Nineteen people died and many more were injured. In Reading, the greatest devastation was caused by the third bomb which made a direct hit on a popular town centre restaurant called the 'People's Pantry' where more than forty people died. There were more than one hundred other casualties in Reading that day, many of them serious.

Above: Friar Street, Reading, where the 'People's Pantry' was destroyed.

Painted in oils on canvas. 2000. 500mm x 750mm

'Monty's Messenger'

Although this painting jumps our story forward by a year or so, it serves
to give a foretaste of the dramatic weeks following the assault on Hitler's
'Fortress Europe' in which the airfields of Berkshire played a major part.
Although General Montgomery didn't use his Messenger to cross to
Normandy the first time, it was certainly one of the first Allied aircraft to
land there intentionally, apart from the thousands of gliders of course.
Air Vice Marshal Portal, the Allies' deputy supreme commander,
also used a Messenger as his personal air transport.

Right: General Montgomery (left)
appears to be telling his passenger to
jump and avoid stepping onto the
Messenger's external flaps.

D-Day. 6th June 1944.

After months of planning, training and almost unbelievable feats of organisation, the largest and most powerful invasion force the world has ever seen was launched against the claimed invincible 'Atlantic Wall' of German-occupied France.

This huge force was assembled predominantly in the South of England over the preceding weeks, in the harbours, rivers and creeks, on the airfields and in vast camps in the countryside for the troops. The fact that the enemy was so totally unprepared for its arrival serves to illustrate how ineffective Luftwaffe reconnaissance had become by that time.

What the reaction of the Luftwaffe would be to the massive D-Day assault, Allied leaders could only guess. However, there would be many thousands of aircraft in the skies in the days to come and it was vital that 'friendly' aircraft were quickly recognised. That is why, late in the day on 5th June, every single Allied aircraft was painted with broad black and white stripes.

Berkshire's main role in this historic assault was to be one of the main launching points for the initial landings by the British and American airborne forces and, by the time dawn arrived on D-Day, the county's airfields had been playing their part for many hours.

The British assault from Berkshire began when, just before midnight on 5th June, six Armstrong Whitworth Albermarles left Harwell to drop sixty 'pathfinder' paratroops of the 6th Airborne Division. Their task was to clear any obstacles from the designated 'drop zones' and to set up beacons to guide in the rest of the division following close behind. The first wave comprised twelve more Albermarles carrying paratroopers and twenty-eight towing Horsa gliders. On returning to Harwell, after a brief rest, the crews were next tasked with towing more Horsa gliders to the drop zone. Harwell's squadrons were in action for the next week or so with supply drops for Special Operations units.

Albermarles had originally been designed as a bomber but were never used as such and the British airborne forces, in preference to slow and outdated aircraft such as Whitleys which they had been forced to use for training, were happy to use them until four-engine aircraft became more widely available.

Painted in oils on canvas. 2001. 400mm x 500mm.

'Pathfinders Go!'

Harwell-based Albermarles were among the first aircraft to drop the British Airborne Forces over Normandy on D-Day. Close behind the six which carried specially trained 'pathfinder' paratroops were twelve more carrying paratroopers and a further 28 towing Horsa gliders.

Above: In the last hours of daylight on 5th June 1944, thousands of American paratroopers from the 101st and 82nd Airborne Divisions board their aircraft at Greenham Common. At Membury and Welford, similar scenes were being enacted, as the greatest invasion force the world has ever seen, prepared to go into battle in France .

For Berkshire's American airfields, operations also began one hour before D-Day, when the first of well over two hundred C47 Skytrains flew out of Greenham Common, Membury and Welford with paratroopers from the US 101st and 82nd Airborne Divisions. Eleven seconds separated each aircraft as they took off, in the dark of course, to link up with the specially equipped 'pathfinders' among them, which led the formations over a course of varying heights and directions, with specially positioned ships acting as marker beacons. The target drop zones had also previously been marked by beacons, dropped by specially trained C47 crews. It took approximately ninety minutes for the Berkshire-based C47s to reach the drop zones and it was just fifteen minutes into D-Day when the first American paratroopers to leave Greenham Common, jumped into Normandy, to an area close behind the 'Omaha' and 'Utah' beaches where, at dawn, their sea-borne colleagues would be fighting their way ashore.

Painted in oils on canvas. 2008. 300mm x 380mm.

'Skytrain'

On the morning of D-Day, there could not have been a more appropriate name for the C47 Skytrain transports that dropped thousands of American paratroops into Normandy. Taking off at an interval of just eleven seconds from Greenham Common, Membury and Welford and following the specially equipped 'pathfinder' C47s leading them, they could perhaps be seen as a two-hundred-mile-long 'train' carrying their passengers into battle.

Painted in oils on canvas. 2001. 500mm x 600mm.

'American Armada'

As dawn broke on the morning of D-Day, C47 Skytrains from Greenham Common arrived over the designated landing zones behind the Omaha and Utah beaches for the second time that day, this time bringing glider-borne troops of the 101st and 82nd American Airborne Divisions to join their paratrooper colleagues who had been dropped by the same C47s a few hours earlier. At dusk, C47s from Membury and Welford, which had also dropped paratroopers in the early hours, returned with yet more glider-borne troops to help consolidate the hard-won beach-heads.

Aldermaston's role on D-Day was different from Berkshire's other American bases. Soon after the paratroopers left the other three bases, an anti-aircraft battalion comprising some seven hundred men, plus their weapons and equipment, embarked on Hadrian gliders lined up at Aldermaston. With their C47 Skytrain tugs, fifty-two combinations took off in the early hours of the morning to a landing zone about a mile inland of Omaha beach where, before daylight, the gliders cast off their tow-lines and were committed to a landing.

In fact, only a handful of the gliders succeeded in reaching the designated zone, causing problems in establishing effective anti-aircraft cover. However, although the Luftwaffe was certainly unaware of the true scale of the invasion they faced, it was not even able to take advantage of the American problems in those first vital hours. Later on, overwhelming air superiority by the Allies ensured the enemy was invariably at a disadvantage. The majority of the American paratroopers landing earlier had also missed their designated zones and were widely scattered over much of the Cherbourg peninsula. Although this also caused problems in quickly establishing cohesive fighting units, it certainly served to confuse the enemy still more. There were just too many different reports of small numbers of parachutes coming down over such a wide area.

Having dropped their paratroopers, the C47s returned to Greenham Common and the aircraft that were still serviceable were immediately hooked up to waiting Horsa and Hadrian gliders full of troops and equipment destined for the landing area behind Omaha beach. It was nearly dawn when the first Greenham Common gliders landed in Normandy. Membury's and Welford's C47s also followed their paratrooper drops with tows of Horsa and Hadrian gliders, departing in the evening of 6th June and arriving over the landing zone as darkness fell.

For all Berkshire's American bases, supply-drops by parachute and additional small-scale glider tows were carried out in the following days and, when landing areas became available, their C47s flew in freight and evacuated casualties. It appears that, from Greenham Common alone, some ten thousand sorties were carried out between 5th and 7th June.

There was, of course, a heavy cost in terms of men and aircraft, to offset the eventual success of the American airborne assault on Normandy. In addition to the three bases in Berkshire, eleven others were involved, in Wiltshire, the West Country and the Midlands. More than thirteen thousand paratroopers and over four thousand troops in gliders, as well as jeeps, artillery and other equipment were transported to Normandy. More than sixteen hundred aircraft and five hundred gliders were used, with forty aircraft and nine gliders lost and over four hundred aircraft damaged. Of the 101st and 82nd Airborne Divisions themselves, it is thought that around 20% were casualties on the first day and, by the end of August, when the enemy had been driven out of Normandy, the two Divisions suffered losses of over three thousand five hundred men killed and four thousand five hundred men wounded.

With the hectic days and nights of the Normandy airborne assault behind them, it was not long before the C47s from Greenham Common, Membury and Welford were in action again. In July, they were flown to Tarquina in Italy for the planned air and sea assault on Southern France and, on 15th August dropped paratroopers from a combined American, British, Canadian and French Airborne Division.

In a similar operation to the Normandy landings, the paratroopers preceded a massive assault by a sea-borne force and the C47s then towed in Horsa and Hadrian gliders bringing in reinforcements. The operation was a success and, by the end of August, the entire coastline and a huge area of Southern France was liberated. The Berkshire C47s remained in France throughout August, hauling freight, then returned to resume supply sorties to Normandy.

While the American squadrons were playing their part in the South of France, the British squadrons at Harwell were gradually having their twin-engine Albermarles replaced with four-engine Stirlings, which were soon being used for supply drops to Normandy. However, the biggest ever airborne assault was being planned at that time and all the Berkshire airfields used on D-Day would be at the forefront again.

Below: This photograph showing C47s and Horsa gliders at Aldermaston has been published a number of times, usually with a caption such as 'waiting for D-Day'. Research generally agrees that Aldermaston's contribution to D-Day in June involved the smaller Hadrian gliders and no other large scale glider operations were mounted there until Operation 'Market Garden' in September 1944. Almost certainly this photograph was taken on the second day of this massive assault.

Operation 'Market Garden', largely conceived by General Montgomery, was a bold attempt to capture a series of bridges over rivers and canals on the Dutch/German border, one hundred and fifty miles behind the enemy lines. The furthest of these bridges, at Arnhem, crossed the Rhine itself and its capture would allow a decisive thrust by the Allies into the very heart of Germany. It has been estimated that its success would have shortened the war by six months and, in allowing the Allies in the West to reach Berlin before the Russians, to have dramatically changed subsequent world history.

The operation began, in the early hours of Sunday 17th September, with devastating attacks on enemy airfields and anti-aircraft sites across a broad swathe of country approaching the target area, by bombers of the RAF and USAAC. This was followed by the biggest aerial assault in history, with over twenty thousand American, British and Polish troops parachuting in and fourteen-and-half thousand landing in gliders. Around fifteen hundred aircraft and five hundred gliders were employed and more than seventeen hundred vehicles and two hundred and sixty artillery pieces, plus ammunition and other supplies were also landed in gliders.

The air assault operation, which was carried out entirely in daylight hours, involved twenty-four airfields in Britain, the aircraft from them forming up into two columns which took different routes to the drop zones. It was reported that the columns were over ninety miles in length and three miles wide. Air cover was provided by swarms of fighters, while light bombers continued to attack anti-aircraft sites ahead of the advancing transport aircraft. Despite this, losses were quite heavy, with some seventy transports and seventy gliders downed, as well as twenty fighters, mainly by anti-aircraft fire.

British and American aircraft from the Berkshire bases were all part of these massive columns. More than forty of Harwell's Stirlings transported British and Polish paratroops to Arnhem. Aldermaston saw forty-five of its C47s fly paratroopers of the 82nd Division to Nijmegen. From Greenham Common, Membury and Welford, one hundred and seventy C47s, and thirty Hadrian gliders flew men of the 101st Division to Eindhoven. All the Stirlings returned safely to Harwell, but ten C47s failed to return to their Berkshire bases and many more were damaged.

Shortages of aircraft had caused the original plan to spread the airborne assault over to the second day, which saw most of the glider tows. Unfortunately, unexpected changes in the weather conditions caused delays to this second phase of operations. Nevertheless, thirteen of Harwell's Stirlings towed Horsa gliders carrying troop reinforcements, while around thirty others dropped supplies by parachute. In the following days re-supply drops became vital for the beleaguered British paratroops at Arnhem, a story that the film 'A Bridge Too Far' was to tell many years later.

Day two of Market Garden, had seen eighty C47s from Aldermaston towing Horsa gliders with more troops of the 82nd Division with vehicles, artillery and other equipment to Nijmegen. The following day, another eighty tows were undertaken, including Hadrian gliders and, on Day three, over fifty re-supply missions were flown from Aldermaston. The other American bases continued with re-supply missions but it was becoming obvious that, overall, Operation Market Garden was failing.

From Day two onwards, fog had made glider tows increasingly dangerous and also meant that fighter cover was unreliable. Approaching a drop zone, the transports had to fly a fixed course and anti-aircraft fire was beginning to take an increasingly heavy toll.

It would be another four months before the Rhine was crossed and the battles moved onto German soil. However, that was not before the enemy had made a surprise offensive and trapped many American units near Bastogne — what became known as the 'Battle of the Bulge'. Berkshire's bases were called into action again and flew a number of re-supply missions. However, the American's tenure of its Berkshire bases was coming to an end and February 1945 saw the Troop Carrier Groups move to France. Harwell's Stirling squadrons had also moved on to a new base in East Anglia and a new role for the airfield was underway.

Looking back to those six months from June to December 1944, it can be seen how the direction of world history could have swung either way. Had it been successful , 'Market Garden' might have brought about major political differences in the years to come. However, Hitler too came frighteningly close to changing the course of the war at that time.

Since 1942 the Germans had been working on the first of Hitler's much vaunted 'secret weapons', the V1 flying bomb. In fact, it hadn't remained secret for long and, from the spring of 1943, massive air raids had been mounted on Peenemunde, where it was being made and on its launching sites in France and Holland. It is thought that these raids delayed the deployment of these weapons for at least six months. Nevertheless, just a week after D-Day, the first V1 hit England and a new and frightening phase of the war had begun for Britain's civilian population — at least, those in London and the South East. In two weeks, around sixty V1s, or 'doodlebugs' as they became known, were hitting London every day and, very soon, well over one million frightened people left the city. It is thought nine thousand five hundred V1s were aimed at London and the South East, but half were destroyed by RAF fighters, anti-aircraft guns and barrage balloons and, by August, only 20% were reaching their target. Nevertheless, more than six thousand civilians were killed by V1 flying bombs, many thousands more were injured and thousands of properties were destroyed or damaged.

By early September, the launching sites in France had been captured and a Government minister went so far as to say that the 'Battle of London' was over. He was wrong. A few days later, on 8th September, two massive explosions rocked London, at Chiswick in the west and Epping in the east. These were the first of the V2 rockets, Hitler's other 'secret weapon'. Unlike the V1, there was really no defence against the V2 and over five hundred fell on the Greater London area in a few weeks, mostly on Boroughs situated to the east and outlying more rural areas of Kent and Essex. In built-up areas they caused terrible damage and loss of life. Some two thousand civilian deaths were added to the grim carnage of Hitler's 'vengeance' weapons and many thousand more were injured and families made homeless. However, Operation Market Garden did succeed in forcing the Germans to pull the V2 launch sites further back to where they could no longer reach central London and, although eastern counties were fired on for a short while, their rural landscape meant there were fewer casualties and damage. Until all firing sites were overrun, Antwerp, which was being used by the Allies as an important port for supply operations, as well as already-liberated Paris were attacked.

Like the dark days of bombing in the early years of the war, Berkshire was relatively untouched by Hitler's vengeance weapons. The only recorded incident involving a V2 rocket was in early 1945, at Pinkneys Green, near Maidenhead, when one exploded in mid-air just before hitting the ground. A row of houses was damaged and twelve people were slightly injured.

V1 flying bombs were limited in their range and, to some extent, also in their efficiency. London was obviously a nearer and easier proposition where, if specific targets were missed, considerable damage and casualties would still be caused. However, it does appear that at least some of the 'doodlebugs' that reached Berkshire, might have been aimed at specific targets.

The first doodlebug to hit the county landed near Streatley on the Thames above Reading, on 21st June, a week or so after the V1 attacks began. The same day another came down close by, near Nuffield, on the Oxfordshire side of the river. Both the important photo-reconnaissance airfield at Benson and also Harwell were a few miles further along their track.

On 1st July, Windsor was hit by a doodlebug. Could it be Windsor Castle was the target? Instead it fell on a corporation refuse plant. Sixty people were hurt, mainly by flying glass and three hundred and fifty properties were damaged. It could have been much worse. It was Maidenhead's turn soon after when a doodlebug landed in the garden of a house in Cookham Road. Luckily, nobody died, but there were sixty casualties and over nine hundred properties were damaged.

Benson or Harwell might have been the target again on 5th July, when a doodlebug came down at Checkendon, on the Oxfordshire side of the Thames near Reading. Again, they were in the flight-path when, on 20th August, one fell at Stonor, near Henley-on-Thames. Both being villages deep in the countryside, no serious damage occurred. Finally, on 30th August, Harwell airfield itself was hit and three parked aircraft were destroyed, but there were no casualties.

So, as the Allied troops moved ever deeper into Germany during the early months of 1945, attacks on London and other parts of the South East ceased and the end of the European war was in sight again.

'V1 killer'

Fighters, anti-aircraft fire and barrage balloons were all used to combat the V1 flying bombs. Fighters brought down more than any other type of defence and Spitfires, Mustangs, Meteors and, particularly at night, Mosquitos were all successful. However, easily the most successful fighter against the V1 was the recently introduced Hawker Tempest Mk.V, whose pilots shot down nearly half of all V1s brought down by the RAF.

Painted in watercolours. 2008. 330mm x 250mm.

Left: By early 1941, FG Miles felt that the enemy could well develop a 'flying bomb' and would not hesitate to use it if the 'tide of war' turned against them. He felt it would be wise to design similar pilotless weapons in great quantities and hold them in reserve as a deterrent against the enemy's possible use. The Miles team designed the 'Hoopla' seen here, a small, very cheap aircraft that nevertheless could carry a 1,000lb bomb, the largest available at the time. Taking the technology further than the Germans ever did, a lightweight automatic pilot, then being developed at Woodley, was fitted (see page 128), as well as radio-control which guided it all the way to the target. When he presented the idea to the Ministry of Aircraft Production, it was rejected and the 'Hoopla' never went into production. Nevertheless, when the German V1s were being hurled against the UK in 1944, people were beginning to ask why we didn't have a similar weapon. The Ministry response was perhaps predictable. In Don Brown's words, "Miles received an urgent telegram saying that in no circumstances whatsoever was he or his staff to reveal – least of all to the Press – that this idea had in fact been put forward to the Ministry some years previously and had been summarily rejected."

In the village of Shaw, near Newbury, where many of the victims of the 1943 bombing had been buried, a new Spitfire production facility had been built. Some of the workers from the Reading factories had transferred to train their new colleagues. Now finished components from both Reading and Shaw were being taken to a new hangar at Aldermaston for final assembly and test flight. The Americans had handed over Aldermaston to the British, with a branch of RAF Technical Training Command now installed there.

At White Waltham, some of the ATA pilots were now flying aircraft across the Channel carrying vital medical supplies

At Woodley, Miles Aircraft was nearing the end of its contract for some eighteen hundred Martinets. Surprisingly, in view of the MAP's previous attitude, a contract for two hundred and fifty M38 Messengers for Army AOP work had been placed. However, the MAP soon cancelled it and, at the same time, savagely cut the large contract for the Monitor and, eventually, when just twenty had been completed, cancelled that too. Despite all this change and uncertainty in the factory, the Miles brothers and their small design team were working at the absolute pinnacle of their considerable design skills and experience, although very few people, even their own employees, knew of the secret project on which they were working.

To understand the sequence of events that brought this project about, a trail must be followed back to the end of 1942. At that time, despite the outcome of the war still being far from certain, the Government had set up the 'Brabazon Committee' to consider the likely post-war needs for civil transport aircraft and the MAP had gone as far as to issue a specification for a trans-Atlantic airliner to just one company — Bristol. Miles Aircraft was among several companies interested in building such a project and FG Miles had tried unsuccessfully to obtain a copy of the specification.

When FG Miles personally approached the Minister and informed him that Miles Aircraft would, in effect, produce its own specification for such an aircraft and go ahead with a project design, he was assured that it would be accepted or rejected solely on the basis of its estimated performance. Another manufacturer, Shorts, also developed a design and was, presumably, given similar assurances.

Don Brown, who was project manager for the Miles X11, describes in his much later book and with much more technical detail than space allows here, all the various machinations of the MAP in finally rejecting the Miles design. What became apparent was that, despite the Minister's assurances, Bristol had already been given the contract and no other manufacturer's design was to even be considered.

Summing up, the eventual Bristol Brabazon that appeared had a wingspan of two hundred and thirty feet, a cruising speed of 270mph and weighed one hundred tons. Yet, in the final MAP specification issued, it called for it to carry just twenty-five passengers. The Miles X11 was just under 70% of that size and weight, was around 30% faster and would have carried twice that number of passengers.

The final justification of the Miles team's design expertise came fourteen years later when another Bristol design, the Britannia, became the first British aircraft to successfully perform the trans-Atlantic role. Very different from that company's ultimate 'white elephant', the Brabazon, the Britannia was remarkably similar to the Miles X11 in size, weight, power, speed, fuel capacity and 'payload'.

In his book, Don Brown, with some justification, was often scathing about the senior personnel in the Ministry of Aircraft Production, especially perhaps since he himself was one of them until he joined Miles Aircraft in 1941. Nevertheless, looking back and trying to be fair to the MAP, the Woodley factory and, in particular, the airfield, was not suitable for the expansion needed for the construction of an aircraft such as the X11. Neither was the company's workforce in any way experienced enough for the construction of large aircraft in metal. FG Miles and his team had often infuriated and embarrassed the MAP but, grudgingly, these civil servants eventually had to acknowledge their supreme design skills and experience. Their next project proved that at least.

'Trans-Atlantic contender'

The Miles X11, designed in 1943, as a direct competitor to the ultimate 'white elephant' of British aviation, the Bristol Britannia.

Painted in oils. 2007. 300mm x 400mm

Arguments with the MAP about the X11, continued through most of 1943, with Rolls Royce, whose new engines had been specified, joining in on the side of Miles. No valid technical reasons for its rejection were ever presented by the Ministry but, in October of that year, FG Miles received a letter telling him a contract for the X11 would not be forthcoming. However, he was invited to the Ministry to be briefed on a new contract for his company. In Don Brown's own words, it was *"the most ambitious and advanced research project ever attempted in the history of aeronautics, in that it called for the design and construction of what was to be the world's first supersonic aircraft"*.

The 'sound barrier', as it was popularly known, had been a talking point in aviation circles ever since high speed aircraft such as the later Spitfires had experienced vibration and control problems when approaching the 'speed of sound' in a steep dive. Once again in Don Brown's words, *"the advent of jet and rocket propulsion made it clear that within a few years it should be possible to attain and indeed exceed the speed of sound. Before that stage was reached, it was equally clear that many problems associated with 'compressibility' would be encountered and would have to be overcome."*

Frank Whittle and his team at Power Jets were to be responsible for the aircraft's powerplant and new technology would be required to sufficiently increase the power of their existing engine designs. Close co-operation would be required between the two companies. For FG Miles, the controversy about the X11 was quickly forgotten as he briefed the small team at Woodley that would be responsible for the design and construction of the airframe. It was led by his brother, George, chief designer, and Don Brown, his assistant, Dennis Bancroft, chief aerodynamicist, HS Wilkinson, chief stressman and Walter Capley, project engineer.

The host of 'technological firsts' that flowed from this talented team to conceive the M52, have impressed aviation historians to the present day. Space limitations do not allow full coverage of them here. More information can be found in Don Brown's book 'Miles Aircraft since 1925' and Julian Temple's much later 'Wings over Woodley'.

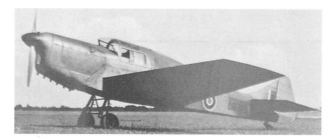

Top left: No aircraft wing like the M52's had ever been flown before and, to establish its performance characteristics at slow speeds, an exact replica was made in wood. It was fitted to a Falcon which, due to the sharp edges of the wing, soon became known as the 'Gillette Falcon'.

Top right: This model of the M52, of approximately four foot wingspan, was made in steel and aluminium. It was one of a number of different models made for windtunnel testing, as seen here, and is now on display at the Museum of Berkshire Aviation.

Middle left: This view of the wooden mock-up of the M52 clearly shows the way in which the pilot's pressurised capsule was attached by 'pylons' to the main fuselage. If the pilot had to eject at high speed, 'explosive bolts' on the pylons would allow the whole capsule to detach and be slowed by a parachute until it was safe for the pilot to bail out in the normal way.

Middle right: The mock-up of the M52 showing the 'all moving' or variable incidence tailplane. Miles Aircraft did not originate this idea, it was part of their original brief from the MAP. It therefore seems that British scientists at the RAE, by 1943, had already proved that this would be the key to going through the sound barrier.

Julian Temple also records that a Miles Aircraft report said that, *"by February 1946, so much information had become available that detail design of the aeroplane was 90% completed …. construction of all assembly jigs was finished and component assembly well in hand. Practically all the items required to complete construction were in stores and the engine was already available".*

Design work was in hand for further versions of the M52 using different power plants. In the 1980s, George Miles said that the Miles team were confident the M52 would have flown in six months.

Above: The Miles windtunnel built inside an existing farm building at Davis Farm, Woodley in 1943. Other buildings that can be seen were part of the Miles Aeronautical Technical School, built at the same time. This photograph was taken in 1985, just before the buildings were finally demolished to make way for yet more housing.

Despite this undoubted success, on 13th March 1946, FG Miles was informed the M52 contract had been cancelled. He was so shocked that, for some time, he couldn't tell his colleagues. But, when he queried this decision with the MAP director-general of Research, Sir Ben Lockspeiser, he was told "Any idea of supersonic flying being just around the corner was completely erroneous."

There were two official reasons given for the cancellation at that time. The first, that recent access to German research into swept-back wings showed "their value in delaying the onset of compressibility at high subsonic speeds". In vain, Miles pointed out that, for an aircraft designed to achieve *supersonic* speed, delaying compressibility by swept-back wings was virtually irrelevant.

'What might have been'

Sadly for British aviation, this is a painting of something that never happened – the first flight of the Miles M52. Unlike the rocket-powered and air-launched Bell X1, the M52 was to be capable of sustained flight, taking off under the power of its Whittle jet engine and climbing to around fifty thousand feet. It was also envisaged that it could continue its active service life for some decades, its simple main fuselage shape being an effective 'test bed' for different power plants and wing and tail shapes.

The second reason was that "it was unfair to ask any pilot to accept the risks involved in flight testing the M52". Again, Miles knew this was wrong. He had a queue of test-pilots, including his own, who desperately wanted to fly this revolutionary aircraft. At the time of the cancellation, all Miles Aircraft's work in solving the huge challenges of supersonic flight had cost British taxpayers £100,000. What is certain is that British taxpayers didn't benefit by the M52's cancellation. However, two other companies certainly were to benefit by that decision.

The first was the American Bell company. As early as the autumn of 1944, on instructions from the MAP, a delegation from Bell Aircraft was allowed to visit Woodley when they were given full details of the M52's moving tailplane and bi-convex wing. At the time, the Miles team were under the impression that this was the beginning of a two-way exchange of information. It wasn't. Then, when Miles was told of the cancellation, he was also instructed to hand over all drawings, research material, windtunnel data, jigs and other 'hardware'.

According to Dennis Bancroft, all this material was still at Woodley in July 1946 when the Bell Aircraft delegation made a second visit, but he was unsure what then happened to it. It was fifteen months later, in October 1947, when the Bell X1, with unswept wings like the M52, but powered by a rocket motor and dropped at high altitude from a bomber, became the first aircraft to exceed the speed of sound.

An interesting footnote to the Bell X1 story occurred nearly sixty years later, in a television programme about the 'sound barrier' broadcast in 2003. 'Chuck' Yeager, the X1's pilot, referred to the instability of the aircraft in its early flights, as it neared the speed of sound. He told how the Bell engineers then developed the all-moving tailplane which cured the problem, a secret so important to the success of supersonic flight that the Americans "kept it from the rest of the world" for five years. Reputedly, Yeager was a good engineer but, perhaps, in 1947, as just the 'jockey' of the X1, he was genuinely unaware that British scientists at the RAE had discovered that particular 'secret' by 1943.

The other company to benefit was Vickers, which was given a £500,000 contract to build various designs of rocket-powered, radio-controlled models, air-launched from a Mosquito bomber, to investigate high-speed flight. Starting with models of the M52, problems with the rocket motors and radio control meant that it was the third attempt before a model actually flew successfully. This it did, accelerating smoothly for one minute to a speed of 1.4 Mach, without any of the instability 'experts' outside the Miles team had been forecasting. When the radio telemetry again failed, contact was lost with the model M52 at a range of some seventy miles, as it sped westward towards America. As Don Brown wrote, *"the design of the M52 was finally and irrefutably vindicated"*. Ironically, this last flight of an M52 model was on 9th October 1948, almost exactly one year after the Bell X1 had gone through the 'sound barrier' and five years to the day after FG Miles was asked if his company could undertake the project.

As Julian Temple wrote, *" The model trials were eventually suspended due to their extremely high cost and very poor return. ….. the total cost amounted to more than had already been spent on the partially completed full-size M52 prototype by February 1946."*

Painted in oils. 2003. 450mm x 600mm.

So, why was the M52 contract cancelled?

Various explanations for the cancellation from official sources were contradictory and conjecture by 'aviation experts' over the years did little to clarify the confusion. Even in the late 1990s, when official papers became available under the 'fifty year rule', in the Minutes of the Government Committee that dealt the fatal blow to British aviation, and Miles Aircraft and Frank Whittle in particular, the 'facts' are surprisingly missing.

One man who was at the heart of the M52 saga from the very beginning — Dennis Bancroft, chief aerodynamicist at Miles Aircraft — prepared an amazingly detailed and well argued report, first published in 1997 with an addendum in 1999, which can be seen in the library of the Imperial War Museum. In this he examined all the official documents available, plus various articles and reports from 'experts', as well as his own documents and recollections. His conclusions would do justice to Sherlock Holmes who said, "When all else is impossible, that which remains must be so." In November 2008, Dennis was happy to approve this brief summary of his conclusion.

Imagine a boxing ring with four protagonists. In one corner was Frank Whittle, inventor of the jet engine, a hero to the press and public and someone who, to achieve his eventual success, had fought many battles with 'authority'. The company he had started, Power Jets, had the greatest concentration of jet engine skills and experience in the world and, when it was 'nationalised' in April 1944, the Ministry of Aircraft Production had agreed it would continue to design and produce new engines for other firms to put into production.

In the opposite corner of the ring were the powerful private-sector engine manufacturers, led by Rolls Royce who, when they had heard of the proposed nationalisation of Power Jets, had been given assurances by the Ministry that, as a Government company, it would not compete with the private sector.

Between these two protagonists was the Ministry, with its mixture of politicians and civil servants, as well as its outside advisors known as the 'Supersonic Committee', one of whom, originally, was Frank Whittle, although he resigned in April 1945.

Painted in oils. 2003. 400mm x 500mm.

'Supersonic dream'

The Miles M52, a sight that could have been seen above Britain a year before the American Bell X1, piloted by 'Chuck' Yeager, became the first aircraft in the world to fly through the 'sound barrier', a dream that had challenged the aviation industry since the invention of the jet engine by Britain's Frank Whittle. Just six months before the M52 would have flown, the Government of the day cancelled the contract. It was the first of many such decisions that would decimate the British aviation industry.

In January 1946 he also resigned from the Power Jets Board, the reason for both resignations being that he fundamentally disagreed with him and his team becoming merely 'research scientists'. From then on, the 'knives were out' for Whittle and his career was virtually ended.

In the meantime, in the fourth corner of the ring, the small team at Miles Aircraft was nearing completion of their 'top secret' aircraft. When, probably later that year, the M52 'broke the sound barrier', powered by a Whittle engine, the 'hero' would become a 'super hero' in the eyes of the press and public.

In the mind of the bureaucrats and their advisors, that couldn't be allowed. For peace with the private-sector engine manufacturers and, no doubt, a 'quiet life' at the Ministry, not only was the 'hero', Frank Whittle, sacrificed but, unjustly and unbelievably, so was the M52. Dennis Bancroft believes no other 'reason' stands up to knowledgeable scrutiny.

When the technological problems of supersonic flight were first beginning to be solved by the small project team at Woodley, a very different aircraft from the M52 had its beginnings. Miles 'folklore' pinpointed this to the spring of 1944 when George Miles caught a chill and had to stay at home for a week or more. He returned with sketches and calculations for a number of aircraft designs, the most notable of which eventually became the M57 Aerovan, the prototype first flying in January 1945.

Despite the disappointment of the X11's rejection, followed by the euphoria of the M52 contract, Miles was still determined to play a part in the post-war market for transport aircraft. Don Brown led the development of three such designs at this time, the M54, M56 and M59. These eventually led to the M60 Marathon, a four-engine airliner designated the Brabazon Type 5a, ordered in October 1944.

Returning to George Miles's M57 Aerovan, this was a very different type of aircraft, in fact, it was quite unique in the industry. Official policy seemed to be to use gliders for freight-carrying in military operations, but George had always advocated the use of low-powered aircraft, specially designed for the purpose, which could be used over and over again. He felt the M38 Messenger had excelled in the Army role for which it was first designed. Now, he envisaged an aircraft of about twice the size and power of the Messenger, but with similar attributes when it came to operations into small areas of rough ground. Looking even further ahead, he also saw this new design as a 'flying scale model' of larger types of freighters. Indeed, in the post-war era, he could see such aircraft being very popular as economical freighters or short-range passenger aircraft.

Once again, it was Ray Bournon at Liverpool Road who became the project engineer and oversaw the Aerovan's design and construction there. In January 1945, it first flew at Woodley, in the hands of Tommy Rose, now the Miles chief test pilot. The pod-shaped fuselage was of plastic-bonded wooden construction and the rear end was hinged to form a large loading door. A metal boom carrying the tailplane was fixed directly to the main spar of the one-piece fifty foot span wooden wing. It proved very easy to fly and, even with full fuel tanks, could carry almost a ton of freight, a feat never previously achieved with an aircraft of this power.

Above: The prototype M57 Aerovan, seen at Woodley in 1945.

George was so convinced of its demand by the military that he submitted it to the MAP and began work on construction of a second aircraft. Needless to say, the Ministry disagreed and, once again, reprimanded Miles Aircraft for building an aircraft without permission. When the war ended a few months later, there was such a demand for the Aerovan from the civil market, that orders were coming in faster than the company could build them.

Before leaving the wartime activities of Miles Aircraft, recognition should be given to the company's development of a variety of different products, well over one hundred being patented.

Among them is the TORA Monoplane Air Tail, a classified secret weapon developed at the Liverpool Road factory in late 1940 for the Fleet Air Arm's torpedo bombers. Little had ever been known about TORA until Julian Temple uncovered information in 1985, during his research for 'Wings over Woodley', where he provided the first details made public. Basically, it provided a gyroscopic control to an air-launched torpedo, allowing it to 'fly' for a few seconds and then ensure that it entered the water at the correct angle. Thousands were made throughout the war and, indeed, long after, being manufactured first at Liverpool Road, then at the Miles-controlled Park Royal facility where Magister components were made and, finally, at the Miles subsidiary factory in Northern Ireland.

Auto-pilots, generally known as 'George' on the wartime bombers, had been developed in the UK in the 1930s. However, they were heavy, some 90lbs, and limited in use. In 1941, in a typical FG Miles way, he gave two young draughtsmen the task of developing in two years, a more versatile all-electric auto-pilot, suitable for installation in light aircraft.

Allowed to purchase any books or equipment for basic research, they were soon breaking into the pioneering business of aviation electronics. Their initial experiments in 1941 produced a single-axis machine controlling just the aircraft's rudder and this was test flown in a Whitney Straight. Soon this was developed into a three-axis machine, power being provided by two small servo-motors. More flight trials followed in different aircraft, including an Airspeed Oxford loaned by the MAP, and various 'teething problems' were overcome. By July 1945, their ultimate, three-axis model was installed in the prototype Aerovan. Now known as the Miles Co-Pilot, it weighed just 45lbs, half the weight of 'George'. A gyroscope sensed any deviation of the aircraft's height or direction and electric actuators, linked to the aircraft's control surfaces, maintained it in perfect flight. Despite the three-axis Co-Pilot's undoubted success, the version approved for production by the Air Registration Board in 1946 was a two-axis model controlling just the ailerons and elevator of an aircraft.

The Miles Electric Actuator, which resulted directly from the quest to find an improved auto-pilot, was undoubtedly the most successful of the many aircraft accessories developed by the company in those war years. A simple device, the actuator was both small and lightweight and 'pigmy power' was coined as a catchphrase for advertising, because this small device could exert a considerable force with apparent ease. Two types were produced, providing linear or rotary motion from a small electric motor. A linear model operated a ram via a screw mechanism. In a rotary model, the electric motor turned an epicyclic gear around the central axis. Eight different models were eventually made, from a small linear model weighing just 1lb 6oz, providing a force of 50lbs, to one weighing 6lb 8oz providing a force of 1,000lbs.

Actuators were used to control ailerons, elevators, rudders, flaps and trim tabs, as well as for retractable undercarriages, cooling gills and ventilators on a number of Miles aircraft designed at that time. When the war ended they were soon in demand by other aircraft and engine manufacturers and found applications elsewhere for tasks such as operating windows and ventilators in buildings when they were situated in inaccessible places.

Unlike Woodley, many of Berkshire's other airfields, particularly those used by the Americans, were virtually non-operational by the end of the war.

Greenham Common, Membury, Welford and Aldermaston had all seen their Troop Carrier Groups transfer to France as landing strips there became available. After VE-Day, for some nine months, Greenham Common became home to around eight thousand RAF new recruits, as they undertook their eight week 'square bashing' course. Then, in June 1946, it closed, but was retained as an inactive site under the care of RAF Welford. Membury was also put under the care of RAF Welford in April 1946, having previously been used by Dakotas of RAF Transport Command for long range troop-carrying to the Far-East. With the introduction of four-engine transports, Dakotas were deemed unsuitable for this task and the Membury Dakotas took up more local 'mail and newspaper runs', with up to nine flights each day, until October 1946, when the airfield was declared inactive. Welford was taken over by RAF Transport Command at the end of June 1945 and, for some eight months, conversion courses were run there, mainly using Dakotas and Horsa gliders. Apart from two short spells under 'care and maintenance' Welford has remained an active site.

Of all Berkshire's American bases, Aldermaston was to face a very different future. The Vickers' site, where Spitfire components manufactured in Reading and Newbury were brought for final assembly and test flying, had opened in July 1943. Production ceased when the European war ended in the spring of 1945. Soon after, the Americans finally left and, for a few months, a unit of RAF Technical Training Command moved in. The airfield lay dormant for almost a year until BOAC opened its Training HQ there in May 1946. Soon Dakotas, Oxfords and Yorks were flying there, followed by Haltons, Vikings and Halifaxes and, by the end of 1947, there were nearly ten thousand aircraft flights every month. At the beginning of 1947, Aldermaston was loaned to the Ministry of Civil Aviation as a temporary civil airport and, about the same time, BOAC joined with BEA to form Airways Training there, the school continuing until November 1948. In August 1949, British Eagle set up its headquarters at Aldermaston. However, within a few months, the whole airfield became the site for the Atomic Weapons Research Establishment.

The airfield at Grove had a chequered career even before the Americans arrived. However, it was one of the last bases they relinquished, handing over to the RAF in February 1946. The extensive storage facilities there remained in use for many years.

The RAF airfields at Hampstead Norris, Great Shefford and Theale were quickly closed down when the war ended. Shellingford's role as No.3 EFTS continued beyond the end of the war and in September 1945, included refresher courses for glider pilots. The School and the airfield closed in 1948.

Watchfield's Beam Approach School continued its work until 1947 and, in the six years it operated, a total of eight thousand five hundred pupils trained there. Records show that one of its aircraft alone had flown almost one hundred thousand hours yet, despite the number of flights, there was only one accident involving injury. Between 1946 and 1950 the School of Air Traffic Control was sited at Watchfield and, afterwards, it became a site for parachute training and a dropping zone for heavy loads from RAF transports.

Berkshire's two pre-war RAF airfields, Abingdon and Harwell, were to have very different futures. Soon after their involvement with the Market Garden operation in 1944, Harwell's Stirling glider tugs moved to a new base and the airfield again became an OTU, mainly operating Mitchell light bombers. This didn't last long and, although other RAF units considered moving in, at the end of 1945, Harwell was chosen to be the site of Britain's Atomic Energy Research Establishment.

Abingdon's role as a bomber OTU had continued throughout the Normandy landings and, by the spring of 1945, there were fifty Wellingtons operating there. However, Abingdon's link with bombers of well over twenty years was soon to be broken and, in October 1946, the airfield was taken over by RAF Transport Command. For about a year, Dakotas operated from Abingdon, to be replaced at the end of 1947 with Avro Yorks. When, in 1948, the Russian blockade of Berlin was answered by the British and Americans with the astonishing Berlin Airlift, the first York to arrive in the beleaguered City was one from Abingdon and soon Abingdon's York squadrons moved to West Germany. Although other roles descended on Abingdon in the early '50s, the main user remained RAF Transport Command.

The RAF presence at Woodley continued after the war, although the flying instructors school did not last long and, in 1947, No. 8 Reserve Flying School replaced it. By the early 1950s de Havilland Chipmunks made their first appearance at the school, replacing the ancient Tiger Moths. However, in 1953, as part of a general cut-back in RAF training, the school was closed, thus ending Woodley's eighteen year continuous direct involvement with the training of RAF pilots.

The RAF Training Command's communications flight, which had been based at Woodley since the early 1940s, also left in 1953, relocating to White Waltham.

In 1945, another long-running link between Berkshire and the RAF was established when the RAF Staff College was transferred to Bracknell. It was eventually absorbed into the Joint Services Command and Staff College in 1997, which moved to Shrivenham in 2001.

Station Badge of the RAF Staff College, Bracknell, 1945 – 1997.

At White Waltham, in the last year of the war, ATA pilots extended their area of operations and made many flights in their Ansons throughout Western and Southern Europe, carrying vital medicines and vaccines. But the end of the ATA was already in sight and a Farewell Air Pageant and Gala Day was held in September 1945 at White Waltham and, on 30th November 1945, the ATA was officially disbanded. However, in a subsequent magazine article, one of the airfield controllers from that time remembered about forty ATA pilots being seconded to the RAF to continue ferrying and, from his tale of a typical day's flying, White Waltham was still a centre for ferrying and an 'air-spotter's paradise' well into 1946.

He also mentioned some of the 'funnies' being flown at White Waltham by the R Malcolm Company at that time. 'Ronnie' Malcolm, before joining the ATA, had joined forces with Marcel Lobelle, the former chief designer of Fairey Aviation. However, financial problems brought the Mobbs family into control of the Malcolm company and Eric Mobbs became managing director, with Lobelle, as chief designer. Soon after, the company moved to a small site at White Waltham and, in 1946, changed the name to ML Aviation. During the war years, the Malcolm company made canopies for RAF Mustangs but a 'funny' that has gone down into aviation history is the Rotajeep, which can still be seen today at the Museum of Army Flying.

Designed by Raoul Hafner and first flown in November 1943, it is essentially a Jeep with a detachable autogiro-type rotor and simple tailplane, which would be air-towed with paratroopers to their drop-zone. In fact, the Rotajeep was not ready by D-Day and Jeeps were generally flown into battle in the larger gliders.

By the end of the war, White Waltham was the largest grass airfield in the UK and it was destined for a busy and varied future. The RAF returned there in October 1946, when it became headquarters of the Reserve Command. About the same time the West London Aero Club set up its operations at White Waltham and would eventually grow to be the largest private flying club in the UK.

The following year, having surrendered their airfield at Heston to the future Heathrow Airport, Fairey Aviation moved their final assembly and flight testing operations to White Waltham. Fairey Air Surveys, with its fleet of six Dakotas, also moved to White Waltham that year, the whole of Fairey's operations being set up in the buildings formerly occupied by the ATA.

At the other end of Berkshire, Chilton Aircraft had considerably expanded during the war years when it operated as a sub-contractor, ironically mainly for unsuccessful aircraft such as the Defiant, the Manchester and the Whirlwind. No doubt, throughout his time in the ATA, 'Reggie' Ward had kept in close touch with his partner Andrew Dalrymple, who ran the company in the war years. When, in 1944, the MAP authorised aircraft manufacturers to spend a limited amount of time planning post-war civil aircraft, the two partners leapt at the chance. Fearing that a lack of suitable engines may be a problem, their thoughts turned to sailplanes and, soon, a well known pilot persuaded them to build him one based upon the pre-war German Olympia Meise design.

Left: R Malcolm's 'Rotajeep'.

Another Berkshire company, Elliotts of Newbury now comes into the story. Elliotts was a pre-war furniture maker which became involved with production of Horsa gliders and, it is thought, produced about one third of the total built. They also made components for Spitfires and Oxfords and were keen to extend this aviation experience into their peacetime activities. Chilton sub-contracted Elliotts to build the wing of their Olympia and this had been delivered. However, a cruel blow was about to devastate the Chilton company.

In 1945, Denys Phillips, a designer with Chilton who had previously flown with the RAF, received permission from the MAP to go to Germany to study certain aspects of aircraft manufacture. It seems he did not have permission to bring a complete aircraft back but, on Christmas Day 1945, he arrived at Chilton Foliat with an ex-Luftwaffe Fieseler Storch on which, it transpired, he had carried out repairs to the starboard wing. Phillips thought the company would be interested in using the Storch as a glider-tug and suggested Andrew Dalrymple join him in a short flight. Having made a few circuits, the starboard wing suddenly appeared to fold upwards and the aircraft side-slipped into the ground and caught fire. Both men were killed instantly.

Effectively, this tragedy brought an end to aircraft manufacture at Chilton, although their Olympia sailplane was delivered to the pilot who had ordered it and, with the aid of ATC cadets to launch it, was first flown from Theale airfield in August 1946. Later, the owner flew it to Dunstable and, subsequently, flew it many times in competitions.

By 1946, Chilton had diversified into the design and manufacture of electrical products, starting with an electric shaver and, later, electric clippers, shaver sockets, rechargeable torches and the UK's first spin dryer. Their success with electrical products soon led to expansion and new premises in Hungerford. Chilton was never again involved with aviation.

Earlier in 1946, there had been a disagreement between Chilton and Elliotts over the jigs for the Olympia's wings. However, this was eventually resolved and Elliotts purchased the right to manufacture the Chilton-designed Olympia, their first one flying in August 1947. In fact, they took the brave decision to set up a production line and, within a year or so, had built one hundred.

Painted in watercolours. 2007. 220mm x 280mm.

Painted in watercolours. 2007. 220mm x 280mm.

'A Welford maiden'

The Newbury Eon, designed and built by Elliotts of Newbury, made its maiden flight from Welford airfield in August 1947.

Unfortunately, Elliotts had over-estimated the post-war demand for sailplanes and many of these remained unfinished in their factory. However, their ambitions extended beyond sailplanes and, in August 1947, their powered four-seat cabin monoplane made its first flight from Welford airfield. Generally known as the 'Newbury Eon', it appears to have been quite a successful aircraft but, although the prototype was demonstrated widely, it failed to achieve any sales.

For Berkshire as a whole however, a future in aircraft manufacture seemed assured. In the west, at Newbury, despite their lack of success with a powered aircraft, Elliotts were beginning to build a good reputation for their Olympias and, later, for training gliders.

Right: The Firefly, the first Fairey aircraft to be assembled and test-flown at White Waltham, was to see service with the Fleet Air Arm in the Korean War in the 1950s.

In East Berkshire, at White Waltham, the newly named ML Aviation had already built a name in aviation for innovative ideas and products. Also now at White Waltham, Fairey's long-established reputation for designing aircraft for the Fleet Air Arm had continued with the Firefly, which was now, in increasing numbers, being assembled and test-flown there. At their main factory in Hayes, the next generation of Fleet Air Arm aircraft was already 'on the drawing board'.

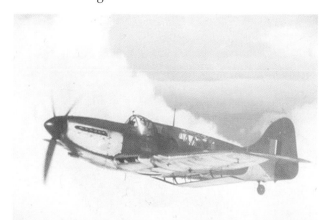

At Woodley, Miles Aircraft was facing the post-war future with very much more confidence than many others in the UK aircraft industry. Indeed, early in 1947, with so many aircraft under construction at Woodley and Northern Ireland, two other manufacturers, Boulton & Paul and Follands, were approached with a view to either of them being purchased by Miles. At the time, neither company was building an aircraft of its own.

However, the financial stability of Miles Aircraft itself was then under threat from an accumulation of factors stemming originally from the fact that the war years had seen a seven-fold growth in its workforce, which was spread around twenty-six dispersal sites. Thanks to the 'Excess Profits Tax' which, incidentally, had brought down Sopwith Aircraft at the end of World War I, Miles had not been allowed to retain proportionate profits from its work and build up capital reserves.

When the atomic bombs were dropped on Japan, the war ended far more quickly than even the Government expected. As a result, the planned 'Break Clause', whereby industry was allowed a twelve-month period to prepare for peacetime conditions, was not forthcoming. Companies such as Miles Aircraft were therefore denied the chance to rationalize their vastly expanded workforce with its inflated costs, before being thrown on their own financial resources to face a competitive market for civil aircraft. Further complications were caused by wartime legislation for all companies to guarantee twelve months employment for former employees returning from the Services.

Despite these undoubted problems, the Miles Aircraft management remained optimistic and were confident that they had a solid foundation for success in the civil aviation market with their existing designs. It was felt that these could be in full production within eighteen months and, in the meantime, a range of non-aircraft products, many already in production, would provide a financial 'cushion' until the major income from aircraft sales became available. Foremost among these were the Biro pen and the world's first photocopier known as the Copycat.

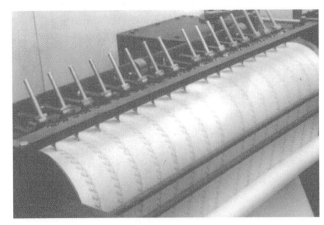

Top: Test-rig for the original Biro pens developed at the Miles Aircraft factory at Woodley. In 1943, FG Miles met an American named Martin who had exclusive patent rights to the Biro pen in North America. Eventually, Miles obtained sole manufacturing rights for the Biro pen outside America and formed the Miles Martin Pen Company.

Middle: The 'Copycat' photocopier, first developed at Woodley by the Miles Aircraft Photographic Department.

Below: A concept for a 'light car', notably similar to the early Volkswagens, prepared by the designers at Miles Aircraft soon after the end of the war.

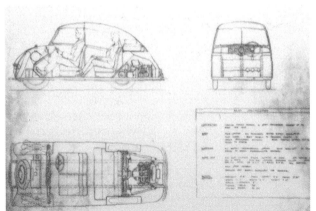

Products such as the aircraft-inspired automatic pilot and actuators, already described, quickly made contributions to profitability. Diversification into the temporary housing market and even the making of a light car were examined. However, it was the development by Miles Aircraft of the Biro pen and the very first photocopier that were significant steps towards profitability. By the end of 1945, a healthy annual profit of more than £50,000 had been made and, by the end of 1946, this had more than doubled to £107,000.

Ever since Rolls Royce had sold its interests in Phillips & Powis to the Miles family in 1941, FG Miles had been assisted and advised on the Board of Directors by the financier, Gatty Saunt, who had introduced a new firm of Accountants, Hogg Bullimore. Samuel Hogg had become senior auditor and, eventually, an adviser in whom the Miles family placed great trust. For instance, Hogg vetted all speeches FG Miles made as chairman of the Board. When Gatty Saunt retired at the end of the war, Miles had invited Sir William Mount to the Board and, in January 1946, he had become financial executive. It was felt that his pre-war experience with Barclays Bank would be particularly valuable. One of his first tasks was to raise further capital to offset the loss of regular progress payments for Government contracts. His negotiations with London & Yorkshire Trust and the merchant bank, Erlangers, were encouraging and it was agreed with the financial advisers that a new share issue of £400,000 would be made in the spring.

Putting all this into context with the design and production of the aircraft at this time, it is necessary to return to 1945. When the war finally ended in August, the main assembly line at Woodley was still hard at work on the Monitor even though the contract for some two thousand aircraft had just been slashed to only two hundred and sixty. When just twenty had been completed in January 1946, the whole contract was cancelled and even these were ignominiously broken up at Woodley by 1947.

The end of the war also saw the end of Spitfire refurbishment in the old repair & service hangars. However, the department was soon hard at work, refurbishing ex-RAF Magisters for sale to overseas airforces, flying clubs and private owners. By far the largest order, for one hundred and forty eight, came from the Argentine government. Others went to Egypt, Lebanon, New Zealand, South Africa and Ireland and sales of this pre-war favourite continued well into 1947.

Despite the assault on Miles Aircraft's hoped-for short-term profitability by the Monitor cancellation, the contract for the three M60 Marathon prototypes, awarded by the MAP in 1944, was the great hope for the Company's future in the post-war civil aviation market. Supporting this were the three types produced in the war years but destined, it was thought, for real success in post war aviation, the M28, the M38 Messenger and the M57 Aerovan.

'The price of peace'

A sad sight for employees of Miles Aircraft was the breaking up of around twenty Monitors at Woodley Airfield during 1947.

Painted in watercolours. 2007. 225mm x 275mm

The factory in Northern Ireland, which the Government had asked Miles Aircraft to open to help local unemployment, was now in operation, managed by Charles Powis who, after service in the RAF, had 'returned to the fold'. It looked as if this factory would play a big part in the production of all three of these types until the Monitor contract was cancelled. In practice, just the Messengers were built there, nearly sixty in total. The bare aircraft was built in Northern Ireland and was then flown to Woodley for painting and upholstering -- a practice that led directly to Miles Aircraft's most successful post-war design, the M65 Gemini.

The frequent flights in single-engine aircraft across the Irish Sea when the factory was being established, as well as the transfer of Messengers for completion at Woodley, made George Miles think of the added safety offered by a small twin-engine aircraft. He quickly designed what, in effect, was a twin-engine Messenger and the first flight of the prototype Gemini was made by FG Miles on 26th October 1945. The Gemini was an immediate success and, eventually, one hundred and fifty would be built, with sales being achieved all around the world. Plans for mass production of the M28 were abandoned. British buyers of the Gemini included the Ministry of Civil Aviation, BOAC and 'Flight' magazine. The well known motor racing driver, Prince Bira of Siam, flew his Gemini to race meetings all around Europe and Douglas Bader, in his post-war job with Shell, was a regular visitor to both Woodley and White Waltham in his.

Above: Douglas Bader in the Miles M65 Gemini he flew in post-war years, when working for Shell Aviation

Miles Aircraft had developed the concept for the M60 Marathon early in 1944, when it was presented to the MAP and became the basis for the official specification later designated the Brabazon Type 5a. However, the MAP decided to issue it competitively to other companies and it was October 1944 before Miles received an instruction to proceed with the design and construction of three prototypes. It was to be the company's largest aircraft to date, the first with four engines and the first all-metal design. It was the great hope for the future, joining the new Gemini, the Aerovan and the Messenger in a collection of civil designs to rival any other British manufacturer.

The future of Miles Aircraft did indeed look very bright. But the best laid plans......

The winter of 1946/47 turned out to be the worst for many years with temperatures below freezing week after week. At the same time, there was a crippling fuel shortage throughout the country and, soon, the Government announced compulsory electricity cuts. Rather than reduce total working hours, Miles workers voted to work one whole day without heat in the factory. Ingenious temporary power supplies were rigged up to keep machinery in operation. However, serious production problems with Aerovans and Geminis resulted from the crisis due to the shortage of materials and the low temperatures affecting both timber and glue. The factory was back in full production in early March but £100,000 was estimated to have been lost.

The best laid plans for the M60 Marathon, the great post-war hope for the future, had also suffered badly. Again, this was through no fault of Miles Aircraft and, to fully appreciate the problems they faced, no better source can be found than Don Brown. What follows is an extract from his excellent book, written some twenty-five years later.

"While the Marathon had been taking shape, it was found that the technical problems involved in its design and construction were as nothing compared with the long and wearisome arguments and negotiations with the various authorities who, in the modern order of things, had individually and severally to be satisfied and every one of whom had conflicting ideas and instructions with no central authority to co-ordinate them.

"There were, for instance, the Ministry of Aircraft Production, the Ministry of Aviation, the Air Registration Board, the Aeronautical Inspection Directorate, the Royal Aircraft Establishment and, very much last, the operators for whom the aircraft was intended. In the early stages of the design, the latter had very little to say and were forbidden to have dealings with the firm.

"It took no less than six months to convince the Ministry of Aircraft Production that the complete engine installation could not, as they were trying to insist, be made interchangeable with that of the de Havilland Dove, an aeroplane of totally different layout.

"Next came criticism on the score of tyre pressures. The Ministry said that the pressures proposed were far too high and quite unacceptable. This meant a major design alteration to the engine nacelles, but it had to be accepted. No sooner was this done than the Royal Aircraft Establishment demanded to know why such low pressures were being used. The figure they suggested was the one originally proposed.

Next, the RAE laid down their requirements as to the structural strength of the fuselage required for ditching. It was clear that to meet these requirements was impossible and would have resulted in the fuselage being considerably stronger and heavier than the hull of a flying boat! Again, many weeks were wasted in argument.

"Then the Ministry insisted on the cabin being pressurised, ignoring the fact that the rated height of the engines was well below that at which pressurisation would be necessary. In vain George Miles pleaded, but the Ministry remained adamant. In the meantime, however, the Minister of Civil Aviation paid a personal visit to see how the job was progressing and immediately took the firm to task with great severity (and sound common sense) for making an aircraft of this type pressurised. Learning that this was being done on instructions, he promptly cancelled the instructions, ordering the firm to delete pressurisation and to start the design of the fuselage all over again.

"Later, Miles received a sharp letter from the Ministry of Aircraft Production, reminding him that the design of the Marathon was their responsibility, no matter what opinions or instructions might be issued by other authorities. As had been the case of the Messenger, there is nothing like an inter-Ministerial war for uncompromising bitterness. All the public hears, of course, is a tale of continually escalating costs which, in the absence of facts, they attribute to the inefficiency of an irresponsible and pampered industry. So time went on."

With all these frustrations it is not surprising that design and construction of the first Marathon took longer than anticipated and it was more than eighteen months from receipt of the order to its first flight—on 19th May 1946. A few weeks later Miles received authorisation to 'tool up', based upon a forthcoming order for one hundred aircraft including the M69 version, the third prototype ordered. Known as the Marathon II, this was to be powered by twin turboprop engines which had been allowed for when the Marathon was first conceived, even though this type of engine was not then available.

Although 'tooling up' had been authorised in June, it was another eight months before the new Ministry of Supply authorised Miles Aircraft to go ahead with the construction of fifty Marathons, thirty for BEA and twenty for subsidiary companies of BOAC. Ten days later, on 27th February 1947, the second prototype made its first flight and, by then, construction of the turboprop Marathon II was well underway. In the meantime, flight trials of the first prototype had proceeded smoothly and successfully.

The Marathon had already made an impact in the airline business, being the first aircraft in the world to meet all the safety standards of the new ICAO, a body representing most of the world's civil airliner operating countries.

In Don Brown's words again. *"Meanwhile the firm still awaited the production order on which the future of the factory depended, but it took yet another year of discussions with the various authorities before the pre-contract document, known as Instructions to Proceed, was received and even then argument continued as regards price. Based on a production order, the firm estimated the actual cost of the aircraft would be £37,500. We supplied full details as to how this figure was determined and suggested a contract price of £40,000, a modest enough profit and but a small margin in the event of an underestimate. The Ministry offered a price of £32,000, giving no details beyond a statement that they could get a Vickers Viking for this."* The Viking was a completely different twin-engine design based largely upon the old Wellington bomber and was already in large-scale production by Vickers.

It is difficult to see what the Ministry hoped to achieve by all this. Was it sheer incompetence or, with the whole British aircraft industry under threat of nationalisation, did the bureaucrats think that relatively small firms like Miles no longer mattered?

Although, as chief designer, George Miles would have been heavily involved with the 'saga' of the Marathon, his fertile aviation brain was always full of new ideas and, early in 1946, when the Aerovan had been flying for more than a year, he had come up with a novel development, the M68 Boxcar.

At the time, containers were not the familiar sight seen today on ships, trains and lorries. But that is exactly what he envisaged being used in the air freight business. Cleverly, the design of the Boxcar maintained the vital 'centre of gravity' exactly in position whether the aircraft was flown with or without the container in position. Four engines were fitted, doubling the power of the standard Aerovan, which had always had a bit of a problem with being under-powered. About this time also, a four-engine Aerovan, the M72, was conceived but, sadly, it was destined never to be built.

Another new design, the M71 Merchantman had actually been conceived back in 1945 and grew out of discussions between George Miles and Don Brown about a larger and more powerful follow-up to the Aerovan, a basic design concept that both felt had a big future in both freight and passenger transport.

During 1946 the design office was fully occupied with both versions of the Marathon and, although the project design of the Merchantman was completed by the end of 1945, detail design could not begin until October 1946. Nevertheless, less than ten months later, on 7th August 1947, the prototype Merchantman was first flown.

In his book, Don Brown makes the following comment. *"During the design period, the number of design draughtsmen averaged twenty, giving a total effort of 800 man-weeks compared with the 4,000 man-weeks spent on the Marathon. Admittedly, the Merchantman used, in effect the Marathon wing and, while it was a less complex aircraft, the disparity in the figures for design effort gives some idea of the cost of working under the control of a government department."*

In simple terms, the M71 Merchantman was a larger, metal-built Aerovan but, having four engines. it was more powerful. Another version, the M71A, was projected to have two larger radial engines such as Armstrong Siddeley Cheetahs or Alvis Leonides. An additional variant of this design was based upon the container-carrying M68 Boxcar.

Even 'on the drawing board', the Merchantman immediately impressed a Woodley-based company, Air Contractors, which already operated Aerovans. Just a month after detailed design work on it had started, on 7th November 1946, a draft agreement was signed between Miles and Air Contractors for the construction of fifty M71A Merchantman. Twenty of these were to be the Mark I version with a standard fuselage and thirty were to be a Mark II 'container' version based upon the M68 Boxcar.

Under the agreement, construction would be funded by progress payments from Air Contractors, guaranteed by associated merchant banks. In fact it was agreed that 10% of the total price for twenty aircraft, amounting to £40,000, would be paid when the Merchantman prototype first flew.

When the Manager of Barclays Bank was informed of this Agreement, he insisted his bank should provide the additional capital required for the Merchantman production. Barclays had indeed been the Company's bankers ever since the P&P days in the early 1930s. Substantial overdrafts had previously been made available and the Miles Aircraft directors assumed this good relationship would continue. Indeed, in Don Brown's book, he claimed that a figure of £800,000 was agreed but, because of Government restrictions at the time, this would be made available in two stages.

Below: The M68 Boxcar, with and without its container. Its specially arranged registration G-AJJM reflected the honour given to Charles Powis in 1935 by Reading Aero Club. In this case, it was the initials of Jeremy John Miles, the son of Blossom and FG. At the time, he was fourteen and being taught to fly.

Painted in oils on canvas. 2005. 450mm x 600mm

'Post-war hopes'

Within a year of the war's end, Miles Aircraft faced the future with a great deal more confidence than many other British aircraft manufacturers. Hopes for the M60 Marathon four-engine airliner were particularly high, even if the Ministry of Aircraft Production had once more caused many problems during the design stages. The M57 Aerovan was, as George Miles had forecast, an immediate success in the post-war civil aviation market as a versatile freight or passenger carrier. Bigger and more powerful versions were already at the design stage in a sector of the civil market in which Miles dominated. The M38 Messenger had fulfilled all the potential that its wartime predecessors had promised. Even more success seemed promised for the twin-engine M65 Gemini with sales beginning to materialise from many overseas countries.

Even before the agreement with Air Contractors for the M71A Merchantman, Barclays had been party to the decision that the production programme for existing aircraft demanded the re-financing of Miles Aircraft, hence the new share issue planned for the spring of 1947.

Despite this, did Barclays' attitude change soon after when, not only Erlangers, but also the other merchant banks introduced by Air Contractors, showed interest in providing Miles Aircraft with finance? This will, no doubt, never be known, but the stark fact is that, within a year, Barclays Bank played a major part in the company's destruction.

In his book 'Wings over Woodley' Julian Temple devotes a whole chapter to what he termed the 'Financial collapse of Miles Aircraft'. He gives a comprehensive, balanced and unbiased account of what, after all, was a complicated series of events. Lack of space here will limit the detail that can be examined and, bearing in mind the author's youthful affiliations with Miles and the fact that the word 'destruction' was used in the previous paragraph, it will perhaps be no surprise that this account is not so unbiased.

Sadly, the central character in the destruction of Miles Aircraft was Samuel Hogg, the previously mentioned 'trusted' financial adviser to the company Board. Looking back, Hogg appears not to have been the type of financial adviser that a company like Miles Aircraft required. One that could envisage *future* finance requirements and assist in finding them. Critically, he seems to have been, to use a more modern Americanism, a 'bean counter'.

Hogg must have been aware that Miles had recently experienced a financially disastrous few weeks due to the freezing weather. He must also have known that the prevarications of the Ministry on the Marathon contract, including overdue payments, were putting a severe strain on the company's cash flow. All this was recent history or actually happening when he audited the accounts for the previous financial year. Yet, like a typical 'bean counter', he happily 'signed off' the accounts ready for the AGM in August 1947, showing a healthy profit of £107,000. Surely today, a really competent financial adviser would make suitable allowances, or at least include a warning for the directors and bankers of 'exceptional future losses'.

Even worse, within days of the AGM, he was put into a position of enormous power by Barclays Bank when, following a meeting with FG Miles at which the manager complained about the escalating overdraft situation, Hogg was asked to prepare a special report on the company's financial situation before the bank would allow further advances. At the time, still trusting Hogg had Miles Aircraft's interests at heart, FG was happy to put the entire accounts department at his disposal for the two weeks he required. However, when the report was finished, Hogg made sure it was delivered to Barclays without FG or any other Miles Aircraft director really having time to study it properly or make any comments.

Julian Temple wrote in 1985, *"Quite why Samuel Hogg acted in this manner remains a mystery…..despite concerted efforts, it has not been possible to locate a copy of this infamous report, so unfortunately we must remain ignorant of the majority of its findings."* A later reaction by FG Miles, Julian records as being *"This is the first attempt to present views which should in common justice be considered in the light of a situation which has done us very serious and possibly irreparable harm. There are many other questions that should be considered before we are condemned of such carelessness as the report implies. I believe that if we had been given time to get a further enquiry, we could have handled things more gently and certainly less destructively. I hope that some part of Miles Aircraft can be saved – after 15 years of success and praise, one hasty, ill-considered report and the circumstances arising therefrom have almost entirely destroyed it."*

Yet, on that one "ill-considered report", without any of the Miles directors being allowed to counter it, Barclays withdrew finance for the manufacture of aircraft. By the end of October, even Erlangers had joined with Barclays in insisting Hogg was made manager of Miles Aircraft with full executive powers.

As FG Miles claimed later, there were even accounting errors which allowed Hogg to show a massive loss of more than £300,000 for the first six months of 1947, attributed exactly where Hogg wanted it to appear. Basically, additional overheads caused by the winter chaos were written against production of just Aerovans and Geminis. None of it was shown as additional overheads for the Marathon and Merchantman.

Trying to understand Hogg's thinking at the time, it must be remembered that, ever since he first began acting for Miles in 1941, he had seen profits from aircraft manufacture decimated by excess profits tax and Government contracts cancelled after materials had been purchased and expensive 'tooling up' costs incurred. He probably could not envisage a time when the company could deal direct with the customer instead of an interfering Ministry. He no doubt thought, how much better are the more recent products such as actuators, pens and photocopying machines. They could be manufactured in bulk and put on a shelf until customers bought them at a pre-determined profit.

That would be 'music to the ears' for a 'bean counter' like Hogg and Barclays were no better. It can be assumed that his report to them set out his ideas for a small range of non-aircraft products from a much smaller workforce and premises, resulting in considerably reduced overheads. A large part of the existing factory and offices would become 'lettable'. The manufacture of some of the new non-aircraft products could be set up as separate companies and, perhaps, sold on. Even the big Ministry contract for the Marathon could perhaps be passed on profitably. He offered a small company with a steady income from regular-selling products, an additional income from rentals and, behind it all, enormous assets in land and property. It was a banker's dream. Their own money would never be at risk.

Of course, Barclays had been backing aircraft manufacture at Woodley for over ten years and, even Hogg probably felt they would not be happy to see it brought to an end on his word alone. He promised a report from an 'independent aviation expert' and, two months after his own report, delivered it. Whether Hogg already knew the 'expert' or had to find him, is not known. But RH Mayo's report could not have been better if Hogg had written it himself! Julian Temple wrote, Mayo was *"generally very critical of the design, performance and potential market for the wooden-built Gemini, Messenger and Aerovan, but was full of praise for the Marathon for which he predicted a great future."* Certainly, at that time, a few 'experts' could still be found who supported the 1937 view of the Air Ministry on the unsuitability of wooden aircraft, despite the subsequent success of the Magister, the Master and its variants and, of course, the magnificent de Havilland Mosquito.

Mayo showed complete ignorance of recent developments at Miles, such as the use of plastic-bonded wooden structures, resins and advanced adhesives. He also seemed to know nothing of the metal-built Merchantman and its variants, the prototype having already flown by then. Probably, he knew nothing of the first flight of a Gemini with more powerful engines, which research had shown promised good sales in North America, as well as an all-metal Gemini being designed at that time.

Unlike Hogg's, Mayo's report did survive and, nearly forty years later, Julian Temple gave George Miles the chance to read it for the first time. Under all the circumstances, his comments were restrained to say the least, the final one being *"most, if not all, of Mayo's conclusions have since been proved wrong."* But, the fact remains, Mayo's report was accepted by Barclays without further discussion.

As if there were not enough cash flow problems in those crucial months, completely unexpected production problems made them worse. In July it was found that a large number of the Blackburn engines that powered Geminis were faulty and had to be replaced, causing major delays in delivery to customers. A claim for damages was made against Blackburn, but it was not resolved in time to affect the apparent losses. Earlier it was found that a new aluminium alloy used for the Marathon wing spar was faulty. Expensive rebuilding of spars caused yet more delays. Government restrictions on foreign currency even caused problems when it was found almost impossible to collect debts from overseas customers because of 'exchange control regulations'.

Even the money due from Air Contractors was never taken into account or, indeed, ever paid. With Hogg and Barclays having made certain that Air Contractors would never get the fifty aircraft they had ordered, they could hardly be blamed for keeping quiet about details of the agreement.

The epilogue to this sad tale of Miles Aircraft's destruction is that FG Miles and Sir William Mount were eventually singled out for criminal prosecution. It was claimed that they had persuaded people to buy shares "through the dishonest concealment of material facts or by reckless statements". At the trial at the Old Bailey in May/June 1950, when the full facts were presented, both men were acquitted.

Painted in oils on canvas. 2008. 600mm x 500mm.

'Flights of imagination'

It is difficult to believe that Miles Aircraft could have been forced to cease trading, with an order for fifty of these aircraft on its books, complete with promised financing. Yet that is what happened and the M71A Merchantman aircraft seen here, powered by Alvis Leonides engines, were never built. Coming in to land is the 'container version' based on the M68 Boxcar and behind it, on the airfield circuit, is a similar aircraft flying without a container. The standard version could carry up to ten passengers and a big future was also predicted for models adapted for the transport of racehorses. Continuing with the Berkshire theme, the horsebox is one built by Vincents of Reading, back to their traditional business after the building of hundreds of Spitfires in the war years at their premises in Reading. For Miles Aircraft enthusiasts, the aircraft about to be boarded by the racehorse owner and his wife is an imagined metal-built Gemini, which was being designed when the company ceased trading.

It was in 1947, that critical year at Woodley, that Fairey Aviation moved its final assembly and test flying operations to White Waltham and it brought an exciting new phase to the airfield's life.

The Fairey Firefly had first flown in 1941 and, as a reconnaissance fighter and anti-submarine aircraft was still making a major contribution to the Fleet Air Arm. In the post-war years it was being exported to other countries such as Australia, Canada, Denmark, Holland, Sweden and India. Indeed one of Fairey's first photographs taken at White Waltham showed a line-up of Fireflys destined for the Dutch navy.

At their Hayes factory, Fairey's designers were working on the next generation of naval aircraft. However, they were also working on what was a completely new breed of aircraft—a 'compound' helicopter, in effect a combination of helicopter and fixed-wing aircraft. The Gyrodyne I, as the first of these new aircraft was called, made its first flight at White Waltham in early December 1947. Some six months later, on 28th June 1948, over a 3km course above White Waltham, it established a new speed record for helicopters of 124mph.

Below: A cut-away illustration of the second Gyrodyne clearly shows the layout of these pioneering aircraft. In the first aircraft, the Alvis Leonides engine transmitted its power in variable ratios to the three-bladed rotor and the anti-torque propeller mounted on the stub-wing. At slow speeds, it flew like a helicopter. However, the propeller provided enough thrust to produce speeds at which the rotors virtually 'free-wheeled' like those of an autogiro. The more luxurious interior suggests this cutaway was an early projection of the second aircraft used for passenger demonstrations.

The second Gyrodyne flew in September 1948, in time to be demonstrated at the SBAC Farnborough air show. The first, having been dismantled, carefully inspected and rebuilt, in April 1949 was about to make an attempt on the 100km closed-circuit speed record for helicopters when disaster struck. Just two days before the attempt, in a test flight near Reading, fatigue failure of the rotor head caused it to crash, killing the pilot and observer. As would be expected, the second aircraft was grounded for a complete investigation and did not fly again until 1953.

Unfortunately, in May 1948, the prototype Miles Marathon had also crashed during official trials at Boscombe Down, due to 'pilot error'. This happened just at the time when Handley Page, one of Britain's longest established aircraft manufacturers, gained responsibility for the former aircraft interests of Miles Aircraft. They became the first tenant of Hogg's reorganised company, taking over the final assembly building at Woodley and soon calling themselves Handley Page (Reading) Limited and the Marathon the HPR1. In his 1985 research, Julian Temple discovered that, as well as the contract for fifty Marathons and completion of the part-built third prototype, Handley Page gained some forty other contracts varying from supplying spares for Miles aircraft still in service to providing technical drawings and even unspecified work on a Lancaster. The second Marathon prototype, built by Miles, was soon being used by Handley Page for demonstration flights for potential customers and the press.

The Berlin Air Lift was at a peak in the summer of 1949 and Handley Page Hastings transport aircraft were heavily involved. This resulted in the parent company's servicing facilities at Radlett becoming overstretched and assistance was requested from the new Woodley subsidiary, although it was recognised that the relatively small grass airfield was marginal for a large aircraft like the Hastings. When the first one arrived it was parked on the grass overnight and, in a scene reminiscent of a certain Lancaster a few years before, sank into the grass up to its axles. Julian Temple records that very few Hastings were serviced at Woodley during the time of the Air Lift, but refurbishment work on them did continue for some years after.

In the meantime, the Marathon II, the third prototype, originally the Miles M69, was nearing completion and, on 21st July 1949, made its first flight in the hands of Hugh Kendall, a former Miles test pilot. Powered by two Armstrong Siddeley 'Mamba' engines, it was Britain's third turbo-prop transport to fly. The same month, an article in 'Flight' described the Marathon I as being "Britain's most promising four-engine feeder liner". Its performance certainly exceeded that of the DC3 Dakota it was designed to succeed, but which was still available as low-cost, war-surplus. With an increase in speed of some 40% over the Marathon I, the twin-engine 'Mamba' Marathon appeared to offer so much more, but would potential operators agree?

When the Ministry originally ordered the fifty Marathon Is, twenty had been destined for BOAC subsidiaries and thirty for BEA. The unbelievable arrogance of Ministry officials in telling experienced aircraft designers what to do was certainly matched by their dealings with the two national airlines, neither of whom was consulted on the aircraft ordered for them to use. Indeed, they were even forbidden to talk to the manufacturers and, although BOAC ignored this and arranged for Miles Aircraft's Don Brown to visit the African countries where their subsidiaries operated, BEA appears to have let the Ministry's behaviour rankle, deciding to be totally uncooperative. They preferred to use war-surplus DC3s and even ex-Luftwaffe JU52s, rather than have Marathons foisted on them. So the future of Handley Page's HPR I Marathon began to look much less promising than 'Flight' had predicted.

'Variations on a theme'

The first production Marathon G–ALUB, built by Handley Page, was painted in BEA livery and flew many thousands of miles looking like this. However, its service with the airline extended to just a three-month trial on their Scottish Islands route. The 'Mamba' Marathon, designed by Miles as the M69, was half-built when Handley Page took over Miles' work at Woodley. They completed this fine aircraft, which deserved a great future with many post-war airlines, but sadly never saw service with BEA, as this painting suggests, or any other airline.

Throughout the first half of the 1950s, production staff at Handley Page worked hard to complete all the Marathon contracts and, indeed, to carry out work for the parent company on major components for their new Victor bomber. The notable Miles-built windtunnel, as well as laboratory facilities at the old Technical School site, also played a part in the design of this unique aircraft. The English Electric Canberra bomber, in which Handley Page were also involved, brought more work to their Woodley subsidiary.

The Handley Page design staff at Woodley had begun work on the first of their own aircraft early in 1949, to a Ministry of Supply specification for an RAF basic trainer to replace the Percival Prentice. Alternative engines were specified—an Armstrong Siddeley Cheetah and the more powerful Alvis Leonides. The HPR2, as it was known, made its first flight at Woodley on 1st May 1950 and, from that very first flight, when its cockpit canopy became detached and flew off, it was an aircraft beset with problems. The Ministry had actually ordered three prototypes of the HPR2, as well as three of a Percival design, for comparative trials. When the second HPR2, even with the Leonides engine, still had many of the same problems as the first, it seemed obvious that the similar looking, but very different behaving, Percival Provost would come out on top at the official trials, as indeed it did.

Below: The ill-fated Handley Page HPR2 seen at Woodley in 1950.

When the first production Marathon appeared at the end of 1949, it was indeed finished in BEA livery and carried the name 'Rob Roy'. It soon departed on a forty-thousand-mile sales tour of Australia and New Zealand. Demonstration tours of many African and European cities followed and, in the spring of 1951, after the apparent 'climb down' by BEA in accepting twelve aircraft, 'Rob Roy' left for evaluation and a three-month trial on the Scottish Islands routes.

Despite the Marathon's genuinely low operating costs, BEA claimed they preferred to keep using their pre-war DH Dragon Rapides on the routes and, having already rejected the 'Mamba' Marathon as being "too noisy", BEA were eventually 'let off the hook' completely by a new Government. Thus, in perhaps a foreseeable outcome of their original arrogance, but a disappointment none the less for Handley Page, the Ministry was left with thirty unwanted Marathons on their hands.

A number of Marathons ordered for BOAC did see service overseas and, in the early 1950s, six went to West African Airways. Two later returned to the UK, being bought by Derby Aviation. Three others were purchased by Burma Airways and two more by Japan's Far East Air Lines. Another became King Hussein of Jordan's personal transport. Two went to Farnborough's RAE for special duties and one to the German Civil Aviation Board. In total, forty of the Marathon Is were built by Handley Page.

The company then reaped the benefit of the Ministry's original arrogance when the decision was taken to convert the unwanted Marathons to RAF Navigation Trainers, thus keeping the Woodley factory busy for a few more years. In fact, RAF Marathons were not popular in the Service, probably because they were appreciably heavier than the original Miles design but, with the same Gypsy Queen engines, were by then underpowered.

Painted in oils. 2008. 400mm x 300mm. Original painting in the collection of Mr F Clayton.

'Airborne Aldermaston'

The prototype Fairey Gannet anti-submarine aircraft was taken by road from Hayes to Aldermaston in early September 1949 because it was felt that its first take-off should be from a concrete runway. At this time, although much of it was beginning to look derelict, it still showed all the signs of a large wartime airfield. Since the American airborne forces had left in 1945, it had been used by BOAC and BEA as a training school and, for a few months had served as a civil airport with as many as ten thousand flights a month. By 1949, it was just being used by British Eagle who had recently moved their headquarters there. However, within a short time, it would become, and remain, the main home of Britain's Atomic Weapons Establishment.

At White Waltham, the 1950s were to see the development of Fairey Aviation's most successful post-war aircraft—the Gannet. It has sometimes been called "the ugliest aircraft in the world", but it is also remembered as "an unsung hero".

By the end of 1945, many wartime advances in electronics and radar had persuaded the Admiralty that a high-performance anti-submarine aircraft they were contemplating should carry much more of such equipment and a new specification was issued.

Since 1935, Fairey had been experimenting with a twin-Merlin-engine installation driving co-axial contra-rotating propellers. However, final success had eluded them. By 1945 they were working on an observation aircraft design built around their twin-Merlin layout. Their designers realised that the new Armstrong Siddeley 'Mamba' turbo-prop engines could replace the heavier and now outdated Merlins, making the new aircraft able to carry the equipment required by the 1945 contract. So the Fairey Type Q design evolved, in time to compete with a new Blackburn design for the Admiralty contract and, in August 1946, the Admiralty ordered two prototypes of both aircraft to be built.

Three years later, in early September 1949, the first prototype Type Q was completed at Fairey's Hayes factory and then dismantled for transport to Aldermaston where the concrete runways were preferred to White Waltham's grass. The Type Q was a big aircraft for transport by road and it must have been an impressive sight for the people of Slough, Maidenhead and Reading as it crawled its way along the A4, through the narrow streets of their towns.

The first flight was made on 19th September at Aldermaston and test flights followed in which the Type Q was found to have a number of aerodynamic problems. Modifications to its ailerons, elevators and rudder cured these problems and, from then on, all test pilots reported excellent flying characteristics. Deck-landing trials began soon after being followed by the first actual deck-landing on HMS *Illustrious* on 19th June 1950. Indeed, it was the first carrier landing by any turbo-prop aircraft. The future looked bright for the Type Q, until the Admiralty changed its mind again. They now required radar installed in the rear fuselage, an extra crew member to operate it, plus a larger weapons bay.

With the second Type Q prototype much too far advanced for the required alterations to be made, a third prototype was ordered. By the time this was flying, the name Gannet had been selected and one hundred aircraft had been ordered. The first Gannet AS1, as it was known, flew in May 1951, but the new radar radome, when lowered beneath the fuselage, was found to cause instability, which was cured by the addition of two small 'finlets' to the tailplane.

By 1953, Gannet AS1s were in full production at the Fairey factory at Hayes, where more than one hundred would eventually be built, as well as their factory at Stockport, where more than sixty were constructed. All Hayes-built aircraft went to White Waltham for final assembly and test flying and the first deliveries were made to the Fleet Air Arm from there in April 1954.

The Gannet offered a unique advantage for an aircraft in the anti-submarine role. The 'Double-Mamba' installation allowed either engine to be stopped and its propeller 'feathered' to allow the aircraft to cruise for many hours with optimum fuel economy. When both the engines were engaged, full power became available for take-off or attack.

The Gannet was the first anti-submarine aircraft to combine the 'hunter/killer' role. Previously, a 'hunter' had located the target for a 'killer' to attack, but communication problems, both visual and by radio, often reduced efficiency. However, the Gannet carried a complete specialist team working closely together. Its exceptionally deep fuselage also made it the first British-built operational naval aircraft to carry its major strike weapons—torpedos, bombs, depth charges and sonar bouys—internally. Air-to-surface rockets could also be carried beneath the wings, as well as additional sonar bouys.

When the Navy crews began flying the Gannet—their first turbo-prop aircraft—it was soon recognised that a trainer version was required. By August 1954, the prototype Gannet T2, the trainer version, first flew and deliveries to the Fleet Air Arm began early in 1955. In service, it became apparent that both the Gannet AS1 and T2 were slightly underpowered and, after development of an uprated 'Double Mamba' giving improved performance, the Gannet AS4 and T5 versions came into service although, by 1958, Whirlwind helicopters began to be used for the anti-submarine role. A new role awaited the Gannet.

Above: A Gannet AS1 at the 1953 Farnborough Air Show.

The next variant of the Gannet was the AEW3 Airborne Early Warning aircraft, the prototype flying in August 1949 and the first production aircraft being delivered in December 1949. The Admiralty had wanted a radar unit 'cannibalised' from a different aircraft to be installed in a Gannet AS1 but this proved impossible and a completely new fuselage had to be designed. In this, the radar unit was housed in a large radome fixed underneath, with the two operators seated within the fuselage.

More than forty AEW3s would eventually be supplied to the Navy and would prove to be one of its most effective aircraft. Indeed, on a number of occasions, Gannets also provided operational Army and RAF units with early warning support. It is probable that many more would have been built had not an incoming Government been making 'defence cuts'. For many years after, critics argued that the Navy was left vulnerable without the Gannet AEW3 and the Falklands conflict perhaps proved these comments justified.

Below: Gannet AEW3 Airborne Early Warning aircraft. Note the large radome permanently fixed under the fuselage, which resulted in it being known as the 'Guppy' version.

At White Waltham then, the 1950s was a time of increasing activity and diversity. Indeed, this could be applied to Berkshire's other main airfields – Woodley, Abingdon, Welford and also Greenham Common, the latter becoming an 'active' station again as the Cold War became decidedly chillier. Activities at all of them grew rapidly over a decade or more and, as a result, it would be confusing to try to tell all their stories in strict chronological order.

So, back to White Waltham where local people perhaps thought the hectic wartime days of the ATA had returned. Coincidentally, one ex-ATA pilot, Lettice Curtis, by then an employee of Fairey and a resident of Berkshire, was part of the team that took part in the Gannet's 'tropical' trials in Egypt.

Fairey Air Surveys had moved to White Waltham in 1947 with their fleet of six Dakotas fitted out for aerial surveying. Over the following years, the company operated many other types, such as the Dove, Auster, Anson, Rapide and Islander. Their crews could expect to be away from home for up to six months in a year and to be operating in any one of more than fifty countries.

Despite the loss of the first Gyrodyne, Fairey's helicopter division remained active. After thorough inspection, the second Gyrodyne flew again in 1953. However, although it generally resembled the first and used a similar Leonides engine, it had been extensively modified and now became known as the 'Jet Gyrodyne'. This was because a new two-bladed rotor had small fuel-burning jet units at the tips. The main engine no longer directly powered the rotor and, instead, drove two centrifugal compressors inside the rotor-head which supplied compressed air to the jets where it mixed with the fuel. The engine also powered two variable-pitch 'pusher' propellers situated at the end of stub wings, which provided the main forward thrust.

A number of tethered flights were made at White Waltham before the first free flight in January 1954. It was March 1955 before a full transition was made from vertical to horizontal flight but, by September 1956, some 190 transitions had been made. What was to become Fairey's 'signature' jet-helicopter principle had been well and truly tried and tested. Today, the airframe and rotor of this unique aircraft can be seen at the Museum of Berkshire Aviation.

Left: The Fairey Ultra Light helicopter

1956 also saw the first flight of Fairey's second helicopter using the 'rotor tip jet' principle – the tiny two-seat Ultra Light – which was exhibited at the Farnborough Air Show in September. Small enough to be flown from a three-ton lorry, it was designed to meet two duties for the Army – 'air observation' and 'air-runabout'. Powered by a Blackburn Turbomeca gas-turbine engine, forward flight was created by the usual helicopter 'tilting rotor' principle.

The RAF had returned to White Waltham in 1946, when it became home to Reserve Command. In 1950, the name changed to RAF Home Command and it was joined by RAF Flying Training Command, its communications flight moving over from Woodley. In the early 1950s, service aircraft to be seen at White Waltham included Mosquitos, Ansons, Balliols, Chipmunks, Dakotas, Mosquitos, Valettas, Vampires and even training gliders from the school originally at Bray.

Two other companies based at White Waltham regularly contributed to the variety of aircraft seen at the airfield. Personal Plane Services, run by Doug Bianchi, moved there from Blackbushe in 1950 and, until the 1960s, carried out a conventional business restoring aircraft. For him, the best was yet to come.

ML Aviation and its 'funnies' have gone down in aviation history, none more so than their inflatable wing aircraft, sometimes known as the 'Durex Delta'. Twelve different sized wings were developed by the RAE at Cardington. In August 1955, ML received a contract to design and build three aircraft to use the wings. This product of the Cold War, can be seen today at the Museum of Army Flying.

In November 1957, what could have been one of Britain's most important post-war airliners made its first flight at White Waltham – the Fairey Rotodyne.

For some years, Fairey had put forward various designs for a 'BEA Bus' and eventually won funding from the Government for further development. Then, in 1953, a contract was awarded to build a prototype. The four-seat 'Jet Gyrodyne' which flew again in 1953 after extensive modifications, can be seen to be part of the development programme.

Like its predecessor, the 24-seat Rotodyne had tip-jets on the end of the four rotor blades. It also had fixed stub-wings, under which two Napier 'Eland' turboprop engines were mounted. The four tip-jets were powered by compressors driven by the main engines and were used for take-off and landing, the turbo-prop propellers providing thrust for forward flight while the rotor auto-rotated. It was, in fact, one of the first large aircraft in what was to become a new class, the 'convertiplane', for which, in January 1959, it set a new world speed record of 191mph over a 100km closed circuit.

Indeed, from its very first flight, the Rotodyne performed well up to expectations and, as well as being fast, proved very safe. It could hover with one engine shut down with its propeller 'feathered' and many times made landings as an autogyro.

At that time many potential users were interested in the prospect of direct city-to-city transport by air and the Rotodyne was clearly a 'front runner' in this market. It could take off vertically from an inner-city 'heliport', with all lift coming from the tip-jet driven rotor, then make the transition to forward flight and, with all power from the main engines transferred to the propellers, the rotor would be auto-rotating. By this time, the rotor would be taking approximately 60% of the aircraft's weight, with the stub wings providing the rest of the 'lift'. On arrival at its destination the tip-jets would be re-started and the Rotodyne would land vertically like a helicopter.

In a demonstration flight, the Rotodyne flew from the centre of Brussels to the centre of Paris in just under one hour. In 1960, the fastest time using a fixed wing aircraft between the cities' airports, with road transfer to the city centres, was more than three hours. The fastest trains at the time took just under three hours.

Left: ML Aviation's 'Durex Delta'.

BEA announced that it was interested in buying six Rotodynes, with an option on up to twenty. The RAF ordered twelve military transport versions. New York Airways agreed to buy five, and possibly more. The US Army was interested in buying two hundred specially adapted Rotodynes to be manufactured by Fairey's American licensee. Government funding depended upon a firm order from BEA and, indeed, all the orders from civil operators were dependent upon noise problems being resolved. The tip-jets had proved to be somewhat noisy at low level, but Fairey were confident of reducing this problem. Even larger and more powerful versions of the Rotodyne were, by then, 'on the drawing board'.

In fact, the main problems faced by the Rotodyne were not technical but political. Seeking to cut costs, the Government decided that the number of aircraft companies must be reduced and demanded mergers among all airframe and engine manufacturers. By simply delaying or withholding defence contracts, the Government soon got its way and Westland took over Fairey Aviation, as well as the helicopter divisions of Bristol and Saunders Roe. However, the Rotodyne's future still seemed secure.

The larger version, fitted with Rolls Royce 'Tyne' engines was being developed to take between sixty and seventy-five passengers with a cruising speed of 230mph, or it would be able to carry nearly 7 tons of freight. This now was the version BEA said they wanted and a Government contract worth some £4.5 million was placed with Westland. However, the expected RAF and BEA orders never materialised, costs rose, delivery dates slipped and the American orders were cancelled. The Rotodyne project finally ground to a halt in February 1962 and, by 1964, the previous Fairey operation at White Waltham was closed.

Fairey Air Surveys' flying operations remained at White Waltham for many more years, although its offices moved into Maidenhead.

'Inter-City Express'

For more than a century, steam trains had provided the fast, comfortable means of travelling between major cities in Britain and, indeed, with certain major cities in Continental Europe. However, in the late 1950s, steam was being phased out by British Rail and replaced by diesel. In the air too, it was a time when inter-city travel, particularly with Europe, seemed set for dramatic changes and the Fairey Rotodyne, seen here at White Waltham , was in the forefront of this new technology which combined vertical take-off and landing advantages of helicopters with the higher cruising speeds of fixed-wing aircraft.

Painted in oils. 2007. 400mm x 300mm.

Painted in oils. 2007. 300mm x 400mm.

'Chasing thermals'

Two Elliott 'Olympia' type 401 sailplanes, built in 1954, are seen in the pursuit of thermals, the ever hopeful pilots 'feeling their way' towards even greater height and, of course, distance.

The type 401 was followed by a virtually annual flow of other improved models of the original German Olympia Meise design adapted by Chilton Aircraft in 1945 and taken over by Elliotts the following year. They culminated in the type 465, specifically designed for the 1965 World Championship.

Painted in watercolours. 2007. 180mm x 240mm.

Left: The Elliotts training glider was also based on an original German design, being an improved version of the Grunau SF 38 training glider. Countless ATC cadets gained their first taste of flying in this simple but very effective little flying machine.

For Elliotts of Newbury the 1950s was a decade when they gradually established themselves as one of the leading British manufacturers of sailplanes.

Their one attempt to break into the competitive market for powered light aircraft, the Newbury Eon, had won no customers. Indeed, in 1950, when it was being used as a 'tug' for a sailplane, it came to an ignominious end when it was wrecked in a rather bizarre accident on the ground. It seems the pilot attempted to start the Eon by swinging the propeller himself, but failed to get in when the aircraft suddenly moved forward. The pilot of the sailplane attached behind managed to jump out before both aircraft went through a boundary fence and were damaged beyond repair.

Although Elliotts made no more powered aircraft, they prospered as a sub-contractor for other aircraft manufacturers, including de Havilland, Vickers and Folland and, also, for the RAE at Farnborough.

However, their main claim to aviation fame was as a very successful manufacturer of sailplanes. Their 1946 decision to go straight into mass production of the Olympia meant sales took some time to catch up with stocks but, by 1948, two other German designs had been improved upon and added to the Elliott range. These were the DFS Grunau 'Baby' sailplane and the SF 38 training glider.

In 1954 Elliotts produced an improved version of the Olympia, known as the 401 and, in subsequent years, further improved types were made. Then, in 1961, the completely new Elliotts 460 'Standard Class' sailplane was introduced which became their most popular design and, in 1965, led to a special version, the type 465, which was built specifically for that year's world championship.

However, that year, Elliotts' managing director, HHC Buckingham, died suddenly. He had long supported the worldwide gliding fraternity, always trying to provide them with the very best sailplanes. It seems that this may not always have been with the company's financial interests in mind and, soon after his death, the Elliotts Board decided to cease sailplane production due they said, to its "increasing unprofitability". Elliotts' sailplane interests were taken over by the long-established Slingsby company but, effectively, another of Berkshire's 'brushes with aviation' had passed into history.

The Cold War of the 1950s brought the Americans back to Berkshire and both Greenham Common and Welford became active stations of the USAF again. Greenham Common was designated a strategic bomber base and the aircraft to be deployed there dictated a considerable upgrading of the runways, hangars and support facilities. This work mainly took place in the summer of 1951 starting with the demolition of wartime hangars and other buildings to allow the building of a massive ten thousand foot runway on top of the old east-west runway, although it extended well beyond this at both ends.

Rebuilding work was still not completed in September 1953, when the now completely reshaped airfield was declared ready for what were known as 'rotations' by American strategic bombers. However, it was March 1954 before well over two thousand personnel and the first B47 bombers arrived and, very soon, a problem became evident. The new runway wasn't strong enough for the large and heavy B47s and it began to break up.

It was April 1956 before the reinforced runway was completed and Greenham Common became home to a squadron of KC-97G Stratotankers, which soon showed up another problem. Somehow, flint stones kept working their way up to the surface of the runway and taxiways, often resulting in damage to propellers. From then on, runway sweeping was virtually a way of life for the American personnel at Greenham Common.

Yet more problems awaited them in October 1956 when it also became a permanent base for the B47 bombers. These were very noisy aircraft, both when taking off and landing, whilst the ground-running of engines and the almost constant noise of generators at the base led to growing protests by the people of Newbury. Opposition to the American base at Greenham Common reached a peak in March 1958 when a B47 experienced difficulties on take-off and had to jettison two full under-wing fuel tanks. These missed the designated 'safe area' at the airfield, one destroying a parked B47 and the other going through the roof of a hangar. Two US personnel were killed and eight were injured. The resulting fire burned for sixteen hours, despite the airfield fire crew being assisted by specialised fire crews and equipment from USAF Welford, RAF Odiham and civilian crews from as far as Reading and Hungerford.

Painted in oils on canvas. 2008 300mm x 380mm.

'Noisy neighbour'

When the large American B47 bombers moved onto the upgraded airfield at Greenham Common in 1956, there were immediate complaints from the residents of nearby Newbury about the excessive noise from the base. Changes to operating patterns for the resident aircraft reduced some of the noise.

The following month, American Strategic Air Command operational patterns were changed so that neither the B47s or their tankers flew so often. Nevertheless, local concerns were again voiced when yet more strengthening of the runway and taxiways began, this time to allow Greenham Common to handle the massive B52 bombers. In fact, no B52s were ever stationed there although, from 1960, they made periodic training visits. The early 1960s were critical years in the Cold War with the building of the Berlin Wall and the Cuban Missile Crisis. Greenham Common was on a high state of readiness, closed to the outside world, with fifteen B47s loaded with nuclear bombs, ready and waiting.

Berkshire's other active military airfield at Abingdon, continued its main post-war role with RAF Transport Command. Hastings and Valetta transports were the most common aircraft to be seen there in 1950. However, the following year, when the No.1 Overseas Ferry Unit transferred to Abingdon, Mosquitos, Oxfords and Harvards arrived for crew training. Soon after, American-built Sabre jet fighters flew in frequently, having been ferried across the Atlantic by the unit. In 1953, Abingdon took on an operational transport role, with a Hastings squadron flying troops out to Kenya. Then, in 1956, the giant Beverley transports arrived, beginning an association with Abingdon that would last more than ten years.

For Handley Page (Reading) at Woodley airfield, the 1950s began with the debacle of the HPR2 trainer. However, this was soon forgotten and their design team turned to a type of aircraft for which, over many years, their parent company had established a world-wide reputation—an airliner. It was, in fact, a 'private venture' aimed at the most competitive of all aviation markets—the 'Dakota replacement'. Before design work began, the company management had undertaken a comprehensive investigation into the requirements of airlines currently operating Dakotas. Although early turbo-prop engines were already in production, the investigation appeared to show that most operators, particularly those in the more 'primitive' parts of the world, would still prefer to have piston engines.

Above: At Woodley, one of the great pioneers of British Aviation, Sir Frederick Handley Page, stands in front of the wooden mock-up of the four-engine Leonides-powered Herald, when he introduces it to potential customers and the world's Press.

Largely based on the 1947 Miles M73 design, which had projected the use of four of the new Alvis Leonides piston engines, the HPR3 'Herald' was a forty-four-seat, pressurised 'feeder' liner. In January 1954, the Handley Page Board gave the go-ahead for two aircraft to be built at Woodley and authorised £1.5 million expenditure over three years, including the cost of jigs and tooling. The wooden mock-up was shown at the Farnborough Air Show in September, while a brochure of the time stated that *"Handley Page, convinced of the universal need on the world's short route and feeder line services of a work-a-day general-purpose airliner of good money-making potential for the operator, is building two prototypes of the Herald…... Basically the Herald is a pressurised high-wing monoplane of all-metal stressed skin construction with a single fin and rudder and twin tricycle undercarriage."*

In August 1955, the first prototype, having been built at Woodley, made its first flight at the Handley Page airfield at Radlett, where it had been taken by road for final assembly. Ominously, as it turned out, the new Vickers Viscount and Fokker Friendship, which was very similar to the Herald, were already flying with Rolls Royce Dart turbo-prop engines, but Handley Page were still convinced that the Leonides piston engines were what most potential customers wanted. At first, the company's confidence seemed justified and around thirty Heralds were on order when the fully-fitted second prototype was flown at the 1956 Farnborough Show in Queensland Airways livery. Flight tests for both prototypes continued apace at Woodley and the Leonides was proving very reliable. Success for the new aircraft seemed assured and a first production batch of twenty-five was begun at Woodley and a total of one hundred had been authorised by the Board. It should be remembered, of course, that this was a private venture for Handley Page and there was no Government funding.

Early in 1957, the success of the rival Friendship turbo-prop airliner was making Herald customers think again about their orders and, by April, the decision was taken to re-design the two prototypes for Dart turbo-prop engines. Although announced as an alternative to the Leonides-powered Herald, the Dart-Herald, as it became known, was eventually the only one to go into service.

The original prototype was converted to a Dart-Herald in about ten months and made its maiden flight from Woodley in March 1958, in the hands of the Handley Page chief test pilot, Sq Ldr Hazelden, who reported considerable improvements in both handling and performance. In just five weeks, around fifty hours of test-flying were completed without problems but, in August, after nearly two hundred hours of flying, disaster struck. Just thirty minutes into a flight from Woodley for photography on the way to Farnborough for the 1958 Air Show, with Hazelden at the controls, a fire broke out in the starboard engine nacelle. After a rapid descent and a skilful crash landing, the aircraft completely burnt out. However, the pilot's prompt action undoubtedly saved the life of everyone aboard, including his wife. A gold watch from Sir Frederick Handley Page and a Queen's Commendation for 'valuable services in the air' were subsequently awarded to Hazelden.

Crash investigators concluded that the fire that destroyed the first Herald resulted from a fault in the Dart engine. The second converted Herald made its first flight in December and the Woodley team went into 1959 hard at work on its flight-test programme and, also, on construction of the first of a production line of ten Heralds. Official confidence in the new turbo-prop Herald was shown when the Ministry of Civil Aviation ordered three for BEA to use on its Scottish Highlands and Islands routes.

Optimism at Woodley in 1959 changed within a year or so, when it became apparent that their parent company was in trouble. Handley Page had always depended heavily upon Government contracts and these seemed more and more unlikely without the company merging with another manufacturer. Sir Frederick Handley Page fiercely opposed this, but the reality of the problem was demonstrated when a contract for further Victor bombers was cancelled.

Sadly, within two years, Sir Frederick died and Handley Page found itself in financial difficulties. The decision had already been taken to move Herald production to Radlett and Cricklewood and it was planned to close Handley Page (Reading) by 1963. Within a short time the Herald was the main hope for Handley Page's future and, during the 1960s, around fifty were to be built but, in the long run, it could not save the company.

After thirty years of aircraft manufacture at Woodley, the Herald was the last aircraft to be built there and, within a short time, the airfield was being used for gravel extraction.

'Prince among Pilots'

One of the last tasks carried out at Handley Page (Reading) was the conversion of Herald G-APWA ('Whiskey Alpha') from standard BEA layout with forty-four seats to an executive twenty-one-seat layout for the personal use of HRH Prince Philip on his forthcoming eleven-country promotional tour of South America early in 1962. BEA also provided Herald G-APWC in its standard layout, as well as the crews for both aircraft. The Heralds were fitted with long-range fuel tanks for their flight across the Atlantic. In February 1962, Prince Philip and his entourage flew out to British Guiana to begin the tour, during which 'Whiskey Alpha' flew thirty-four out of the fifty-five days, with a total flying time of one-hundred and-twenty-seven hours. Prince Philip was at the controls for ninety-nine out of the one-hundred-and-twelve hours he spent on board. 'Whiskey Alpha' was re-converted to standard layout after the tour and, over a long career, flew with many different airlines. In the early 1990s, it returned in pieces to Woodley, to the Museum of Berkshire Aviation where a small group of Handley Page enthusiasts rebuilt it. Over thirty years after he flew it, in April 1997, Prince Philip visited the Museum to officially unveil 'Whiskey Alpha' to the public again.

Painted in oils on canvas. 2000. 500mm x 600mm. The original painting is now in the personal collection of HRH Prince Philip.

By the mid-1960s, the demise of Miles, Fairey and Handley Page (Reading) had brought an end to some thirty years of large scale aircraft manufacture in Berkshire. However, the mid-1960s was also the time when Doug Bianchi's Personal Plane Services at White Waltham became a manufacturer and, under a new name, Bianchi Aviation Film Services, began a career, the results of which can still be seen in some of the best aviation films ever made.

It was 1962 when Doug was approached by Twentieth Century Fox to build and operate replicas of veteran aircraft for their proposed film to be called 'Those Magnificent Men in their Flying Machines'. When it appeared in 1965, the film was a huge hit and probably did more than anything else to make the general public aware of aviation history and to 'kick start' the subsequent big business of aircraft refurbishment and replica building.

Most of the aviation sequences for 'Magnificent Men' were filmed at or near Booker airfield near High Wycombe and, in 1965, Doug Bianchi moved his operations there permanently. 'The Blue Max', which appeared in 1966, was also associated with White Waltham. Other well-known feature films such as 'Indiana Jones and the Last Crusade', as well as 'A Bridge Too Far' and 'The Eagle Has Landed' included aviation sequences by his company. Although its founder died some years ago, Bianchi Aviation Film Services exists still and many films and television productions feature on its credits list.

'Those Magnificent Men in their Flying Machines' also involved two people who have already played important roles in the story of Berkshire aviation. The first was Joan Hughes, the ex-ATA pilot and, by the early 1960s, chief flying instructor at the West London Aero Club at White Waltham. When Doug Bianchi's company built one of the undoubted stars among the film's actual flying machines—the tiny Demoiselle, supposedly flown by the amorous French pilot—it was found to be so small that the 'petite' Joan Hughes was the only pilot who could actually fly it. Not only did she make its first test flight at White Waltham, but she then went on to be the pilot in all of its actual flying sequences.

It is understood that three versions of the main aircraft were built, although only one of each could actually fly. The other two were used for close-ups and crash sequences.

Painted in oils on canvas. 2008. 400mm x 500mm.

'Those Magnificent Men (and Woman) in their Flying Machines'

Two 'stars' of the successful 1965 film that helped to 'kickstart' today's public interest in aviation heritage. The biplane Bristol Boxkite dwarfs the tiny monoplane 'Desmoiselle', which was originally designed by the diminutive Brazilian, Alberto Santos-Dumont, for his own use. The exact replica of the Desmoiselle was too small to be flown by most male pilots and it was test flown and then flown in all flying sequences in the film by Joan Hughes.

The other Berkshire personality to make a major contribution to the film's flying sequences was George Miles. By the 1960s he was working with his brother again, designing and building aircraft where they had first started, at Shoreham in Sussex. It was there that they had returned in 1952 after a few years in Redhill, where the reconstituted FG Miles Limited went back to work. In 1962 George Miles was contacted by the film-makers and finished up being responsible for another of the film's flying 'stars'. It was actually a Bristol Boxkite but, in the film, it played the aircraft flown by the American 'hero', Orvil. Presumably he was named Orvil with a nod in the direction of the Wright brothers, even though the first brother to actually fly spelt his name Orville.

Above: George Miles, about to make the first flight in the Bristol Boxkite which he designed and built. It was to be one of the 'stars' of the 1965 film 'Those Magnificent Men in their Flying Machines'.

For the Miles brothers, following the destruction of their Berkshire activities, the '50s and '60s were productive and yet, often frustrating years. FG Miles had established a new company with a small nucleus of former Woodley employees at Redhill airfield. His first project there was the M75 Aries, a Gemini with more powerful engines. Just two were built.

In December 1950, another piece of Berkshire history re-surfaced when the M5 Sparrowhawk, G-ADNL, originally designed by Blossom Miles for FG to fly in the 1935 King's Cup, came to Redhill for a major re-design. G-ADNL had been with various owners since its 'war service' and, the current one, Fred Dunkerley, saw its potential as a 'jet age' racer.

A year or so later FG Miles moved his company to Shoreham airfield, where his aviation career had begun and there he was joined once again by his brother George. The 'Sparrowjet', as it became known, was first flown at Shoreham by George Miles in December 1953 and it was his first flight in a jet.

G-ADNL enjoyed its finest moment in 1957 when, twenty-two years after its first attempt to win the King's Cup, it did just that, flown by Fred Dunkerley. Even more remarkable perhaps, Miles designs took four of the first five places, repeating the record-breaking achievement of the 1935 race. A Falcon Six was second, a Monarch third and a Magister fifth. It was a 'clean sweep' again for Miles designs and no other manufacturer ever achieved it even once.

Soon after George first flew the Sparrowjet in 1953, the Miles brothers decided to design and build a jet trainer, hoping to gain orders for the Services. This would be a difficult task because the Percival Jet Provost had already been ordered for the RAF, but George felt they could produce a competitive aircraft at about half the cost and offering significantly better fuel consumption. Although a unique design with many outstanding features was completed quickly, limited resources meant that its first flight did not take place until May 1957, too late for consideration by the Services. The M100 Student, as it was called, certainly lived up to the Miles brothers' expectations and could have been a very successful Services trainer. Later, it was fitted with a more powerful engine and plans to build a version in South Africa for their Air Force had to be abandoned when the UK Government embargoed the supply of any aircraft to that country.

Painted in watercolours. 2008. 230mm x 270mm

'King's Cup encore' *The Sparrowjet version of G-ADLC was the first jet-powered aircraft to win the prestigious King's Cup Air Race, twenty-two years after the first version raced with distinction in the 1935 race. In both races, Miles designs took first, second, third and fifth places, a feat never equalled by any other manufacturer.*

'Bright Student' *The M100 Student, as it appeared at Duxford in a striking red, white and blue livery some thirty years after it first flew. Unfortunately, at a display, an engine cut-out was followed by a high-speed forced landing. This resulted in severe damage to the fuselage and ended its flying days. Subsequently, a team of enthusiasts at the Museum of Berkshire Aviation undertook to rebuild this unique aircraft to display standards.*

Painted in watercolours. 2008. 220mm x 290mm

Painted in watercolours. 2008. 170mm x 250mm.

'The French Connection' *The HDM 105 research aircraft was a joint venture with the Hurel Dubois company.
It incorporated the French company's 'high aspect ratio' wing design with a fuselage obviously derived from the Miles M57 Aerovan.*

'Pioneering again in Sussex' *The attractive Miles B218 four-seater incorporated a high proportion of glass fibre in its
construction, a pioneering aviation use for this now commonly used material around 1960 when the design was conceived.*

Painted in watercolours. 2008. 230mm x 280mm.

After the war, the French company Hurel-Dubois had pioneered aircraft designs with 'high aspect ratio wings', essentially long, narrow, thin wings like those used on high-performance sailplanes. These contrasted with almost every Miles design, which had tended towards 'low aspect ratio wings', that is to say quite wide and thick relative to their span.

In 1955, George Miles became interested in the French company's work, particularly with regard to freight aircraft designed for a low cruising speed. This led to co-operation between the two companies in the design and construction of the HDM 105, a research aircraft based on a Miles Aerovan fuselage. This first flew in March 1957 and flight trials proved so successful that a joint company was formed in order to exploit derivatives of this type of aircraft. The HDM 106 was a design based on the larger Miles Merchantman but, for reasons unknown, was never put into production. Instead, the design was sold to Shorts, eventually becoming the basis for their very successful Skyvan model.

During the late 1950s a steadily increasing flow of foreign-built light aircraft, mainly American, was coming into the UK. George Miles was well aware of this fact and was working on competitive designs to reduce these imports and hopefully gain much needed export earnings. He had developed three designs by 1960, the smallest being a cheap, simple two-seater with a fixed tricycle undercarriage. This was the M114 Mk I and was designed as a flying-club trainer or a cheap private-owner aircraft to be powered by a 100hp Rolls Royce Continental engine. The other two designs were comparable with George's 1940s Messenger and Gemini four-seaters. Rolls Royce Continental six-cylinder engines were to be fitted, a 145hp model specified for the single-engine M114 MK II and two 100hp models for the M115. Unlike the wooden construction of the 1940s designs, the new aircraft had an aluminium load-carrying structure, with the rest of the airframe mainly in glass fibre. Indeed, glass fibre was used for some 60% of the aircraft's surface area, representing a pioneering aviation use for this material at the time. Detail design work for these three aircraft was underway at Shoreham when, in February 1961, the aviation work of FG Miles Ltd was acquired by a new British company.

British Executive and General Aviation had been formed by the directors of Pressed Steel at Oxford, who had recruited Peter Masefield from the Bristol company to run it, specifically to target the light aeroplane market. Two of the leading exponents in this field, Miles and Auster, were quickly acquired by Masefield and the expanded organisation was eventually renamed Beagle Aircraft Limited.

The Board of the new company gave priority to a design originating at Bristol which it hoped would win a large Ministry contract and it was not until October 1961 that construction of prototypes of the M114 MkII and the M115 was authorised, the latter being re-designated the M218 to fall in with Beagle numbering for a twin-engine aircraft. To improve the performance of the M218 when flying fully-loaded on just one engine, George Miles now specified the more powerful 145hp Continental engines, thus making the new aircraft more comparable with his brother's M75 Aries of 1951, rather than the Gemini.

The first flight of the M218 was made in August 1962, with George himself at the controls. It proved to be an outstanding aircraft but, frustratingly, never went into production because the limited resources of Beagle were fully committed to their B206 design and that illusive Ministry contract.

It was around this time that George Miles became involved in, at least for him, a completely new type of aircraft—an autogyro. RAF officer, Ken Wallis had been building and flying autogyros at Shoreham when George Miles suggested they co-operate on a design for an Army Air Corps contract. The result was the WA 116, three of which were built by Beagle-Miles for evaluation and, over a number of years was flown by Wallis at military and civilian air shows and broke many records for the type. Success prompted Wallis to leave the RAF and concentrate on building autogyros, most famously the one in the James Bond film 'You only live twice'.

George next turned his fertile design brain to a class of aircraft in which no British manufacturers were attempting to compete. 'Executive jets' were a virtual monopoly of the Americans with just a few European designs also in the reckoning.

Existing or projected designs for jet or propeller-turbine aircraft varied considerably in terms of their performance, as well as the number of passengers and the price, resulting in the important 'price per seat' factor. Examining data for eighteen different designs, George arrived at a combination of these variables that he was sure would attract the widest market. Eventually, he opted to design an eight-seater with a relatively high performance and a low cost, his target price being approximately £80,000.

What evolved was the Century, an attractive high-wing monoplane, sitting low on the ground, with a tricycle undercarriage. With an all-metal construction, it would be powered by two French-built Turbomeca engines. A maximum speed of 450mph was projected with an economic cruising speed of 350mph. Its maximum range would be sixteen hundred miles, reducing to thirteen hundred miles when carrying its maximum payload. If the target price of £80,000 was achieved, the Century's price per seat would be just £10,000, compared with from £15,000 to £50,000 for its competitors.

A full-size wooden mock-up was built and George wasted no time in presenting his design to the Ministry of Transport. Don Brown reported in his book that there it was "received with enthusiasm" and a Government grant of 50% of the development cost was immediately offered, with the manufacturer providing the other 50%. Great interest was being shown in the Century in both the UK and America but, despite this, in the financial climate of that time, the money was simply not available and perhaps the most promising design George Miles ever created slipped into obscurity.

Although George Miles continued to be involved with aviation projects for some twenty years after 1964 when the Century was projected, it can perhaps be seen as the very last of the remarkable succession of designs created by the Miles brothers, many of them being built in appreciable numbers and flown with distinction in both war and peace. The story of their work up to the time of the Woodley Company's destruction in 1947 has been covered exhaustively in this book and in others over the years. Sadly, it is probable that, if Samuel Hogg and Barclays Bank hadn't done the job for them, the Government of the time would have forced Miles Aircraft into a merger that would have stultified the individuality that made them unique in British, if not world aviation.

As stated earlier, their designs for large aircraft, no matter how enterprising and advanced, were beyond their company's ability to manufacture. However, the work back at Shoreham cemented the well-proven ability of Miles to design aircraft in the categories of the Messenger, the Gemini, the Merchantman and, without Ministry interference, the Marathon.

The destructive Mayo report of 1947 criticised the Miles wooden-built aircraft, although George Miles always maintained that, at the time, relative to its weight, wood was the strongest material and the easiest to work and repair. Mayo, of course, was also unaware of further developments at Woodley in glues and the resin-bonding of moulded wood. It was, no doubt, beyond his imagining that, just three years down the line, FG Miles would form a Plastics Division which developed a load-bearing aircraft skin from a phenolic/asbestos material, stabilised with a paper honeycomb. Or that George Miles would later use a combination of aluminium and glass fibre in a pioneering aircraft design.

Looking back, it can be suggested that, if Miles Aircraft had been able to secure adequate funding in 1947, they would have been capable of developing, like no other British manufacturer, into a world-beater in the lighter end of the civil aircraft market, reversing the flow of imports that grew year by year in that post-war period.

Could it have happened? Perhaps, on a level playing-field. But, with a Government intent on its blinkered vision of what the aviation industry should be, perhaps that is a fantasy just too far.

Painted in watercolours. 2008. 180mm x 310mm.

Left: The Miles Century project from the early 1960s.

Painted in oils on canvas. 1999. 450mm x 600mm.

'Croydon's sunset'

After an eventful life of some forty-four years, London's famous Croydon Airport was finally to close on 30th September 1959. By the time the final scheduled flight arrived – a Morton Airways' de Havilland Dove from Newmarket – there was a sizeable crowd witnessing the last sad moments of this once great airport. As the famous clocks on the control tower showed 18.39, the final scheduled flight departed. It was another of Morton Airways' fleet, a de Havilland Heron bound for Rotterdam. Ironically, it was piloted by Captain Last. Soon after, the few remaining small airliners also departed – empty – and the crowd began to disperse. Very few took any notice of a small bonfire by the hangars some way from the main terminal and hangars. On top of the bonfire was an effigy of the Minister of Transport, the final gesture of protesters who had fiercely opposed Croydon Airport's closure. Among them was Christopher de Vere, later the first secretary of the Croydon Airport Society. It was almost dusk when he climbed into his Miles Gemini, G-AJWE. As it sped across the grass runway, bound for Gatwick*, just a few miles away, the sound of its engines echoed weirdly in the empty hangars. The very last aircraft had left Croydon. In 1959 there were more than fifty Geminis still on the British Register of Civil Aircraft and many more flying overseas. There were also nearly as many Messengers on the Register, in a total of some one hundred and fifty Miles aircraft, which included many pre-war designs, such as Magisters, Falcons, Whitney Straights and Monarchs.

Postscript. *This story originated in a small book, 'Croydon Airport Flypast' by Peter Cooksley, published in 1984 by the London Borough of Sutton Libraries and Arts Services. Among many other excellent colour profiles of historic aircraft flown from Croydon was an elevation of G-AJWE. The painting seen here, 'Croydon's Sunset', was completed many years later and, with an interpretation of Peter Cooksley's original text was included in the geoffbeckett.com website. In December 2008, having seen the website for the first time, John Prytherch sent an e-mail saying that, on that evening in September 1959, G-AJWE was actually flown to Biggin Hill and not Gatwick. He should know. He was one of the passengers!*

Returning to Berkshire, what was happening at the remaining active airfields, Abingdon, Greenham Common, Welford and White Waltham through the 1960s and beyond?

By the early years of the decade, Abingdon had become one of the busiest airfields in the UK, with over two thousand aircraft movements every month, many of these being overseas flights. Transport Command had operated Blackburn Beverleys out of Abingdon since the late 1950s. These one-hundred-and-sixty-two-foot wingspan giants, which could carry bulky loads but were also able to operate from small rough airstrips, were in the forefront of the RAF's research into movement of heavy freight and large scale air movements. This was completed by 1967, by which time Abingdon had become the training base for the RAF's new Andover aircraft, before they were moved to a new base in 1970.

Two years earlier, Abingdon had been chosen as the venue for the 50th Anniversary celebrations of the RAF. The Queen lunched in the Officer's Mess and inspected a display of historic RAF aircraft, many of which were destined for the new Hendon Museum. However, the celebrations were generally low-key because, at that time, the RAF 'top brass' was unhappy with the Government which seemed to want missiles rather than aircraft and most felt was unsympathetic to the Service and its traditions.

Further changes were underway at Abingdon by 1974, when the changes to the county boundaries transferred the airfield to Oxfordshire, along with a number of Berkshire's other historic aviation sites. From the mid-1970s Abingdon became one of the RAF's most important bases for the overhaul and repair of aircraft. Jaguars, Hunters and Hawks were mainly to be seen there, but most RAF fixed-wing

types could also be seen over the years, including the ex-British Airways VC 10s destined for conversion. A particularly interesting major service carried out at Abingdon was for the RAF's sole Lancaster 'City of Lincoln' from their historic Battle of Britain Flight. Bulldogs of the University of London Air Squadron and Oxford University Air Squadron were also residents of Abingdon beyond 1993, when the RAF finally abandoned the airfield.

Above: In September 1990, Abingdon was the venue for an air display to commemorate the 50th Anniversary of the Battle of Britain.

Painted in watercolours. 2008. 250mm x 320mm.

'Reverse thrust'

A watercolour version by Geoff Beckett of a David Shepherd original oil painting 'Reverse thrust at Beihan, West Aden Protectorate', featuring an RAF Blackburn Beverley. Until Abingdon closed, David Shepherd's original oil painting hung in the Officer's Mess there.

Painted in watercolours. 2008. 160mm x 250mm.

'Landing with a clutch of records'

Excitement among air-spotters in the Newbury area was intense when, on 16th October 1963, a B58 Hustler bomber landed at Greenham Common. In fact, this was the end of a record-breaking flight over Tokyo, Alaska, Canada, Greenland, Iceland and London, in eight hours thirty-five minutes at an average speed of 938mph. Five hours were spent at supersonic speeds, five aerial re-fuellings were carried out and a total of five world records was established on the flight. The highly advanced delta-wing Hustler was the only bomber of its time that could fly at more than twice the speed of sound and at an altitude of sixty thousand feet.

In the Cold War, the high drama of the 1962 Cuban Missile Crisis had been replaced by a sort of sullen watchfulness by East and West. The USAF had been building up its fleet of strategic bombers such as the B52 and both sides had developed and deployed intercontinental ballistic missiles. Though still a formidable aircraft, Greenham Common's B47s had aged in terms of technology and new types such as the swing-wing F111, were being developed.

In 1963, the USAF announced that the B47 was to be withdrawn from service and, in November of that year, a joint statement by the Air Ministry and the USAF indicated that the Americans would be leaving Greenham Common the following year.

The people of Newbury paid tribute to their American neighbours when, on 5th May 1964, thousands lined the streets of the town centre as two hundred and fifty airmen from Greenham Common marched by in a farewell parade. In the Market Place they were addressed by the mayor and, in return, the base commander presented a banner bearing his group's emblem and a leather-bound book telling the history of the USAF units that had been stationed at Greenham Common over the years.

A month later, on 4th June, the last B47 left and, on 1st July 1964, the airfield was formally handed back to the RAF.

In fact, it was not long before the Americans were back. In 1966, to the surprise of all the other nations in NATO, the French president announced their intention to withdraw and ordered the closure of all American bases in France. A number of USAF units quickly moved to British bases and, in January 1967, it was announced that it was also to move back to Greenham Common, although some time would elapse before flying operations were resumed.

Although the Cold War remained distinctly chilly, there were moves toward Strategic Arms Limitation Talks and, in 1968, a major arms control exercise took place at Greenham Common with the aim of building up experience of arms control verification procedures and techniques.

In 1970 the base was reactivated for regular flying operations. Air Traffic Control was re-established for twenty-four hour operations and, in the autumn, the Flintlock 1970 exercise saw well over two hundred flights by some ninety transports from other USAF bases fly in and out of Greenham Common. A similar scale exercise was held at the base a year later and, although the Flintlock 1972 exercise moved to another USAF base, many interesting transports visited Greenham Common at that time, including the first visit by a giant C5 transport. 1976 saw the Flintlock exercise return to Greenham Common.

1976 also saw Greenham Common reactivated as an operational base for three months, for the first time in thirteen years. USAF F111 swing-wing bombers were redeployed from Upper Heyford while runways there were resurfaced. The following year, it looked as if Greenham Common might be the UK home of the large and noisy Boeing KC135 Stratotankers and work began on extending and refurbishing the runways and taxiways. A storm of protests from local people resulted and, eventually, the Government rejected the plan on the grounds that aircraft could, too easily, fly over the nearby Aldermaston Atomic Weapons Establishment.

Then, from 1978 to 1980, Greenham Common was the venue for an exercise involving many different US Army helicopters from units based in West Germany. These exercises often included a chance for crews to carry out live firing at the Salisbury Plain ranges.

1973 saw the first of Greenham Common's many International Air Tattoos which, over the next ten years, went on to become Europe's leading military air show and even began to 'steal' visitor numbers from the long-established Farnborough Air Show. Some sixty thousand eager spectators descended on the airfield for that weekend in July 1973. The 1974 show, which hosted fifteen Air Arms from eight countries, attracted even more spectators, special charter flights bringing enthusiasts from Ireland, West Germany and Holland, while six coach-loads came by road from Scotland. By the 1976 show, billed as a Hawker Hunter Meet, spectator numbers had doubled to one hundred and twenty thousand.

However, it was the 1979 show that really proved, although it was still only a 'standby base', Greenham Common was a model of efficiency. In just a few days, aircraft and crews from all over the world were handled and accommodated. Two hundred and sixty aircraft from twenty-two countries took part. The flying programme lasted seven hours and included fifty-five items, whilst there were one hundred and twelve aircraft in the static parks. In fact, the number of aircraft on show was greater than the whole Air Arm of some countries exhibiting there.

Four anniversaries were commemorated at the 1979 show. The venerable C130 Hercules was twenty-five years old and there were twenty-six of them on show in the static park from eighteen different Air Arms. It was the 60th anniversary of the RAF Benevolent Fund and the 30th anniversary of the founding of NATO.

The other anniversary—sixty years since the first non-stop air crossing of the Atlantic—was celebrated by the appearance of two RAF officers and their much decorated Phantom, which had achieved the same feat a week or two before, albeit with the aid of a refuelling tanker. The crew of that historic 1919 flight in a Vickers Vimy were, of course, Alcock and Brown and the 1979 crew were, wait for it, Alcock and Browne. The Phantom pilot was indeed the nephew of the original pioneer but perhaps surprisingly, there seem to have been no Phantom navigators in the RAF at that time with the more common spelling of Brown.

Before going on to recount the final and perhaps best remembered phase of Greenham Common's illustrious military career, there were, around 1980, a number of non-military events at the airfield that are worthy of mention.

The airfield was sometimes used for gliding at that time and it was chosen as the venue for the 1981 National Gliding Championships. Sadly, of the ten days in May allocated, just two were suitable for gliding. An unusual event at the Championship was the competition for the Kremer prize, to be awarded for a figure-of-eight flight in a man-powered aircraft. Over the previous year or so, local people could well have seen the Newbury Man-Flier at Greenham Common being flown by pilot Simon Grant as he attempted this difficult feat. Eventually, both Grant and the aircraft's designer Nick Goodhart were beaten by a structural failure that prevented the Newbury Man-Flier from flying on the crucial day.

Although not one of Greenham Common's many 'brushes with aviation', an attempt on the land speed record must have seemed very much like flying for the driver Richard Noble. Indeed, his vehicle was powered by a 35,000hp Rolls Royce aircraft engine and, in September 1980, he set a new British record, at Greenham Common, with a speed of 248mph. The following year, he broke six more British land speed records there, paving the way for his later jet vehicle driven by RAF pilot Andy Green which, on a dried lakebed in the USA in the 1990s, pushed the world speed record to 633mph.

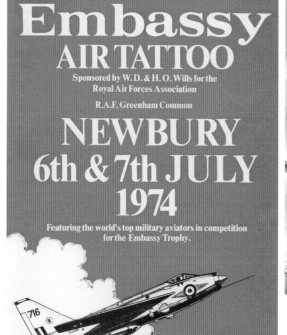

A little known fact is that, in the early 1980s, Greenham Common also played a part in the US space programme when it was chosen by NASA as one of the Trans Oceanic Abort Landing Sites for the Space Shuttle. That role has eventually passed to RAF Fairford although, so far, the UK has never been called upon to help out with a Space Shuttle landing.

Far left: The poster for the very first of eight International Air Tattoos which were held at Greenham Common between 1973 and 1983.

Left: Programme cover for the 5th Greenham Common International Air Tattoo which commemorated four aviation anniversaries.

International Air Tattoo 1979
RAF Greenham Common, Newbury, Berks Saturday 23 and Sunday 24 June
In aid of the Royal Air Force Benevolent Fund and in association with **Nationwide Building Society**

Looking back to the Cold War situation in 1980, it had become evident to NATO that, during the 1970s, while seeming to co-operate in the Arms Limitation Agreement, the Russians had used various loopholes to significantly increase their overall number of nuclear weapons. It was this new threat that had accelerated the development by the Americans of what became known as Ground Launched Cruise Missiles (GLCM) and brought about a new life for Greenham Common.

In December 1979, the NATO Council of Ministers approved the deployment of GLCM in five of their European Member States and, in June 1980, the British Government announced that Greenham Common would be one of two UK bases where they would be stored, with the first arriving in late 1983.

The Government attitude was summed up by Prime Minister Margaret Thatcher in 1981, as follows. *"The British view towards those who resist the Cruise missile is that the effect should be to say to the Soviet Union: Look! You have the most modern, up-to-date, theatre nuclear weapons…. You have them targeted on every country in Europe and you increase their numbers at the rate of rather more than one a week. Do you really expect us to sit back and do nothing? If you don't want us to have Cruise missiles in Europe as a deterrent to you using yours, then dismantle yours. Take them down. Agree to be inspected so that we know what you are doing. I know the worries. I do not like nuclear weapons either, but I value my freedom and my children's freedom, and their children's freedom, and I am determined that it shall continue."*

Cruise missiles would never be fired from Greenham Common, because a major part of the GLCM system were specially designed Transporter/ Erector/Launcher vehicles and, in times of crisis, these would take the missiles to pre-selected launch sites up to two hundred miles away. A regular part of the deployment at Greenham Common were the exercises whereby convoys of these launch vehicles, with their various communications, support and guard vehicles, practised dispersals. Such exercises put the civilian population at minimum risk because actual missiles and warheads were never transported. In terms of noise nuisance for local people, re-opening Greenham Common would also have little effect, because there would only be a few movements each month by transport aircraft.

In 1981, a major development of the base began. Six massive, specially-hardened shelters were constructed to protect the Launcher and support vehicles and the overall security infrastructure of the base was greatly strengthened. Some thirteen hundred USAF personnel were expected to be based at Greenham Common and a building programme for family accommodation was undertaken in Newbury and many surrounding areas as far afield as Reading, Andover and Wantage.

Not surprisingly, in view of their long and close association, the USAF personnel were welcomed back by the majority of Newbury people as old friends. It appears that the same could not be said of the protest groups that began to gather outside the airfield. A book primarily about aviation is not the place to discuss all the politics involved in these final years of Greenham Common's proud time as an airfield. The facts are that the end of the Cruise missile years there had nothing to do with protests in Britain or anywhere else and everything to do with the economic collapse of the Soviet Union, the defeat of its belligerent 'old guard' government and the eventual disintegration of the East European 'Warsaw Pact' empire it had enslaved since 1945.

It was December 1987 when the treaty was agreed to scrap all intermediate range nuclear missiles. The second UK Cruise missile site in Cambridgeshire had not received its full quota of missiles when the new treaty came into force and the decision was taken to remove all equipment from there first. Thus it was that Greenham Common's missiles and associated equipment did not begin to be flown out until August 1989. The last sixteen missiles were flown out in March 1991 and, in May, it was announced that the Greenham Common USAF unit, comprising some sixteen hundred military personnel and one hundred and twenty civilians, would be closed down, with just four hundred airmen remaining on a standby basis to conform to treaty requirements.

Throughout this time aircraft movements at the airfield were just flights in and out by the giant USAF transports used to take the Cruise missiles and their associated equipment back to the US for destruction and the Aeroflot Ilyushin airliners bringing the Russian inspectors on their agreed regular visits to both the UK bases. In June 1992, Greenham Common ceased to be a military airfield. By 1997, the runway and taxiways were being broken up and much of this historic site has since been returned to the common land from which it was created.

Below: A typical scene at Greenham Common around 1990, as a USAF C5 Galaxy transport takes off carrying Cruise missiles and their support equipment back to the US for destruction.

Since the early 1950s, when the Cold War had brought the USAF back to Berkshire, the fortunes of Greenham Common and Welford were closely linked. Welford actually re-opened in September 1955 as a non-nuclear munitions storage area and has remained in this role to the present day, playing its vital role in more recent conflicts. Substantial stocks of ammunition had been held by the USAF since WWII, at a number of former airfields of RAF Bomber Command. This was transferred to Welford, where new ammunition storage buildings were built by the side of the old main runway and a new series of bomb revetments were constructed.

By the end of the 1950s, Welford could boast some fifteen miles of railway track and sixteen miles of paved roads within the huge site, which enclosed eight hundred and fifty acres, within a perimeter fence more than seven miles long. Originally, most munitions arrived at the site by rail from the docks in South Wales via the main line and a specially built three-mile line from the Newbury to Lambourn branch line. The M4 motorway, when constructed in 1972, came close enough to Welford to allow a road to link it directly to the base and this was one reason why the rail link was abandoned.

The M4's Membury Service Area also plays its part in commemorating another of West Berkshire's World War II American airfields. Membury airfield was abandoned by the Air Ministry in 1955 and sold off, much of it reverting to agricultural land, athough enough remained for a small industrial estate and, in the 1960s, another 'brush with aviation'.

It was a company called Campbell Aircraft that, in 1969, designed an autogyro very much like the Ken Wallis design built by Miles in the early 1960s. It was powered by a 72hp Volkswagen four-cylinder engine and was known as the Cricket. It first flew from Membury in July 1969 and, subsequently, over forty were built. Not one remains to be seen today, but a more powerful model, the Cougar, was also built and is now on display at the Helicopter Museum.

Although it seems Campbell Aircraft may have abandoned Membury in the early 1970s because of the construction of the M4 motorway, ten years or so later enough of the original site remained for it to be called Membury Airfield again and to play its part in another of Berkshire's 'brushes with aviation'.

Above: The Chevvron 2-32 and its designer, Angus Fleming.

At Membury, in 1983, the prototype of the AMF Chevvron 2-32 microlight made its first flight. At the time, most microlights were little more than 'hang-gliders' with a 'motorcycle-sidecar' type of fuselage and a simple engine slung beneath. The Chevvron's designer, Angus Fleming, set out to design something very different—an aircraft that combined the low purchase and running costs of a microlight, with the sophistication and practicality of a light aircraft and the gliding ability of a motorglider. In 1987, it was granted full CAA approval— the very first microlight for which Lloyds of London offered insurance.

The Chevvron offered a surprisingly roomy cabin for two people with dual controls, while its 32hp four-cylinder two-stroke radial engine was very reliable and astonishingly quiet. AMF claimed that advanced production techniques and the use of new composite materials gave the Chevvron a very strong but lightweight structure with a high-quality surface finish. The unique Chevvron proved popular, both with flying clubs and private owners and forty were sold around the world.

In 1997, Angus Fleming changed the name of his company to Aviation Enterprises Limited and, still operating from Membury Airfield, now describes its activities as a specialist design, development and manufacturing organisation specialising in the light aviation industry and the application of high-tech composite materials, in particular, design for light-weight and high performance. Although offering a varied range of other products including wind-turbines and water-turbines, Aviation Enterprises maintains the long tradition of Berkshire as a home for aircraft manufacturer, offering a similar, though more advanced development of the Chevvron, known as the Magnum.

So how should this story of Berkshire's 'brushes with aviation' be brought to an end? The fact is, of course, the story still goes on—at Membury, at Brimpton and, of course, at White Waltham.

Brimpton? Yes, a small airfield just a few miles from Aldermaston, perhaps best known to followers of aviation heritage as the home of two 1950s ex-RAF Percival Provosts. Sir William Mount, director of Miles Aircraft, originally owned the land, and had the strip prepared for his own Miles Messenger in the late 1940s. In the 1970s it was used by crop-sprayers and, in 1977, was taken over by Alan House who developed the site to its present thriving state where it is the home of ten or so aircraft and a club of some fifty members. Alan bought the two Provosts in the 1980s. They were restored to full flying condition and have often been demonstrated at air displays. Sadly, in July 2009, one of them crashed, killing the pilot John Fairey.

Right: The logo of Brimpton Flying Club features a Percival Provost.

Flying days are a feature of the Brimpton Flying Club, the beneficiary of these popular events usually having been the White Waltham-based Thames Valley & Chilterns Air Ambulance. Founded in 1999, this worthwhile charity receives no Government or lottery funding and relies entirely on sponsorship, donations and fund-raising activities. In fact, after answering nearly ten thousand call-outs, 2007 saw the end of its time at a Berkshire base. Coinciding with a change of name to the Berks, Bucks and Oxon Air Ambulance, it now operates from RAF Benson and, from the summer of 2008, now uses the larger, more powerful and more versatile EC135 Eurocopter.

Below: The yellow and green Bolkow 105 of the Thames Valley & Chilterns Air Ambulance was based at White Waltham until 2007.

White Waltham also lost the last link with one of its longest established commercial tenants, when the test site of ML Aviation closed in 2004. In fact, from the early 1980s, ML Aviation had been involved in a series of mergers and eventually became part of the Cobham Group, being absorbed into their Flight Refuelling company at Wimborne in 1997.

It is perhaps unfair to describe MLA's Sprite as another 'funny' but it was the last of their flying machines to take to the air at White Waltham and it was certainly unusual. The brochure described it as a *'uniquely manoeuvrable remotely-piloted helicopter for short range civil and military operations'*. It was designed to carry different cameras, imaging devices, laser and electronic devices and it first flew in 1983. Today, an MLA Sprite can be seen at the Museum of Berkshire Aviation.

The difficulty of trying to wrap up Berkshire's 'brushes with aviation' in a neat and tidy way, was demonstrated by items in a 2008 edition of 'Aeroplane' magazine. The first was a progress report on Charles Lindbergh's Miles Mohawk which was then being restored to display standards at the RAF Museum.

Below: The Sprite was a complete fully operational system comprising an Air Vehicle and a Ground Control Console which, together with its two operators, could be carried in a small cross-country vehicle.

The other item recorded that pilot and vintage aircraft enthusiast Peter Bishop had sent his Miles Monarch to France to be restored to flying condition. Until 2006 it had been at a Scottish aviation museum. More surprising perhaps, is that another of his aircraft was also being restored in France. This is the tiny Woodley-built jet racer known as the Somers Kendall SK1, designed by Miles test pilot Hugh Kendall for racing pilot 'Nat' Somers. It first flew in 1955 but could be seen to be a one-off failure and was left out of this book's main story. Perhaps that was a bit unfair to Hugh Kendall because its only real problem seems to have been the unreliability of its engine. Nevertheless, after a heavy crash landing in 1957, it disappeared from public view and spent many years in storage at the Cranfield Institute of Technology. Now, with the reliability of small jet engines much improved over the past fifty years, it is hoped the SK1 will be flying again before too long.

Since one of Berkshire's seemingly lost 'brushes with aviation' has unexpectedly returned, another 'one-off failure' which was, originally, left out, should perhaps be mentioned. The three-engine Aerogypt 1, which first flew from Heston in 1939, was a quarter-scale version of a proposed eighty-seat airliner designed by Egyptian-born Saleh Helmy, who lived in Maidenhead. Later, he based it at White Waltham. The unique design feature was a large retractable flap mechanism on top of the fuselage, although this was removed, along with one of the engines when, in February 1946, the Aerogypt 2 set off from White Waltham on a flight to Eygpt via Northolt. Unfortunately, Northolt is as far as it got and it crashed. It may even then have been able to fly again, if the salvage crane hadn't dropped it! Hey ho.

It never ceases to amaze me how my own' brushes with aviation' still keep happening and, in this instance, the Internet played a part. It was December 2008, when a mistake in my own web-site prompted John Prytherch to contact me. The painting on page 152, which appears in my web-site, was inspired by a story in a small book about Croydon Airport that I was given back in the late 1980s. It said the Miles Gemini G-AJWE, the very last aircraft to leave, flew to nearby Gatwick. John told me that it actually flew to Biggin Hill. He should know because he was one of the passengers!

"'bye for now"

On reflection, perhaps the best way to draw this version of Berkshire's aviation heritage to an end is with another painting, this time an end-of-the-day scene at White Waltham, safe in the knowledge that tomorrow, there and in other places, it will be the start of yet more 'brushes with aviation'. With two classics from the 1930s in the foreground, it could easily be thought to be White Waltham during the time of the de Havilland pre-war Flying School. But members of the West London Aero Club would no doubt point out that their clubhouse wasn't built until post-war days. Then, if you look beyond the Tiger Moth, two very much more modern aircraft clearly set the scene in modern times.

Bibliography

'Miles Aircraft since 1925'   *Don L Brown*
    Published: Putman & Company Limited. 1970.

'Wings over Woodley'   *Julian Temple*
    Published: Aston Publications. 1987

'The mystery of the cancellation
of the contract for the Miles M52'   *Dennis Bancroft*
    Published: DS Bancroft. 1997

'Action Stations 6'   *Michael JF Bowyer*
    Published: Patrick Stephens Limited. 1983

'Action Stations 9'   *Chris Ashworth*
    Published: Patrick Stephens Limited. 1985.

'The Forgotten Pilots'   *Lettice Curtis*
    Published: EL Curtis. 1971/1982

'Patrick Young Alexander'   *Gordon Cullingham*
    Published: Cross Manufacturing Co. 1984

'In Defence of Freedom'   *Jonathan Sayers*
    Published: J J Sayers. 2006.

'Fred & John Holmes
and the Berkshire Aviation Co.'   *Frank Poller*
    Published: Hanney History Group. 2002

'Reach for the Sky'   *Paul Brickhill*
    Published: Collins. 1954

'Bader. The Man and his Men.'   *Michael G Burns*
    Published: Arms and Armour. 1990

'Handley Page Herald'   *Graham Cowell*
    Published: Jane's Publishing Company Limited. 1980.

'Knights of the Air'   *Peter King*
    Published: Constable & Company Limited. 1989

'Pure Luck'   *Alan Bramson*
    Published: Patrick Stephens Limited. 1990

'The Spitfire Story'   *Alfred Price*
    Published: Silverdale Books. 2002

'RJ Mitchell'   *Gordon Mitchell*
    Published: Nelson & Saunders Publishers. 1986

'Balloons and Airships'   *Lennart Ege / Kenneth Munson*
    Published: Blandford Press. 1973

'Blossom'   *Jean Fostekew*
    Published: Cirrus Associates (SW). 1998

'Thames Valley Airfields
in the Second World War'   *Robin J Brooks*
    Published: Countryside Books. 2000

'De Havilland Aircraft Co'   *Maurice Allward & John Taylor*
    Published: The Chalford Publishing Company. 1996

'Miss Winifred Spooner'   *Jim Bell*
    Published: Jim Bell. 2009

Photographs and graphic images

My collection of 35mm slides was started in 1985 when Julian Temple gave me a number of 'spares' from his own collection that he was building up at Woodley at the time. From then on, as my own research into Berkshire's aviation heritage expanded, I took every opportunity to add to the collection. Eventually, it included around two hundred slides, most of which played a part in the numerous presentations I gave in the '80s and '90s. It is possible that some 'corners were cut' in the frantic days of trying to promote the museum and, twenty plus years later, I can only apologise if this was the case. However, this was almost certainly a 'once in a lifetime' collection that never existed before and, because of the unique opportunities I had for research in those years, could never be built up again. With the advent of computers, digital photography and improved copiers, my collection was largely transferred to the electronic medium. Since all of this has taken place over a long, long time, perhaps not surprisingly I am unsure who many of the original holders of the copyright might have been. In any case, as most of the photographs originated well over fifty years earlier, copyright ownership becomes even more questionable. For this reason, if I do not actually know who the original copyright owner was, I have indicated who I think it may have been and, in some cases, included the source of my own copy. My sincere thanks go to the many people who, in some way, have contributed to the inclusion of the photographs in this book. Other photographs have usually been taken by me or Valerie. If mistakes have been made, I can only apologise and promise to correct them in any future edition.

P.1		*Phillips & Powis via Adwest Archives.*
P.2		*Unknown.*
P.4	top:	*Phillips & Powis via Adwest Archives.*
	bottom:	*Air Transport Auxiliary.*
P.7		*Phillips & Powis via Adwest Archives.*
P.8		*Miles Aircraft via Adwest Archives.*
P.10	both	*Miles Aircraft via Adwest Archives.*
P.13		*Western Manufacturing via Adwest Archives.*
P.14		*Julian Temple.*
P.15	hangar	*Julian Temple.*
P.17		*Simonds Brewery.*
P.18		*Phillips & Powis via BAG.*
P.23	bottom right	*British Steel.*
P.24		*The Publicity Mill.*
P.26		*USAAF.*
P.29	top left	*Berkshire Chronicle.*
	top right	*The Publicity Mill.*
P.37 & 38		*via Windsor Collection.*
P.39		*via West Berkshire Museum.*
P.40		*The Rolls Royce Heritage Trust.*
P.41		*Unknown.*
P.42		*de Havilland via BAe.*
P.44		*via West Berkshire Museum.*
P.45		*via Windsor Collection.*
P.46		*Grahame-White Co. and Author's collection.*
P.48		*via Maidenhead Heritage Centre.*
P.49	1st col.	*Daily Mail.*
	2nd col.	*via Windsor Collection.*
	3rd col.	*Imperial War Museum.*

P.50		*Berkshire Chronicle. via A Catton.*
P.51		*RAF Museum.*
P.53 & 54		*via Frank Poller / R Jackson.*
P.55	left	*Berkshire Chronicle. via A Catton.*
	right	*Unknown.*
P.56 & 57		*via Adwest Archives.*
P.60		*via Adwest Archives.*
P.61		*via Andrew McIrvine / Jim Bell.*
P.63		*via Berkshire Aviation Group.*
P.65		*RAF Museum.*
P.67	1st col.	*via Royal Berkshire Hospital.*
	2nd col.	*RAF Museum.*
	3rd col.	*Miles Aircraft. via Adwest Archives.*
P.68		*via Maidenhead Heritage Centre.*
P.69 to 77		*Phillips & Powis via Adwest Archives.*
P.80		*Phillips & Powis via RAF Museum.*
P.82 & 83		*Phillips & Powis via Adwest Archives.*
P.85 & 86		*Phillips & Powis via Adwest Archives.*
P.87	1st col.	*RAF Abingdon.*
	3rd col.	*Phillips & Powis via Adwest Archives.*
P.90 to 93		*Phillips & Powis via Adwest Archives.*
P.94		*RAF Museum.*
P.99 & 100		*Vickers Armstrong.*
P.102 & 104		*Air Transport Auxiliary.*
P.103		*Lettice Curtis.*
P.106		*Air Transport Auxiliary.*
P.110		*Martin Baker.*
P.114 & 115		*Miles Aircraft via Adwest Archives.*
P.116	2nd col.	*Miles Aircraft via Adwest Archives.*
	3rd col.	*Berkshire Chronicle.*

P.117		*War Office.*
P.118		*USAAF.*
P.121		*USAAF.*
P.125	M52	*Miles Aircraft via Adwest Archives.*
	Wind Tunnel	*Julian Temple.*
P.128		*Miles Aircraft.*
P.129		*RAF Staff College.*
P.131		*Fairey Aviation.*
P.132 & 133		*Miles Aircraft via Adwest Archives.*
P.134		*Miles Aircraft.*
P.138		*Fairey Aviation.*
P.139		*Handley Page (Reading).*
P.141	Top	*Fairey Aviation.*
	Bottom	*Author.*
P.142	Top	*Fairey Aviation.*
	Bottom	*ML Aviation.*
P.146		*Handley Page (Reading).*
P.148		*George Miles.*
P.153		*via RAF Abingdon.*
P.155		*via Jonathan Sayers.*
P.156		*Jonathan Sayers.*
P.157		*Aviation Enterprises.*
P.158	1st col. Top	*Brimpton Flying Club.*
	Bot.	*Thames Valley & Chiltern Air Ambulance.*
	2nd col.	*ML Aviation.*
P.159		*West London Aero Club.*

Index (continued)

162

Index (continued)

Numbers in 'bold' indicate an item in the main text, numbers in 'italics' indicate a photograph or painting and its caption

The Berkshire Aviation Heritage Collection